AN INTRODUCTION TO MILL'S UTILITARIAN ETHICS

John Stuart Mill was the leading British philosopher of the nineteenth century, and his famous essay *Utilitarianism* is the most influential statement of the philosophy of utilitarianism: that actions, laws, policies, and institutions are to be evaluated by their utility or contribution to good or bad consequences.

Henry R. West has written the most up-to-date and user-friendly introduction to Mill's utilitarianism available. This book serves as both a commentary to and interpretation of the text. It also defends Mill against his critics. The first chapter traces Mill's life and philosophical background. The second chapter analyzes Mill's arguments against alternative theories. Succeeding chapters address the theory of qualitative hedonism; the question of whether Mill was an act or rule utilitarian; the theories of sanctions and of the relation between justice and utility; and the "proof" of the principle of utility. An appendix reviews in detail the structure and arguments of *Utilitarianism*.

This book is primarily intended as a textbook for students in philosophy assigned to read *Utilitarianism*, but it should also prove helpful to students and professionals in other fields such as political science, history, and economics.

Henry R. West is a professor of philosophy at Macalester College in Minnesota.

An Introduction to Mill's Utilitarian Ethics

HENRY R. WEST

Macalester College

CAMBRIDGE
UNIVERSITY PRESS

PUBLISHED BY THE PRESS SYNDICATE OF THE UNIVERSITY OF CAMBRIDGE
The Pitt Building, Trumpington Street, Cambridge, United Kingdom

CAMBRIDGE UNIVERSITY PRESS
The Edinburgh Building, Cambridge CB2 2RU, UK
40 West 20th Street, New York, NY 10011-4211, USA
477 Williamstown Road, Port Melbourne, VIC 3207, Australia
Ruiz de Alarcón 13, 28014 Madrid, Spain
Dock House, The Waterfront, Cape Town 8001, South Africa

http://www.cambridge.org

First published 2004

Printed in the United States of America

Typeface Meridien 10/13 pt.   *System* LaTeX 2$_\varepsilon$ [TB]

A catalog record for this book is available from the British Library.

Library of Congress Cataloging in Publication Data

West, Henry R., 1933–
An introduction to Mill's utilitarian ethics/Henry R. West.
p. cm.
Includes bibliographical references and index.
ISBN 0-521-82832-5 – ISBN 0-521-53541-7 (pbk.)
1. Mill, John Stuart, 1806–1873. 2. Ethics, Modern – 19th century.
3. Utilitarianism. I. Title.
B1608.E8W47   2003
171′.5′092–dc21   2003051540

ISBN 0 521 82832 5 hardback
ISBN 0 521 53541 7 paperback

To Pat, my wife,
for love, support, and patience

CONTENTS

Acknowledgments   *page* ix

Method of Citation   xi

Introduction   1

1   Mill's Life and Philosophical Background   8

2   Mill's Criticism of Alternative Theories   28

3   Qualities of Pleasure   48

4   Was Mill an Act- or Rule-Utilitarian?   74

5   Sanctions and Moral Motivation   96

6   Mill's "Proof" of the Principle of Utility   118

7   Utility and Justice   146

Appendix: An Overall View of Mill's *Utilitarianism*   169

Bibliography   195

Index   213

CONTENTS

ACKNOWLEDGMENTS

My greatest debt is to John M. Robson and Toronto University Press for publishing the *Collected Works of John Stuart Mill*. Without that, research on the corpus of Mill's writings would have been difficult and limited. Another debt is to *The Philosopher's Index* for leads to secondary literature.

The paradigm of recent scholarship on Mill's ethics is the work of David Lyons, whose careful analysis of Mill texts has been a model to emulate. I have also been influenced by Alan Fuchs, who, through correspondence and conversation, has challenged some of my tendencies in interpretation. Conversations with Wendy Donner have also been helpful. In the early stages of this study, I was helped and encouraged by J. B. Schneewind.

I am thankful to my colleagues Martin Gunderson and Karen J. Warren for reading parts of the script and making helpful comments for revisions. The readers for Cambridge University Press gave useful suggestions for revisions that improved the book. My friend Robert Foy read the entire manuscript, improving its style for clarity.

I became interested in Mill from a prior interest in utilitarianism, initiated by Professor Charles Baylis in a graduate course on Ethical Theory. My interest was furthered by discussions with fellow graduate students such as David Lyons, David Kurtzmann, and Michael Stocker, and I wrote a doctoral dissertation on utilitarianism, with Roderick Firth and John Rawls as advisors. In three years of postdoctoral research at Oxford University I had the opportunity to discuss utilitarianism with R. M. Hare, J. J. C. Smart, Derek Parfit, Peter Singer, Jonathan

Glover, R. M. Frey, James Griffin, and others. I have participated in NEH seminars, on utilitarianism led by Richard Brandt, and on consequentialism led by Jonathan Bennett. I benefited from the participation of others in those seminars, and I have benefited from commentators on papers that I have presented at professional meetings. Finally, my thinking on utilitarianism has been encouraged and kept on track by many years of conversations and correspondence with my good friend Bart Gruzalski.

My research and writing has been supported by Macalester College and by an NEH Fellowship for College Teachers.

METHOD OF CITATION

All page references to the writings of Mill are to the *Collected Works of John Stuart Mill*, 33 volumes, John M. Robson, General Editor (Toronto: University of Toronto Press, 1963–91). There are many reprints of Mill's more popular works; for easy reference to them I have included the book and/or chapter, section, or paragraph in parentheses or brackets even if the paragraph is not numbered in Mill's text.

INTRODUCTION

U TILITARIANISM is the ethical theory that the production of happiness and reduction of unhappiness should be the standard by which actions are judged right or wrong and by which the rules of morality, laws, public policies, and social institutions are to be critically evaluated. According to utilitarianism, an action is not right or wrong simply because it is a case of telling the truth or lying; and the moral rule against lying is not in itself correct. Lying is wrong because, in general, it has bad consequences. And the moral rule against lying can be subjected to empirical study to justify some cases of lying, such as to avoid a disastrous consequence in saving someone's life.

Utilitarianism is one of the major ethical philosophies of the last two hundred years, especially in the English-speaking world. Even if there are few philosophers who call themselves utilitarians, those who are not utilitarians often regard utilitarianism as the most important alternative philosophy, the one to be replaced by their own. Examples of the latter are intuitionists, such as E. F. Carritt[1] and W. D. Ross,[2] early in the twentieth century, and, more recently, John Rawls, whose book *A Theory of Justice*[3] contrasts his principles of justice with utilitarian principles and contrasts his contractarian foundation for his principles with the grounds for utilitarian principles. Some of the most prominent ethical philosophers of recent years have

[1] E. F. Carritt, *Ethical and Political Thinking.*
[2] W. D. Ross, *The Right and the Good.*
[3] John Rawls, *A Theory of Justice.*

1

explicitly considered themselves utilitarians. Examples would be Richard Brandt,[4] J. J. C. Smart,[5] and R. M. Hare.[6] Nearly all introductory courses in ethics include utilitarianism as one important theory to be considered. And public policy is often based on cost-benefit analysis, perhaps not using pleasure and pain as the measures of utility but rather using some proxies for welfare and harm, such as consumer or voter preference or economic goods. Thus utilitarianism has an important place in contemporary ethics.[7]

John Stuart Mill's essay entitled *Utilitarianism*[8] is the most widely read presentation of a utilitarian ethical philosophy. It is frequently assigned in introductory courses on ethics or moral philosophy in colleges and universities and included as an examination topic at both graduate and undergraduate levels. It has been the subject of numerous disputes in books and in philosophical periodicals regarding its proper interpretation, and it has been the subject of numerous attacks and defenses by those who disagree or agree with its conclusions and supporting arguments.

[4] Richard B. Brandt, *A Theory of the Good and the Right; Facts, Values, and Morality*, and other writings.

[5] J. J. C. Smart, "An Outline of a System of Utilitarian Ethics," in *Utilitarianism: For and Against*, by J. J. C. Smart and Bernard Williams, eds.

[6] R. M. Hare, *Moral Thinking: Its Levels, Method, and Point*, and other writings.

[7] A textbook illustrating this is William H. Shaw's *Contemporary Ethics: Taking Account of Utilitarianism*.

[8] John Stuart Mill, *Utilitarianism*. References to *Utilitarianism* will be in parentheses in the text. In quoting from Mill, an effort will be made to add the feminine pronoun when the masculine is used to refer to a representative human being. About this Mill says: "The pronoun *he* is the only one available to express all human beings; none having yet been invented to serve the purpose of designating them generally, without distinguishing them by a characteristic so little worthy of being the main distinction as that of sex. This is more than a defect in language; tending greatly to prolong the almost universal habit of thinking and speaking of one-half the human species as the whole." *A System of Logic, Ratiocinative and Inductive* (bk. 6, ch. 2, sec. 2, n. 837).

2

The present work is conceived as a contribution to those disputes, both of interpretation and of the merits of Mill's philosophical position. It is an effort to present an interpretation of the work as a whole and of its constituent parts, taking into consideration many of the conflicting interpretations found in philosophical literature, and to defend the essay against many of the objections that have been presented against it or its utilitarian philosophy. It is my belief that Mill's version of utilitarianism is far clearer and more consistent than it is often made out to be, and that his version of utilitarianism is a plausible if not a totally defensible ethical theory. A complete defense of utilitarianism would require a refutation of all alternatives to it, or at least a discussion of other serious alternatives to show the superiority of utilitarianism. I am not sure that such a comparison is possible, because alternatives may rest on metaphysical or dogmatic assumptions that are beyond rational discussion; but, in any case, it is not my aim to do that. Nevertheless, it is my aim to answer many of the standard objections to the theory. Thus this is a work of substantive moral philosophy as well as exegesis of a text.

Mill's essay is often read only in excerpts, and that can be misleading. For example, Mill introduces utilitarianism in the following way: "The creed which accepts as the foundation of morals, Utility, or the Greatest Happiness Principle, holds that actions are right in proportion as they tend to promote happiness, wrong as they tend to produce the reverse of happiness" (210 [II, 2]). This formula is ambiguous in several ways. First, it appears to apply to each act that an agent might consider doing, case by case. Such an interpretation is what has been called "act-utilitarianism," in contrast to "rule-utilitarianism" or other more complex versions of utilitarianism. In Chapter 5 of *Utilitarianism* and in other writings, it is clear that Mill is not an act-utilitarian. One chapter of this book will be devoted to a discussion of that issue, drawing on the data in *Utilitarianism* and remarks by Mill in his correspondence. Another ambiguity is what is meant by the expression, "right in proportion as they tend to promote happiness." One interpretation is that a particular act has some consequences that promote happiness and other consequences that produce unhappiness. An act, then, has a net tendency when the tendency to promote unhappiness is subtracted from the tendency to promote happiness or vice versa.[9] Given an act-utilitarian interpretation of the formula, one could then say that an act is right if it in fact has a greater net tendency to promote greater happiness (or less unhappiness) than any alternative. This is the sort of act-utilitarianism defended by J. J. C. Smart in *Utilitarianism: For and Against*. This is not only act-utilitarian but "actual consequence" utilitarianism in contrast to "foreseeable consequence" utilitarianism. But another interpretation of "tends" in the formula is possible. It is that a *kind* of action tends to promote happiness to the extent to which that kind of action *usually* promotes happiness. The tendency, then, is the probability that actions of that kind have been found to promote happiness. Such an interpretation will be defended in this work. Many objections to utilitarianism are directed against act-utilitarianism and against actual-consequence utilitarianism. Mill's theory is much more complicated, and it is not subject to many of those objections.

Sometimes Chapter 2 of *Utilitarianism* is read without the chapter on the "sanctions" that motivate morality, the chapter on the "proof" of hedonism, and the chapter on justice. These are all controversial chapters, but taken together they help to interpret Mill's version of utilitarianism. Understanding the "sanctions" requires an understanding of Mill's psychological theories, which are found in his notes to an edition of his father's psychology textbook. Understanding the "proof" is aided by his comments in a letter to a correspondent. The chapter on justice shows that Mill took rights very seriously.

---

[9] This is the interpretation given by Roger Crisp, *Routledge Philosophy Guidebook to Mill on Utilitarianism*, 104. Crisp also interprets Mill as an act-utilitarian (113) and as an actual-consequence utilitarian (99–100).

In the chapters of this work, these chapters are interpreted in the light of Mill's correspondence and other writings. In *Utilitarianism* Mill gives little attention to alternative moral theories. Chapter 2 is devoted to showing that Mill had reasons to reject other theories, as well as the positive arguments for utilitarianism found in the essay.

Mill derived his utilitarianism from his father, James Mill, and from Jeremy Bentham, the eighteenth-century founder of the utilitarian tradition in moral philosophy. Mill was critical of Bentham in two early essays on Bentham, and in his essay *Utilitarianism* he revises Bentham's quantitative analysis of pleasures and pains by introducing a qualitative dimension to the analysis. The tone of Mill's essay also differs from the tone of Bentham's writings. Bentham writes polemically to attack the current moral thinking that appealed to moral feelings, which he called "caprice." Mill also rejected any appeal to a moral sense, but in this essay, he is out to show that utilitarianism is supportive of most commonsense morality. Many interpreters have been led to emphasize the differences between Mill and Bentham. My reading of Mill, on the other hand, will emphasize the similarities. Mill, like Bentham, was a reformer. He was an advocate of women's rights and of better wages and voting rights for the working classes. He opposed aristocratic privileges. He thought that Christianity was a source of perverted ethical doctrines. And Mill, in spite of the greater complexity of his analysis of pleasures and pains, like Bentham was a hedonist. Mill revised and perhaps broadened and softened Benthamism, but he never deserted it.

Chapter 1 will give a brief statement of biography for those unfamiliar with the life of the man whose *Autobiography* is a classic work of that genre of literature and whose other works were important contributions to philosophy of science, economics, and political theory. This chapter will also place J. S. Mill's work in the tradition of utilitarianism stemming from Jeremy Bentham. Those familiar with Mill's life and Bentham's philosophy may wish to skip that chapter and go on to Chapter 2.

Chapter 2 presents Mill's criticism of alternative ethical theories found, not in *Utilitarianism*, but in other writings. In those writings, Mill attacks the appeal to Nature, to God's commands, and to a moral sense, as the foundation for ethics.

Chapter 3 analyzes Mill's controversial evaluation of pleasures and pains on the basis of "quality" as well as "quantity." Many critics have claimed that Mill has deserted hedonism in making this distinction. I argue that Mill is correct to distinguish between pleasures and pains on the basis of qualitative phenomenal differences and that this is not a desertion of hedonism. But I also argue that he has not successfully made out his claim that those who have experienced pleasures that employ the distinctively human faculties consistently prefer them.

Chapter 4 states Mill's theory of the sanctions that motivate moral behavior and explicates the psychological theory that is their background.

In Chapter 5, the question whether Mill is properly interpreted as an "act-utilitarian" or as a "rule-utilitarian," or as neither, is discussed. My conclusion is that neither formulation captures the structure of Mill's position. Mill wants rule-utilitarian reasoning to be used in some contexts; act-utilitarian reasoning to be used in others; and he has an important role for rights and for a distinction between duty and supererogation (actions that are meritorious, beyond the call of duty).

Chapter 6 sets out and defends Mill's "proof" of the Principle of Utility. Mill's argument for hedonism is usually attacked as committing a number of fallacies. I defend it against these charges and claim that it is a persuasive argument.

Chapter 7 restates Mill's theory of the relationship between utility and justice, showing that, on the analogy of rule-utilitarian reasoning, the role of rights and of justice in Mill's system is consistent with his utilitarianism.

An appendix gives an outline of the structure of *Utilitarianism*, in the order of the chapters of the essay, summarizing Mill's arguments. For those unfamiliar with the work, for those who have read it but without confidence in following the arguments, or for those who want a quick review, a reading of the appendix before reading the remainder of the book will be helpful.

This book is intended for a wide audience, from the reader first becoming acquainted with Mill's philosophy to the professional philosopher or even the Mill scholar who is familiar with the controversies surrounding Mill's work. For those who are unfamiliar with Mill, I strongly recommend that after reading Chapter 1 and perhaps Chapter 2, they read Mill's essay *Utilitarianism* or at least the appendix that summarizes it, before attempting to study Chapters 3 through 7.

1

MILL'S LIFE AND PHILOSOPHICAL BACKGROUND

U TILITARIANISM as a distinct tradition in ethical thought was founded by Jeremy Bentham (1748–1832). The principle of utility, that the production of happiness and elimination of unhappiness should be the standard for the judgment of right action and for the criticism of social, political, and legal institutions, was proposed by many writers in the eighteenth century, but it was Bentham who attempted to build a complete system of moral and legal philosophy upon that basis, and it was Bentham whose doctrine became the basis of a reform movement in the nineteenth century. A brief statement of Bentham's philosophy will be given at the end of this chapter.

John Stuart Mill was a direct heir of Bentham's philosophy. His father, James Mill (1773–1836), had moved from Scotland to become a freelance journalist in London, where he edited two journals, translated books, and in the period of John Stuart's childhood wrote a multivolume *History of British India*. This became the standard work on the subject and earned him a post with the East India Company, which, as a quasi-governmental bureau, managed British colonial interests in India. Soon after moving to London, James Mill became acquainted with Bentham. John Stuart writes in his *Autobiography* that his father was "the earliest Englishman of any great mark, who thoroughly understood, and in the main adopted, Bentham's general views of ethics, government, and law."[1]

---

[1]   John Stuart Mill, *Autobiography*, reprinted in *Autobiography and Literary Essays*, vol. 1 of *Collected Works of John Stuart Mill*, J. M. Robson and Jack Stillinger, eds., 55 (ch. II, par. 11). References to the *Autobiography* in this chapter will be in parentheses in the text.

James Mill became an exponent of the utilitarian philosophy in articles for journals and for the *Encyclopaedia Britannica*, applying Benthamite principles to such subjects as government, education, liberty of the press, and colonial policy. He also did much to define the policy of a group of reformers known as the "philosophical radicals," which included some members of Parliament and various intellectuals, such as the economist David Ricardo and the legal philosopher John Austin. Major works by James Mill, in addition to his *History of British India*, were *Elements of Political Economy* (1821), a presentation of Ricardian economic theory, and *Analysis of the Phenomena of the Human Mind* (1829), a treatise of psychology drawing heavily upon the work of David Hartley (1705–57). But James Mill is most famous for the education that he gave his son John Stuart, which could appropriately be regarded as one of his chief works.

John Stuart Mill was born May 20, 1806, his parents' first child. He never attended school in the usual sense. With the exception of a few months at age fourteen, when he visited Bentham's brother's family in France, and the following year, when he studied law with John Austin, John Stuart was taught exclusively by his father, beginning in infancy. He began learning Greek at the age of three, from vocabulary cards with the English equivalent; so he already at three knew how to read English! By the time that he was eight, he had already read, in Greek, several classics of Greek history, including the whole of Herodotus and six dialogues of Plato. All of this was done in the room in which his father was writing the several volumes of his monumental *History of British India* as well as all else that he wrote to support his family. At twelve, John Stuart began the study of logic, working through Aristotle in Greek and scholastic logic in Latin, which he began to learn when he was eight; and in the year that he reached the age of thirteen, his father took him "through a complete course in political economy" (31 [I, 18]).

All of this is reported in detail in the *Autobiography*. There Mill gives the teaching of political economy as an example of his father's method. His father had him read the works of David Ricardo and Adam Smith, "and in this reading it was one of my father's main objects to apply to Smith's more superficial view of political economy, the superior lights of Ricardo, and detect what was fallacious in Smith's arguments, or erroneous in any of his conclusions" (31 [I, 19]).

Mill praises this method. "Most boys or youths who have had much knowledge drilled into them," he says, "have their mental capacities not strengthened, but overlaid by it. They are crammed with mere facts.... Mine, however, was not an education of cram. My father never permitted anything which I learnt, to degenerate into a mere exercise of memory.... Anything which could be found out by thinking, I was never told, until I had exhausted my efforts to find it out for myself" (33–5 [I, 22]).

The education was no doubt rigorous. "[N]o holidays were allowed, lest the habit of work should be broken, and a taste for idleness acquired..."(39 [I, 24]). And he was kept from any association with other boys to avoid contagion by vulgar modes of thought and feeling.

Because John Stuart was so much under the tutelage of his father, with regard to modes of both thought and feeling, it is of interest to notice his account of his father's moral attitudes. He says that his father's moral inculcations were at all times mainly those of the Socratic virtues as prescribed by Cicero: "justice, temperance (to which he gave a very extended application), veracity, perseverance, readiness to encounter pain and especially labour; regard for the public good; estimation of persons according to their merits, and of things according to their intrinsic usefulness; a life of exertion, in contradiction to one of self-indulgent sloth" (49 [II, 7]). James Mill's standard of morals was utilitarian, taking as the exclusive test of right and wrong the tendency of actions to produce pleasure and pain. But, John Stuart reports, he had "scarcely any belief in pleasure" (49 [II, 9]). He deemed few pleasures worth the price that, at least in the present state of society, must be paid for them. Accordingly temperance – stopping short at the point of moderation in all indulgences – was for him almost the central point of educational precept. He rated intellectual enjoyments above all other, even in value as pleasures, independently of their ulterior benefits. The pleasures of the benevolent affections he placed high in the scale, and he used to say that he had never known a happy old man, except those who were able to live again in the pleasures of the young (49–51 [II, 9]).

Some of these precepts can be seen reflected in John Stuart Mill's own ethical doctrines, such as the low regard for merely sensate pleasures and the intrinsic superiority of intellectual ones. Another feature of James Mill's philosophy reflected in John Stuart's philosophy is the distinction between the rightness and wrongness of an action and the motive of the agent: Actions are judged right or wrong on the basis of consequences, not the motive of the agent, but the motives of agents are all-important in assessing the character of agents. John Stuart says that his father "blamed as severely what he thought to be a bad action, when the motive was a feeling of duty, as if the agents had been consciously evil doers." But honesty of purpose had its full effect on his estimation of characters. "No one prized conscientiousness and rectitude of intention more highly . . ." (51 [II, 9]).

James Mill was not only a disciple of Bentham. He was also a close associate. Each summer he and John Stuart would be visitors at Bentham's summer estate, and in 1813 the Mill family moved to a house near Bentham in London, which they rented from him; so John Stuart from an early age was acquainted with the man. But it was not until he was fifteen that he read Bentham's philosophy itself. In the preceding year he had spent six months visiting Bentham's brother's family in southern France, where he had learned French, had gone to lectures on chemistry and zoology at the Faculty of Sciences at Montpellier, and had private tutoring in higher mathematics. The following winter he read Roman law with John Austin, an acquaintance of his father's who had, according to Mill in his *Autobiography*, "made Bentham's best ideas his own" (67 [III, 2]). At the beginning of this study with Austin, his father put into his hands a French translation of Bentham by Etienne Dumont, entitled *Traité de Legislation*. Mill reports, "The reading of this book was an epoch in my life; one of the turning points in my mental history" (67 [III, 2]). Up to that point his education had been, in a certain sense, a course in Benthamism. The Benthamic standard of "the greatest happiness" was that which he had always been taught to apply. "Yet in the first pages of Bentham it burst upon me with all the force of novelty" (67 [III, 3]). He was impressed with the way in which Bentham treated the common modes of reasoning in morals and legislation, deduced from phrases such as "law of nature," "the moral sense," and the like, as dogmatism in disguise, imposing its sentiments upon others under cover of expressions that convey no reason for the sentiment but set up the sentiment as its own reason. He was struck that Bentham's principle put an end to all of this, that all previous moralists were superseded. He was impressed by Bentham's classification of various actions and the orders of their consequences. And to this intellectual clarity was added inspiring prospects of practical improvement in human affairs. "When I laid down the last volume of the *Traité*," Mill writes, "I had become a different being. The 'principle of utility,' understood as Bentham understood it, and applied in the manner in which he applied it through these three volumes, fell exactly into its place as the keystone which held together the detached and fragmentary component parts of my knowledge and beliefs. It gave unity to my conceptions of things. I now had opinions; a creed, a doctrine, a philosophy . . ." (69 [III, 3]).

Mill as an adult was to write essays in some respects critical of Bentham, and in his *Utilitarianism* he was to make some modifications in Bentham's analysis of the dimensions of pleasure, of the sanctions that can enforce morality, and of other points. But his debt to Bentham cannot be overemphasized. His modifications are refinements of a basically utilitarian view from which he never wavered.

From May of 1823, the month of his seventeenth birthday, Mill worked for thirty-five years for the East India Company, a position secured for him by his father, who had himself become an officer of that firm. John Stuart officially started as a clerk of the lowest status, but from the first he prepared drafts of dispatches and in a few years was promoted to a department head. Eventually he held the second-highest position in the India Company's London office. He retired when the administration of India was reorganized, turning down an invitation to continue on as a government official. Mill claims that he found office duties an actual rest from the other mental occupations that he carried on simultaneously with them. And throughout those thirty-five years, as well as after his early retirement, he was extremely active as a writer of books and essays and for a time an editor of a radical political and philosophical review. He also did research for articles written by his father, and he spent all of his leisure time in the year 1825 taking Bentham's disjointed manuscripts on judicial evidence and rewriting them into a coherent five-volume work, published as Bentham's *Rationale of Judicial Evidence*, with J. S. Mill's name as editor. Mill also organized a reading group of a dozen or so of his young friends, who met together for two hours twice a week to discuss some work that they would agree to read together. They went through works on psychology, political economy, and logic.

In the year 1826–7, when Mill was twenty years of age, there occurred what he labels a "crisis" in his mental history. Some biographers have misinterpreted this as a mental crisis in the sense of mental breakdown. It was rather an extended state of depression, a sense of joylessness in life. His activities up to this time had seemed to him to fill up an interesting and animated existence. But in the autumn of 1826 he suddenly felt himself incapable of feeling the sympathy with human beings that was supposed to be the chief source of happiness of a reformer of the world's institutions and opinions. During this time he continued with his usual occupations, but he says that he went on with them mechanically, by the mere force of habit. After six months, however, on reading a passage in some memoirs that told of a boy's father's death, the distressed position of the family, and the sudden inspiration by which the boy felt and made them feel that he would be everything to them, Mill was moved to tears. From that time the oppression of the thought that all feeling was dead within him was gone, and he gradually found that the ordinary incidents of life could again give him pleasure; he says that there was again enjoyment in sunshine and sky, in books, in conversation, in public affairs, and there was once more excitement in exerting himself for his opinions and for the public good. Biographers have engaged in speculation as to what the incident shows about Mill's relation to his father.[2] Mill himself drew two lessons from it. One was that happiness, as the end of life, could only be attained by not making it the direct end. Those only are happy who have their minds fixed on some object other than their own happiness, or at least this is true of the great majority of mankind. The second lesson was that the "passive susceptibilities" needed to be cultivated as well as the active capacities, feelings as well as intellect. And so the following year Mill found "medicine for his mind" in reading Wordsworth's poetry, and he began to extend his circle of friends to those of a more poetical and less analytical mentality than his own, including some followers of the poet Coleridge. However, he found that they were often as one-sided in their views as his Benthamite friends, and he wanted to be many-sided. It was in this spirit that a decade later

---

[2] A. W. Levi, "The Mental Crisis of John Stuart Mill," *Psychoanalytic Review* 32 (1945): 86–101; Bruce Mazlish, *James and John Stuart Mill*, ch. 10. Michael St. John Packe also raises the question of Mill's attitude toward his mother, in *The Life of John Stuart Mill*, 80. On the other hand, Mill's friend Alexander Bain attributes the crisis to overwork: "That the dejection so feelingly depicted was due to physical causes, and that the chief of these causes was over-working the brain, may I think be certified beyond all reasonable doubt." Alexander Bain, *John Stuart Mill*, 38. Mill had spent all of his "leisure" time of the preceding year editing Bentham's five-volume work.

he wrote essays on "Bentham" and on "Coleridge," emphasizing to his radical and liberal readers some negative aspects of Bentham's views and the positive value of Coleridge's; but Mill says that he later turned back from what there had been of excess in his reaction against Benthamism.

Mill also became acquainted with some of the writings of Continental thinkers, especially those of the Saint Simonians and of Auguste Comte, with their theory of history as characterized by different stages. Later Mill was to become acquainted with the socialist theories of the Saint Simonians and of Francois Fourier, which appeared to him a superior description of socialism than that of the British socialist Robert Owen.

Mill's *Autobiography* recounts other influences upon his life – authors that he studied and persons that he knew. One of the most controversial subjects in the Mill biography is the influence of Harriet Taylor, whom Mill first met in 1830 when he was twenty-five and she was twenty-three. At the time she was married and the mother of young children. Twenty-one years later, two years after the death of her husband, she became Mill's wife. But throughout those twenty-one years, they were frequent companions. Mill praises her intellectual as well as moral virtues without stint, attributing to her coauthorship of much that he wrote, especially his *Principles of Political Economy* and the essay *On Liberty*. Mill accepts credit for being the theorist, in political economy, analytic psychology, logic, philosophy of history, moral philosophy, and political science, but claims that much of the practicality found in his writings is because they are the work of her mind as well. Although it is probably an exaggeration to call her a coauthor, it is apparent from correspondence between them that she made suggestions for topics and how he should treat them, which he carried out accordingly, and that she suggested changes in the manuscripts, which he presented to her before making final revisions.

Mill recounts that from this time in his life, there were only two substantial changes to come in his thought. They consisted in a greater approximation, so far as regards the ultimate prospects of humanity, to a qualified socialism, and a shifting of his political ideal from pure democracy to a modified form of it. The first of these is attributed by some commentators to the influence of Harriet Taylor, and there is evidence of it in their correspondence.[3] The second Mill attributes to his study of Alexis de Tocqueville's *Democracy in America*. The movement toward socialism appeared in successive editions of Mill's *Principles of Political Economy*. The modified form of democracy that he came to advocate is found in his book entitled *Considerations on Representative Government*.

Mill's first published major work, and the book that established his reputation as one of the leading philosophers of the nineteenth century, was his *System of Logic*, published in two volumes in 1843. The research and writing occupied much of his time over eleven years (1830–41). The book had a rapid and wide success, being adopted as a text at both Oxford and Cambridge universities and going through eight editions in Mill's lifetime. Its title is now misleadingly narrow, for it is a fairly complete outline of what would today be called epistemology, philosophy of language, and philosophy of science. Mill's philosophy is in the tradition of British empiricism stemming from Francis Bacon and John Locke in the seventeenth century, with its emphasis upon experience as the source of the materials and much of the form of all knowledge. In *System of Logic* Mill presents a radically empiricist account of syllogistic reasoning and of mathematics, claiming that all inference is from particulars to particulars, deductive inference being only apparent inference; and he analyzes all mathematical truths, including those of arithmetic, as generalizations from experience. *System of Logic* contains an innovative account of induction,

[3]   Gertrude Himmelfarb, introduction to *Essays on Politics and Culture*, by John Stuart Mill, with an introduction by Gertrude Himmelfarb, ed., xix; Josephine Kamm, *John Stuart Mill in Love*, 74–7. See Appendix G, "John Stuart Mill-Harriet Taylor Mill Correspondence," in *Principles of Political Economy*, vols. 2–3 of *Collected Works of John Stuart Mill*, J. M. Robson, ed., 1026–37.

including five "methods" or "canons" of induction that are now known by Mill's name. Mill concluded with a chapter on the logic of the "moral sciences," some of which will be cited in discussing the place of rules in Mill's ethics.

In the years 1830–1, Mill had written some essays on economic topics, which in 1844 found a publisher with the title *Essays on Some Unsettled Questions of Political Economy*. But Mill's major work in economics was his *Principles of Political Economy*, two volumes, written in 1845–7 and published in 1848. This became the most popular treatise on the subject, almost immediately selling out its first edition and going through seven editions in Mill's lifetime. Mill attributed to Harriet Taylor the fact that it is a book not merely of abstract science, but also of application. Mill pays unusual attention to the effects upon the laboring class of various systems of property ownership, credit, allocation of resources, and changes in industrial and agricultural productivity. He attempts to make a distinction between the laws of production of wealth, which he calls real laws of nature, dependent on the properties of objects, and the modes of distribution, which, subject to certain conditions, depend upon human will. It is a matter of institutions and customs that there are distinct classes of laborers, capitalists, and landlords, receiving wages, profits, and rent, respectively. Modes of distribution do not depend on necessities of nature but on those combined with the existing arrangements of society and can be altered by the progress of social improvement.

As indicated previously, the later editions of the book were more sympathetic to socialism and more critical of existing conditions. Mill says that he and Mrs. Taylor came to the conclusion that the social problem of the future would be how to unite the greatest individual liberty of action with a common ownership in the raw material of the globe, and an equal participation of all in the benefits of combined labor.

Mill's *System of Logic* and *Principles of Political Economy* were the major works by which he was best known through most of his lifetime. But his work most widely read in the twentieth century is his essay *On Liberty*, published in 1859. It was written before Harriet Taylor Mill's death in 1858, and Mill says that it was more directly and literally a joint production with her than any other of his writings. It is one of the classics of liberal thought, a sustained argument for the importance of a large variety in types of individual character and for giving full freedom to human nature to expand itself in innumerable and conflicting directions. It contains one of the most eloquent and powerful arguments for freedom of opinion and freedom of expression in speech and press to be found anywhere.

Mill was profoundly fearful that growing democracy in government and equality in society would suppress individuality and override minorities. He was fearful of the "tyranny of the majority," not only through governmental coercion but through the informal social control of opinion and attitude, and *On Liberty* attempts to draw a line as to what is appropriate for social control and what should be left to individual taste. His criterion is against paternalistic interference in adult behavior when it is not harmful to others: "[T]he sole aim for which mankind are warranted, individually or collectively, in interfering with the liberty of action of any of their number, is self-protection."[4]

From 1858, when Mill retired from the East India Company with an adequate pension, he devoted himself full time to writing, with the exception of three years, 1865–8, when he served in Parliament.

In 1860–1, Mill wrote *Considerations on Representative Government*, published in 1861, to present the conclusions of his thoughts over many years on what would be the best form of constitutional government. He advocates representative government in order that laws be made in the interest of the governed but also for its beneficial effects upon the voting population. He felt that electoral participation made people

---

[4]   John Stuart Mill, *On Liberty*, reprinted in *Essays on Politics and Society*, vol. 18 of *Collected Works of John Stuart Mill*, J. M. Robson, ed., 223.

more active and intelligent than even the most benevolent despotism, cultivating public sympathies and stimulating people to look at questions from impersonal points of view. But he wanted to ensure that the voice of minorities would be heard in Parliament and that representatives not simply reflect the ignorance and prejudices of an uneducated majority. To achieve these aims he endorsed a form of what is today known as "proportional representation." In Mill's version, it is a scheme of preferential voting for persons on a list of candidates, without restriction to geographical representation. He favored plural votes for those with more education; and he proposed that there be a legislative commission of specialists to actually draft legislation, which would then be passed or rejected by the popular assembly. Hoping that representatives would be better informed and superior in judgment to the electorate, he opposed binding them to vote the views of their constituents.

It was also in 1861 that Mill published his essay *Utilitarianism*, the primary subject of this book. Between 1850 and 1858 he had written two unpublished essays, on the foundations of morals and on justice. These were combined into one work in 1859 and rewritten in 1861. The essay was first published, in three parts, in successive issues of *Fraser's Magazine* (October, November, December 1861). It was reprinted as a separate work in 1863.[5]

Two of Mill's lengthier but less frequently read works were published in 1865. One, *Auguste Comte and Positivism*, was Mill's effort to sift what was good from what was bad in the French thinker's speculations concerning social progress. On the one hand, Mill thought that Comte's proposals for a "religion of humanity" indicated possibilities for replacing traditional religion with a more enlightened emotional and social equivalent, but, on the other hand, Mill thought that Comte's program to

---

[5] For the composition of the essay, see J. M. Robson, Textual Introduction to *Essays on Ethics, Religion and Society*, cxxiii–cxxvi.

suppress all divergent opinion and behavior would lead to a tyrannical society with even worse consequences.

The other book published in 1865, *An Examination of Sir William Hamilton's Philosophy*, is a source, in addition to *System of Logic*, of Mill's empiricist epistemology and metaphysics. In it he went beyond *System of Logic* in attempting to account for our concepts of matter and of the existence of our own and other minds. He attempted to reduce our concept of matter to its experiential basis, calling matter a "permanent possibility of sensation." The work, however, is primarily devoted to a critical attack on Hamilton as a representative of the intuitionistic school of philosophy, and in *Autobiography* Mill says that the difference between this school and that of "Experience and Association," with which Mill identifies himself, is not a mere matter of abstract speculation. Mill says that a philosophy that is addicted to holding up favorite doctrines as intuitive truths, and deems intuition to be the voice of Nature and of God, speaking with an authority higher than that of our reason, is one of the chief hindrances to the rational treatment of great social questions and one of the greatest stumbling blocks to human improvement. This tendency in social theory had its source in intuitional metaphysics, Mill thought; so he undertook to show the inconsistencies and other weaknesses in one of the ablest representatives of that school of thought.

Another important source for Mill's empiricist philosophy is found in a revised edition of James Mill's *Analysis of the Phenomena of the Human Mind*, published in 1869, edited with additional notes by John Stuart Mill and Alexander Bain. The notes, as extensive as the original text, are designed to bring the doctrine of empiricist psychology up to date. They give J. S. Mill's mature philosophy of mind, arguing for a concept of mind as a series of states of consciousness, but one of an extraordinary kind in that it is aware of itself as having a past and future. This awareness is an inexplicable fact about the self, which distinguishes it from matter, from a mere permanent possibility of experience.

In 1865, Mill agreed to stand as a Liberal candidate for Parliament, but under conditions that made his election surprising. He refused to spend any money campaigning because he objected to it on principle, thinking that a candidate's expenditure amounted to buying his seat. He said that if elected he would not give any time or labor to local interests, and he announced that if elected he would support the cause of women's suffrage and representation in Parliament on the same terms with men. He thought that it was the first time that such a doctrine had ever been mentioned to English electors, and he believed that the fact that he was elected after proposing it gave a start to the movement in favor of women's suffrage.

In Parliament, Mill restricted his efforts primarily to the most unpopular causes and to those that had least support from either of the major parties. He spoke against abolition of capital punishment, which the Liberal party was supporting. Such a position may surprise some twenty-first-century readers, but he gave utilitarian arguments for his view. In other speeches he denounced the English mode of governing Ireland and advocated Irish land reform; he sought prosecution of soldiers and the colonial governor for atrocities against former slaves after a disturbance in Jamaica; he sought to protect political refugees in England from extradition; he supported wider suffrage for the working classes and their right of assembly in public parks; and he proposed to admit to the suffrage all women who possessed the qualifications required of male electors. He also supported working-class candidates for Parliament, including one who was openly antireligious. As a result, when he stood for reelection he got strong opposition from the Conservative party, little support from the Liberal party, and was defeated. His defeat surprised him less than his election in the first place.

In 1869 Mill published a treatise written several years earlier entitled *The Subjection of Women*, arguing in favor of equality in the marriage relationship, first-class citizenship, and greater economic opportunities for women. To the twenty-first-century reader, the book seems dated in its claims on behalf of what is now known as "women's liberation," but at the time its thesis was a radical one.

In his last years, in addition to the notes on his father's psychology text already mentioned, Mill wrote an essay entitled "Theism." This, along with two other essays entitled "Nature" and "The Utility of Religion" written between 1850 and 1858, was published in 1874, a year after his death, as *Three Essays on Religion*. Mill had no religious instruction as a child, growing up an atheist. In these works, he admits that there is the possibility that the universe has an intelligent designer, but, if so, the designer is not benevolent. Nature, when personified, is cruel. He also wrote the remainder of his *Autobiography*, the first part of which had been written and rewritten before his wife's death. It too was published posthumously, in 1873. When Mill died in 1873 he was widely regarded as the foremost intellect of his time. He had a record of acute comments upon controversies of culture and politics, and he had made monumental contributions to philosophy in most of its branches – logic; epistemology and philosophy of science; metaphysics and philosophy of mind; moral, political, and legal philosophy – and to economic theory.

As previously mentioned, at age fifteen Mill read Bentham's utilitarian philosophy as presented in Dumont's *Traité de Legislation*, which had used as its opening the first six chapters of Bentham's *An Introduction to the Principles of Morals and Legislation*.[6] It is useful background to Mill's essay *Utilitarianism* to review the doctrine expressed there. There can be little doubt that this is the doctrine of utilitarianism that Mill has in mind to defend, with modifications, in his essay. Bentham's work was intended as an introduction to a penal code, to give the philosophical foundation for a reform of criminal law. The first six

---

[6] Jeremy Bentham, *An Introduction to the Principles of Morals and Legislation*. The definitive edition is edited by J. H. Burns and H. L. A. Hart. References to this work in this chapter will be given in the text in parenthesis, with the page of this edition followed in brackets by chapter and section numbers.

chapters announce the most general utilitarian principles; the remainder of the text begins to work out the way in which these would be applied to criminal law. Mill, in his essay, is concerned more with morality than with law, but, as does Bentham, he holds that the same principle of utility is the foundation for both.

Bentham's book begins in dramatic fashion, proclaiming: "Nature has placed mankind under the governance of two sovereign masters, pain and pleasure. It is for them alone to point out what we ought to do as well as to determine what we shall do.... The principle of utility recognizes this subjection, and assumes it for the foundation of that system, the object of which is to rear the fabric of felicity by the hands of reason and of law" (11 [I, 1]).

Here Bentham is proclaiming two theses, which have been labeled "ethical hedonism" and "psychological hedonism." The word "hedonism" is from the Greek word *hedone*, which means "pleasure." Ethical hedonism is the view that pleasure and pain are the criteria the production of which makes acts right or wrong. Psychological hedonism is the view that pleasure and pain are the ultimate motivational forces determining action.

These two claims are closely related. As we shall see in discussing Chapter 4 of *Utilitarianism*, Mill thought that psychological hedonism could be the foundation for a persuasive argument for ethical hedonism. But the relationship is not as simple as Bentham's opening sentences suggest. If pleasure and pain determine what we shall do, it seems unnecessary that they should point out what we ought to do. However, choices of actions produce results that range over time. It is possible for an agent to choose acts that sacrifice immediate pleasure for the attainment of greater pleasure in the future, and, vice versa, it is possible to choose an immediate pleasure that results in the loss of greater pleasure in the future. It is similar for pains and for the conflict between pleasures and pains. Acts also affect other people. So Bentham developed a "hedonic" or "felicific"

23

calculus to enable a person rationally to apply his doctrine. This calculus will be described in the following text, after giving Bentham's description of the "principle of utility."

The principle of utility, which he also calls the "greatest happiness principle," is the principle "which approves or disapproves of every action whatsoever, according to the tendency which it appears to have to augment or diminish the happiness of the party whose interest is in question. . . . I say of every action whatsoever; and therefore not only of every action of a private individual, but of every measure of government" (12 [I, 2]).

Bentham thinks of happiness as simply a sum of positive pleasures and negative pains: "A thing is said to promote the interest, to be *for* the interest, of an individual, when it tends to add to the sum total of his pleasures: or, what comes to the same thing, to diminish the sum total of his pains" (12 [I, 5]). An action conformable to the principle of utility can be regarded as one that ought to be done or at least as not one that ought not to be done; it is a right action or at least not a wrong action. "When thus interpreted," Bentham claims, "the words ought, and right and wrong, and others of that stamp, have a meaning: when otherwise, they have none" (13 [I, 10]).

Bentham said that the principle was not susceptible of any direct proof, "for that which is used to prove every thing else, cannot itself be proved: a chain of proofs must have their commencement somewhere. To give a proof is as impossible as it is needless" (13 [I, 11]). But Bentham recognized that some people have opposed the principle. These could fall into three classes. There were those who opposed it, without being aware of it, by the very principle itself, as in calling it a dangerous principle. Second, there might be those who put forward an "ascetic" principle, consistently opposing happiness, but Bentham doubted if anyone had ever done so consistently. And there were those who put forward their own prejudices, their own feelings, as the criterion of right and wrong. Bentham called this the principle of either despotism or anarchy; despotical if their own feelings are thought to be the standard for every other person regardless of that other person's feelings; anarchical if there are as many standards of right and wrong as there are people with differing sentiments.

Bentham's hedonic calculus was to call attention to the dimensions of pleasures and pains and of actions insofar as actions are likely to bring about pleasures and pains. In Bentham's analysis a pleasure or pain has a certain intensity at any point in time and a duration through time. These two dimensions constitute the quantity of a particular pleasure or pain and thus constitute its intrinsic value. But actions have pleasurable or painful consequences beyond their immediate pleasurable or painful feeling. Bentham calls these the "tendency" of an action. In assessing the tendency of an action to produce a pleasure or pain, the degree of certainty or uncertainty must be calculated. An action that has only a 50 percent chance of producing a pleasure of a given quantity has only half the instrumental value of one that is certain to produce a pleasure of that quantity. What would today be called the "expected value" of the former pleasure would be only half as great as the expected value of the latter. Bentham also regarded remoteness from the present in time as a discounting factor. A present pleasure or pain would be calculated at full value; a remote pleasure or pain would be given some fraction of full value. Furthermore, pleasures and pains have a chance of resulting in further pleasures or pains, which Bentham labeled their "fecundity" and "purity." Fecundity is the probability that a pleasure will be followed by further pleasures (or a pain by further pains); purity is the probability that a pleasure will not be followed by pains (or a pain by pleasures). Finally, there is the question of "extent" – the number of individuals affected. Taking all of these into account, Bentham thought it possible to sum up the values of all the pleasures on the one side and all the pains on the other for each individual person affected by an act. The balance, if it be on the side of pleasure, would give the good tendency of the act upon the whole, with respect to the interests of that individual person; if on the side of pain, the bad tendency of it upon the whole. Then, repeating the previously mentioned process for every individual affected, the balance between the degrees of good tendency and the degrees of bad tendency for different individuals would give the general good or bad tendency of the act with respect to the community.

Bentham said that it is not expected that this process should be strictly pursued before every moral judgment or legislative or judicial decision, but he regarded it as the ideal toward which an exact process should approach.

It is fairly clear that by "pleasure" (and by "pain") Bentham is not restricting himself to a particular kind of sensation that feels the same regardless of its source. "Pleasure" and "pain" appear to be generic terms, each of which would have many species falling under them. This is evident when he comes to list, in Chapter 5, "Pleasures and Pains, Their Kinds." There is an extended list of pleasures: of sense, of wealth, of skill, of amity, of a good name, of power, of piety, of benevolence, of malevolence, of memory, of imagination, of expectation, of association, and of relief, and for most of these there are corresponding pains. What Bentham does have to be assuming, however, is that all of these kinds of pleasures and pains are commensurable. They can each be ascribed some intensity and duration as quantitative measures and summed up to give a total amount of pleasure or pain.

Because Bentham holds a theory of psychological hedonism – that pleasures and pains are the motives of all behavior – pleasure and pain are the means, as reward and punishment, by which a legislator must seek to modify individual behavior in socially desirable ways. Bentham enumerates four types of "sanctions," by which behavior can be modified by pleasure and pain: the physical, the political, the moral, and the religious. The first of these is simply causal relations in nature by which people learn that certain things cause pleasure and others cause pain. The political sanction consists of pleasures and pains meted out by judges or other state officials. The moral or "popular" sanction consists of pleasures and pains that are produced by the response to actions by unofficial persons in the community that one has dealings with. And the religious sanction consists of pleasures or pains expected to be experienced in this life or a future one imposed by a superior invisible being.

On many of the details of Bentham's analysis – his analysis of pleasures and pains in purely quantitative terms, his list of sanctions, his abbreviated argument for hedonism – Mill thought either that Bentham was mistaken or that more needed to be said. Mill is also writing in a different historical context. Bentham thinks of himself as providing basic principles of moral and legal philosophy somewhat on the model of Isaac Newton's laws of motion for physics. He has little concern for whether he will be understood or misunderstood by a general reading public. And he is acutely conscious of the need for radical reform of the law. Mill, on the other hand, wants to persuade the general intellectual reader of the plausibility of utilitarianism as a basis for social criticism, and one means of doing this is to show its convergence with intuitive notions regarding fundamental morality and justice. Mill is a social reformer, but he is a conservative regarding ordinary day-by-day morality. He wants the utilitarian foundation for morality to be accepted as the basis for change in attitudes toward the distribution of wealth, retributive punishment, and gender relations; but he wants it to be recognized as upholding honesty, trustworthiness, and other common standards of morality.

2

MILL'S CRITICISM OF
ALTERNATIVE THEORIES

IF one holds a view in moral philosophy, how is it to be supported? Basically, there are two ways. One is to argue in favor of one's own position either positively by stating reasons for holding it or defensively by answering objections to it. The other is to show that there are problems with alternative views.

Most of Mill's *Utilitarianism* is a defense of the utilitarian view. In Chapter 2 he answers a series of objections to utilitarianism and in Chapter 5 answers the major objection that justice is independent of utility. In Chapter 3 Mill analyzes sources for motivation to be moral and claims that utilitarianism has a source of motivation lacking in other theories. In Chapter 4 he gives psychological evidence for a hedonistic theory of ultimate value. It is primarily in Chapter 1 that Mill explicitly criticizes alternative ethical theories, and his remarks are very brief. He says that to show the deficiencies of his opponents "would imply a complete survey and criticism of past and present ethical doctrine,"[1] and that it is not his present purpose to do so. In some of his other writings, however, he goes into greater detail in showing the deficiencies of other views. Those readers who are narrowly concerned with the interpretation and significance of the explicit controversies of *Utilitarianism* may wish to skip or to skim this chapter. For those interested in the status of utilitarianism as a viable ethical theory, however, I believe that this chapter is important.

---

[1]   John Stuart Mill, *Utilitarianism*, 207 (ch. I, par. 4). Citations of this work in this chapter will be given in parentheses in the text.

In this chapter, I shall report some of Mill's criticism of alternative ethical doctrines, as found elsewhere in his writings. In these other writings, Mill recognizes theories of morality that do not fit into the dichotomy that he gives in Chapter 1 of *Utilitarianism* between the *a priori* school and the empirical school. Evidently he does not consider these others worthy of such notice in that context, but elsewhere he also criticizes the "divine command" theory of morality and the theory that morality is based on "natural law."

I shall first summarize Mill's statements in Chapter 1, pointing out assumptions that he makes in criticizing *a priori* theories. These assumptions really presuppose a structure to a moral theory that rules out the kind of theory that he is attacking. They show more a contrary orientation than a refutation of the opposition. I then give Mill's criticism of alternative theories, drawn from his other writings in ethics.

In Chapter 1, Mill presents the main contending schools of the foundation of morality as the intuitive or *a priori*, on the one hand, and the inductive or empirical, on the other. These two schools of thought, he says, go back to ancient Greece, represented in Plato's dialogue, the *Protagoras*, where Socrates is presented as arguing a hedonistic view against popular morality. Mill does not state those arguments, but they can be briefly summarized. Socrates asserts that pleasure and pain are intrinsically good and bad: ". . . I am rather disposed to say that things are good in so far as they are pleasant, if they have no consequences of another sort, and in so far as they are painful they are bad."[2] Socrates then attempts to answer obvious objections to that position. Against the counterargument that people are sometimes overcome by pleasure in eating and drinking, which implies that pleasure is sometimes bad, Socrates argues that the evil is not on account of the pleasure that is immediately given to them but on account of the painful consequences of overindulgence; and goods that are painful are not good for any

---

[2] Plato, *Protagoras*, in *The Dialogues of Plato*, translated by B. Jowett, 120.

other reason except that they end in pleasure (greater than the pain) or get rid of or avert (greater) pain. Socrates says that if you call pleasure an evil in relation to some other end or standard, "you will be able to show us that standard. But you have none to show." And, "if you have some standard other than pleasure and pain to which you refer when you call actual pain a good, you can show what that is. But you cannot."[3]

Mill adopts somewhat the same tactics in *Utilitarianism* in opposing the intuitive or *a priori* school of morality. Mill claims that his opponents unconsciously use the principle of utility and that without it they have no ultimate standard. "... [T]hey seldom attempt to make out a list of the *a priori* principles which are to serve as the premises of the science; still more rarely do they make any effort to reduce those various principles to one first principle, or common ground of obligation" (206 [I, 3]). It is the tacit influence of the utilitarian standard, Mill says, that accounts for "whatever steadiness or consistency these moral beliefs have attained," and whenever they deem it necessary to argue for their doctrines, they find that "utilitarian arguments are indispensable" (207 [I, 4]).

He gives the example of Kant's first principle, "So act, that the rule on which thou actest would admit of being adopted as a law by all rational beings." Mill says of Kant that "when he begins to deduce from this precept any of the actual duties of morality, he fails, almost grotesquely, to show that there would be any contradiction, any logical (not to say physical) impossibility, in the adoption by all rational beings of the most outrageously immoral rules of conduct. All he shows is that

---

[3] Ibid., 123. Mill did an abbreviated translation of that section of the *Protagoras*. He had Socrates conclude: "Then pleasure is the same thing with good, and pain with evil: and if a pleasure is bad, it is because it prevents a greater pleasure, or causes a pain which exceeds the pleasure: if a pain is good, it is because it prevents a greater pain, or leads to a greater pleasure. For, if this were not so, you could point out some other end, with reference to which, things are good or evil: but you cannot." John Stuart Mill, "The Protagoras," 58.

the *consequences* of their universal adoption would be such as no one would choose to incur." (207 [I, 4])

Before going into a deeper discussion of Mill's criticism of alternatives, we should notice some assumptions that Mill makes in his general objections to the *a priori* school. These show that Mill's orientation is to impose a structural condition upon ethics that makes the alternative unqualified to be even a candidate for eligibility.

First, Mill assumes what can be called a "teleological"[4] principle: "All action is for the sake of some end, and rules of action, it seems natural to suppose, must take their whole character and colour from the end to which they are subservient" (206 [I, 2]).[5] Second, he assumes that there must be either a single principle at the root of all morality, "or if there be several, there should be a determinate order of precedence among them" (206 [I, 3]). Third, he interprets the intuitive school of morality as agreeing with the empirical that "the morality of an individual action is not a question of direct perception, but of the application of a law to an individual case" (206 [I, 3]).

The last point misses some of the differences between different schools of intuitive ethics existing before Mill's time as well as since then. For those who think that we have a conscience or moral sense that recognizes what is right or

---

[4] "Teleological" is derived from the Greek word *telos*, which means "end" or "purpose." As a classification of an ethical theory, this term is contrasted with "deontological," derived from the Greek word *deon*, which means "duty," or that which is obligatory in and of itself. More recently, the term "consequentialist" has replaced "teleological" as a name for the class of ethical theories that base the rightness or wrongness of actions upon the end or goal of action, that is, upon their consequences, either actual or intended. See Henry R. West, "Consequentialism," in *The Encyclopedia of Philosophy: Supplement*, 346–7. For an introductory discussion of the distinction between deontological and teleological theories, see William K. Frankena, *Ethics*, 13ff.

[5] Elsewhere Mill quotes with approval from his father's "Fragment on Mackintosh": "But all action, as Aristotle says, (and all mankind agree with him) is for an end. Actions are essentially means...," in James Mill, *Analysis of the Phenomena of the Human Mind*, 262, n. 49.

wrong, this moral sense is sometimes thought to tell us in particular cases that an act is wrong (or right) as well as to tell us what general kinds of rules we ought to follow. William Frankena labels this a distinction between "act-deontologists" and "rule-deontologists,"[6] citing Joseph Butler, an eighteenth-century British moralist, as an example of an act-deontologist.[7] A moral-sense act-deontologist would be one who thinks that one's conscience or moral sense can know immediately that a particular act in a particular situation is right or wrong. And many intuitionists would claim that the moral sense is more like the physical senses than like our reasoning faculty. Mill has not recognized this type of opponent. But, more important, Mill's first two assumptions beg the question against the most fundamental characteristics of intuitive ethics.

Richard Brandt makes a distinction between two basic kinds of ethical theories, calling them "result" theories and "formalist" theories. The labels are to call attention to the fact that for result theories, such as utilitarianism, over-all moral obligation depends entirely on the intrinsic worth of the actual or expected results. To put this in Mill's terminology, actions (or rules) take their whole character and color from the end to which they are subservient. In contrast, formalist theories have in common that the "*nature* of the act (that is, whether it is a lie or a breach of promise – something about it different from the intrinsic worth of actual or expected consequences)" is sometimes an important fact bearing on whether there is a moral obligation to perform or avoid it.[8] The intuitive or *a priori* school that Mill is criticizing falls within the formalist category. To presuppose that rules take their character from the end

---

6 "Deontologist," as indicated in a preceding footnote, is derived from the Greek word for "duty," calling attention to the fact that certain acts or kinds of acts are duties, independently of consequences.

7 William Frankena, *Ethics*, 15. But Frankena seems to think that Butler is not consistently an act-deontologist. On the next page he lists Butler as perhaps a rule-deontologist.

8 Richard B. Brandt, *Ethical Theory*, 354–5.

that they serve is to presuppose that a "result" theory is the proper one.

Assuming that a result theory is the proper one does not limit one to hedonistic utilitarianism. It is worth noting that there are other possible result theories. Even within the hedonistic tradition, Mill differs from Bentham in his analysis of the dimensions of pleasures and pains that are to be analyzed, and there can be other results besides pleasure and pain that are regarded as valuable ends. Some of these are other types of experience, such as the cognition of truth, the appreciation of beauty, or the experience of love, which may be valued in themselves and not merely as means to or necessary conditions for certain types of pleasure. Other candidates are states of affairs that may be valued even when not experienced. Beauty, knowledge, loving relationships, and personal achievements are things that can be experienced, and the experience of them can have value. But some philosophers claim that experience of them does not exhaust their value as ends. Some philosophers claim that the *occurrence* of these things, apart from the experience of them, is intrinsically valuable. Other philosophers claim that if they are among the objects of an individual's deepest desires, then the fulfillment of those desires is constitutive of personal welfare, independent of the experience or even knowledge of the desires being fulfilled. G. E. Moore gives arguments for the intrinsic value of beauty independent of any experience of it,[9] and James Griffin has argued for an extended list of items of prudential well-being.[10] Finally, a result theory could give preference to the agent or those that are in special relations to the agent in counting the significance of the results. What affects oneself, or one's family, or citizens of one's own country, and so on, could count for more than what affects others, thus differing from the impartial weighing that Mill advocates. In claiming that rules and actions take their character from their ends, then, Mill is

[9] G. E. Moore, *Principia Ethica*, 83–5.
[10] James Griffin, *Well-Being*, ch. 4.

not limiting a theory to his version of hedonistic utilitarianism, but he does prejudge the case against nonconsequentialist theories.[11]

In assuming that there must be a single principle at the root of all morality or an order of preference among multiple principles, Mill is prejudging the case against another common feature of intuitive systems of moral philosophy. John Rawls even defines intuitionism as a theory that has multiple principles with no decision procedure for settling conflicts between them: "Intuitionist theories, then, have two features: first, they consist of a plurality of first principles which may conflict to give contrary directives in particular cases; and second, they include no explicit method, no priority rules, for weighing these principles against one another: we are simply to strike a balance by intuition, by what seems to us most nearly right."[12] Thus, in asserting that there must be a single principle or an order of preference among multiple principles, Mill is assuming that an adequate theory cannot be an intuitionistic one in Rawls's sense.

In other writings Mill has more explicit criticism of alternative views, and these do not prejudge the issue. In these writings he subjects the opposing view to more detailed analysis, usually showing one of three things: that the view uses fallacious logic in drawing conclusions; that the view has consequences that are unacceptable; or that the view makes assumptions that are unacceptable. The standard of unacceptability may be moral unacceptability, requiring that one approve of conduct that is so

---

[11] "Consequentialism" is a term that came into use in the twentieth century to refer to those theories, including utilitarianism, that evaluate acts, rules, and so on, on the basis of consequences. This is a more general category than utilitarianism, which is historically associated with hedonistic theories of evaluating the consequences. See Michael Slote, "Consequentialism," in *Encyclopedia of Ethics*, 2nd ed., 304–7.

[12] John Rawls, *A Theory of Justice*, 34. For a discussion of such theories, see J. O. Urmson, "A Defence of Intuitionism," *Proceedings of the Aristotelian Society* 75 (1974–5): 111–19.

far from civilized practice that it is absurd or implausible. Or the standard may be scientific unacceptability, requiring that one reject or suspend belief in some of the conclusions of modern science.

In what follows, I report Mill's criticism of three alternative views: the "divine command" theory of morality; the theory that what is "natural" or in accord with some sense of "natural law" should be the standard of morality; and the intuitionist theory.

The theory that the standard or test of moral obligation is God's commandments may take more than one form. Mill has no objection to belief that a righteous God would command what is morally obligatory and that if one could know the will of such a God, this would be informative of moral goodness. His objection is to the theory that God's commands are *constitutive* of moral obligation and virtue, that there is no standard independent of God's will, that whatever God wills is thereby morally correct. This position is criticized in two early essays, "Blakey's History of Moral Science" and "Sedgwick's Discourse." In these Mill attacks the view that good is whatever God arbitrarily commands and that what we call evil is only evil because God has arbitrarily prohibited it. Mill points out that one of the consequences of this view is that the "countless myriads to whom he has never signified his will, are under no moral obligations."[13] Another is that assertions in scriptures that "God is good, God is just, God is righteous," would then affirm nothing at all but the identical and unmeaning propositions that God is himself.[14] Mill also says that the doctrine takes away all motives to yield obedience to God, except those that induce

---

[13] "Blakey's History of Moral Science," 27. This criticism assumes that one must be informed of one's moral obligations in order to be under such obligations. That could be a controversial point.

[14] Ibid., 27. A clearer way of stating this point would be to say that because God's will is definitive of what is good or just, to say that God is good is to say that God's will is in accord with God's will. Presumably the scripture claims more than that.

a slave to obey his master. Mill says that the question, "Why am I bound to obey God's will?" requires an answer: "'Because he is my Maker' is no answer. Why should I obey my Maker? From gratitude? Then gratitude is in itself obligatory, independently of my Maker's will. From reverence and love? But why is he a proper object of love and reverence? . . . Is it because he is just, righteous, merciful? Then these attributes are in themselves good, independently of his pleasure. If any person has the misfortune to believe that his Creator commands wickedness, more respect is due to him [or her] for disobeying such imaginary commands, than for obeying them. If virtue would not be virtue unless the Creator commanded it – if it derive all its obligatory force from his will – there remains no ground for obeying him except his power; no motive for morality except the selfish one of the hope of heaven, or the selfish and slavish one of the fear of hell."[15]

Another problem with ascribing a supernatural origin to the received maxims of morality, according to Mill in a different treatise, the essay "Utility of Religion," is that such an origin protects them from being criticized. Some doctrines may have been erroneous or not properly limited in expression, or no longer suited to changes that have taken place in human relations, but when thought to be the will of God, they are considered equally binding with the noblest.[16]

One technique of criticism of an opponent's ethical view that we can notice in these arguments is to draw out implications of the doctrine that are absurd or implausible or for some other reason unacceptable. Another procedure is to criticize assumptions or the logic by which these assumptions are made to cohere with conclusions.

One problem with the divine will theory is that it assumes that there is a God and that one can have knowledge of God's will. The grounds for this assumption are subjected to criticism

---

[15] "Sedgwick's Discourse," 53.
[16] "Utility of Religion," 417.

in another of Mill's essays, "Theism." One of the most persistent problems is that of reconciling belief in a moral creator with the "atrocious cruelty and reckless injustice of Nature."[17] Another problem in Christian doctrine is the injustice of the existence of hell, with salvation from it a gift of special grace bestowed on a few but withheld from so many. Because since the worship of the deity of Nature or of the gospel has to ignore so much, Mill claims that it can be done only by sophistication and perversion. The Christian moralist is forced to engage in fallacious logic or to draw conclusions that are morally repugnant. "It may almost always be said both of sects and of individuals, who derive their morality from religion, that the better logicians they are, the worse moralists."[18] Mill also, in private correspondence, denounces the Judeo-Christian Bible as the basis for morality: "How can morality be anything but the chaos it now is, when the ideas of right and wrong, just and unjust, must be wrenched into accordance either with the notions of a tribe of barbarians in a corner of Syria three thousand years ago, or with what is called the order of Providence; in other words, the course of nature, of which so great a part is tyranny and inequity – all the things which are punished as the most atrocious crimes when done by human creatures, being the daily doings of nature through the whole range of organic life."[19]

Mill devoted a complete essay to criticism of ethics based upon an appeal to Nature. Entitled "Nature," this essay was written at about the time that Mill was drafting his essay *Utilitarianism*, but not published until the year after Mill's death as part of *Three Essays on Religion*.[20] The main argument of the essay is given in a summary at the end:

---

[17] Ibid., 423.

[18] Ibid., 425.

[19] Letter to Walter Coulson, November 22, 1850, in *The Later Letters of John Stuart Mill 1849–1873*, vols. 14–17 of *Collected Works of John Stuart Mill*, Francis E. Mineka and Dwight N. Lindley, eds., 52.

[20] The date of the composition of the essay is reported in an "Introductory Notice," by Helen Taylor, Mill's stepdaughter, 371.

"The word Nature has two principal meanings: it either denotes the entire system of things, with the aggregate of all their properties, or it denotes things as they would be, apart from human intervention.

"In the first of these senses, the doctrine that man [i.e., a human] ought to follow nature is unmeaning; since man has no power to do anything else than follow nature; all his actions are done through, and in obedience to, some one or many of nature's physical or mental laws.

"In the other sense of the term, the doctrine that man ought to follow nature, or in other words, ought to make the spontaneous course of things the model of his [or her] voluntary actions, is equally irrational and immoral.

"Irrational, because all human action whatever, consists in altering, and all useful action in improving, the spontaneous course of nature:

"Immoral, because the course of natural phenomena being replete with everything which when committed by human beings is most worthy of abhorrence, any one who endeavoured in his [or her] actions to imitate the natural course of things would be universally seen and acknowledged to be the wickedest of men [i.e., humans]."[21]

Mill gives very convincing examples to back up these assertions. For example, killing, "the most criminal act recognized by human laws, Nature does once to every being that lives; and in a large proportion of cases, after protracted tortures...."[22] Mill concludes that this reduces to absurdity the claim that we should model our behavior on the course of Nature.

He says that if we really believed that all natural agencies were appointed by a benevolent Providence as a means of accomplishing wise purposes, then everything from draining a pestilential swamp to curing a toothache ought to be accounted

---

[21] "Nature," 401–2.
[22] Ibid., 385.

impious. But, he thinks, no one really believes that; people can't hold that the whole of nature is good, and when they try to pick out which part is good, one recommendation is as fallacious as another when it attempts to appeal merely to what is in accord with Nature.[23] He also argues that many virtues go against what is natural. Courage is "from first to last a victory achieved over one of the most powerful emotions of human nature," and "the sentiment of justice is entirely of artificial origin."[24] In correspondence with William George Ward, Mill said, "You ask what are the natural instincts that civilization has strikingly and memorably conquered. I answer, nearly all. E.g. the instinct of taking a thing which we very much wish for, wherever we find it – food, for instance, when we are hungry. The instinct of knocking down a person who offends us if we are the strongest. As a rather different example take the eminently artificial virtue of cleanliness – think what savages are, & what violence must be done to the natural man to produce the feelings which civilised people have on this point. . . ."[25] Later in the same letter, Mill argues against a natural sense of right and wrong: "I am convinced that competent judges who have sufficient experience of children will not agree with the opinion you express that they have a natural idea of right and duty. I am satisfied that all such ideas in children are the result of inculcation. . . ."[26]

In these criticisms of nature as a criterion of morality, Mill's strategy is to clarify the doctrine by an analysis of the concepts involved, then to show the obvious unacceptability, by common standards of morality, of such a criterion.

Mill also thinks that the appeal to what is natural has had terrible social consequences and is a hindrance to progress.

[23] Ibid., 391.
[24] Ibid., 393–4.
[25] Letter to William George Ward, spring of 1849, *The Later Letters of John Stuart Mill 1849–1873*, 26.
[26] Ibid., 30.

Mill does not cite it as an example in this essay, but one of his greatest concerns was the problem of overpopulation. This is an instance where appeal to what is "natural" has devastating consequences and needs to be opposed.[27] In his discussion of the rate of wages in *Principles of Political Economy*, he accepts the Malthusian doctrine[28] that it is the tendency of human population increase to outrun any increase in production of means of subsistence; so to avoid starvation and poverty, it is necessary to have artificial checks upon population increase.[29] Mill cites with approval laws on the Continent that delay marriages, and he thinks that they are not objectionable as violations of liberty.[30] "Poverty, like most social evils," says Mill, "exists because men [and women] follow their brute instincts without due consideration. But society is possible, precisely because man [i.e., the human] is not necessarily a brute. Civilization in every one of its aspects is a struggle against animal instincts. It has artificialized large portions of mankind to such an extent, that of many of their most natural inclinations, they have scarcely a vestige or a remembrance left. If it has not brought the instinct of population under as much restraint as is needful, we must remember that it has never seriously tried."[31] "In Mill's opinion,"

---

27 In the *System of Logic*, Mill gives the principle of population as an example of a disagreeable conclusion that writers fallaciously seek to avoid by opposing the theory of divine benevolence to the evidence of physical facts. See *A System of Logic*, 772 (bk. 5, ch. 3, sec. 8).

28 Thomas Malthus, *An Essay on the Principle of Population*; Thomas Malthus, *Principles of Political Economy*.

29 John Stuart Mill, *Principles of Political Economy*. In bk. 2, chs. 11–13, he deals with wages and the remedies for low wages.

30 The description of the Continental laws is found in Mill, *Principles of Political Economy*, 346–8 (bk. 2, ch. 11, sec. 4). See also 358 (bk. 2, ch. 12, sec. 2), where Mill says, "Every one has a right to live. We will suppose this granted. But no one has a right to bring creatures into life, to be supported by other people." That laws restricting marriage are not a violation of principles of liberty is found in *On Liberty*, 304 (ch. 5, par. 15).

31 Mill, *Principles of Political Economy*, 367–8 (bk. 2, ch. 13, sec. 1).

writes his biographer, Michael St. John Packe, "an uncontrolled birth-rate was all that stood between men and ultimate Utopia. Although he would regret that physical devices should take the place of moral discipline, he would probably have regarded the general introduction of effective contraceptives as the greatest social benefit since the discovery of America."[32] When he was seventeen, Mill was arrested for distributing pamphlets with instructions on birth control, and later in life he asserted that facts regarding birth control should be communicated to married couples by their medical advisers.[33] Here, then, in unrestricted birthrates, is an example where the practice of what is "natural" has consequences unacceptable to Mill, and, in his mind, to anyone who understands these scientific facts and is concerned for the general good. Mill also thought that information about birth control was related to the subjection of women. In a letter to Edward Herford, for example, he says, in discussing the problems of the poor, that emigration "would do no more than push off to another generation the necessity of adopting a sounder morality on the subject of overpopulation – which sounder morality, even if it were not necessary to prevent the evils of poverty, would equally be requisite in order to put an end to the slavery to which the existing state of things condemns women...."[34]

In *The Subjection of Women*, Mill discusses the claim that the subjection of women is "natural." Mill points out that masters of slaves have claimed that their authority was natural, that theorists of absolute monarchy have claimed that theirs was the only natural form of government, that conquering races have claimed that it was Nature's dictate that the conquered should obey the conquerers. In general, those who wield power claim it as a natural right: "... [W]as there ever any domination which

---

[32] Michael St. John Packe, *The Life of John Stuart Mill*, 303.

[33] Packe, 56–9.

[34] Letter to Edward Herford, January 22, 1850, *Later Letters of John Stuart Mill 1849–1873*, 45.

did not appear natural to those who possessed it?"[35] And that which is customary appears to be natural: "The subjection of women being a universal custom, any departure from it quite naturally appears unnatural."[36] Thus Mill sees the appeal to Nature, natural law, or natural rights as a hindrance to moral and social progress.

I turn now to Mill's criticism of the intuitive or *a priori* school of moral doctrine, which he considered his chief opponent.

In discussing intuitionistic theories of morality, Mill distinguishes between the psychological or "metaphysical" question regarding the origin of moral judgments and moral feelings and the different question, what kinds of acts and dispositions are the proper objects of those feelings.[37] Mill says that the theory of a moral sense, as the ground of morality, may be understood to involve answers to both questions, to account for what our feelings *are*, and to provide the standard or test for what our conduct *should be*. It would be possible to hold one of these views without holding the other; for example, to believe in a moral sense that is the origin of moral feelings, and that such a sense recognizes utility as the standard or test of morality. Mill attributes this view to David Hume.[38] But generally, Mill thinks, those who believe in a moral sense "assume the ordinary precepts of morals as of *a priori* authority" (206 [I, 3]). And utilitarians generally accept a theory that moral feelings are acquired by ordinary experience, not due to a moral sense. They arise from sympathetic feelings – the idea of pain of another is naturally

---

35 John Stuart Mill, *The Subjection of Women*, reprinted in *Essays on Equality, Law, and Education*, vol. 21 of *Collected Works of John Stuart Mill*, John M. Robson, ed., 269 (ch. 1, par. 9).

36 Ibid., 270 (ch. 1, par. 9).

37 This distinction is made in "Blakey's History of Moral Science," 26, and in "Sedgwick's Discourse," 50–2.

38 "Blakey's History of Moral Science," 27. This interpretation of Hume (1711–76) as a utilitarian is a subject of controversy. Annette Baier, in discussing it, says that if he is to be seen as any sort of utilitarian, he is not an "act" nor a "rule" utilitarian, but a "character trait" utilitarian. See Annette Baier, "David Hume," in *Encyclopedia of Ethics*, 2nd ed., 812.

painful; the idea of pleasure of another is naturally pleasurable – as well as from inculcation.[39] And from "the sympathetic reaction of these feelings in the imagination and self-consciousness of the agent, naturally arise the more complex feelings of self-approbation and self-reproach ... satisfaction and dissatisfaction with ourselves."[40]

As previously indicated, the intuitionists generally take the received rules of morality as those that are claimed to be given by a moral sense. These may be rules quite similar to those based on the standard of utility, but Mill asserts that when attributed to a moral sense, they are not subject to criticism: "... [U]pon the truth or falseness of the doctrine of a moral sense, it depends whether morality is a fixed or a progressive body of doctrine. If it be true that man [i.e., the human] has a sense given to him [or her] to determine what is right or wrong, it follows that his [or her] moral judgments and feelings cannot be susceptible of any improvement.... According to the theory of utility, on the contrary, the question, what is our duty, is as open to discussion as any other question ... and changes as great are anticipated in our opinions on that subject, as on any other, both from the progress of intelligence, from more authentic and enlarged experience, and from alterations in the condition of the human race, requiring altered rules of conduct."[41]

Thus, one reason for Mill's hostility to the moral sense view is that it prevents rational criticism and reform of existing moral and social practices: "The contest between the morality which appeals to an external standard, and that which grounds itself on internal conviction, is the contest of progressive morality against stationary – of reason and argument against deification of mere opinion and habit. The doctrine that the existing order of things is the natural order, and that, being natural, all innovation upon it is criminal, is as vicious in morals as it

---

[39] "Sedgwick's Discourse," 60.
[40] "Whewell on Moral Philosophy," 185. Mill also discusses the origin of moral feelings in Chapter 3 of *Utilitarianism*.
[41] "Sedgwick's Discourse," 73–4.

is now at last admitted to be in physics, and in society and government."[42]

Mill attached great importance to his *System of Logic* as helping to undermine intuitionism in general and thereby contributing to the battle against intuitionism in moral and social philosophy. In his *Autobiography* he makes explicit the connection: "The notion that truths external to the mind may be known by intuition or consciousness, independently of observation and experience, is, I am persuaded, in these times, the great intellectual support of false doctrines and bad institutions. By the aid of this theory, every inveterate belief and every intense feeling, of which the origin is not remembered, is enabled to dispense with the obligation of justifying itself by reason, and is erected into its own all-sufficient voucher and justification. There never was such an instrument devised for consecrating all deep-seated prejudices. And the chief strength of this false philosophy in morals, politics, and religion, lies in the appeal that it is accustomed to make to the evidence of mathematics and of the cognate branches of physical science. To expel it from these, is to drive it from its stronghold.... [T]he *System of Logic* met the intuition philosophers on ground on which they had previously been deemed unassailable; and gave its own explanation, from experience and association, of that peculiar character of what are called necessary truths...."[43]

Likewise, in correspondence with Theodor Gomperz concerning the latter's offer to translate *System of Logic*, Mill said that his book "was chiefly valued by me as a necessary means towards placing metaphysical and moral science on the basis of analyzed experience, in opposition to the theory of innate principles, ... I consider that school of philosophy [i.e., the one supporting the theory of innate principles] as the greatest speculative hindrance to the regeneration so urgently required, of man and society; which can never be effected under the

---

[42] "Whewell on Moral Philosophy," 179.
[43] *Autobiography*, in *Autobiography and Literary Essays*, 233 (ch. 7, par. 4).

influence of a philosophy which makes opinions their own proof, and feelings their own justification."[44]

These criticisms, while persuasive to those who think that some features of current morality need change, would not be persuasive to those who are intuitionists. The latter would more likely regard any change as degeneration. The argument that a moral sense leaves no room for criticism or improvement is also subject to dispute. Human beings have an innate sense of hearing, but that sense is subject to indefinite improvement in the discrimination of sounds that constitute meaningful language, in the discrimination of sounds that constitute harmonious music, etc. Similarly, all the perceptual senses may give information about the physical world, but the theoretical interpretation of physical appearances (e.g., that the earth is rotating on its axis rather than stationary) shows the possibility of indefinite improvement in knowledge of the external world. Moral sense theorists have not been in agreement about the conclusions to be drawn from their intuitions, but Mill used this only as evidence against the theory.

The intuitionists say that the feelings to which they appeal are not their own individually, but characterize universal human nature. Mill denies that there is such unanimity of feeling. "They assume the utmost latitude of arbitrarily determining whose votes deserve to be counted. They either ignore the existence of dissentients, or leave them out of the account, on the pretext that they have the feeling which they deny having, or if not, that they ought to have it."[45]

Mill takes Whewell's opposition to Bentham's including animal suffering in moral calculation as an example. According to Whewell it is "to most persons not a tolerable doctrine, that we may sacrifice the happiness of men [i.e., humans] provided we can in that way produce an overplus of pleasure to cats,

[44] Letter to Theodor Gomperz, August 19, 1854, *The Later Letters of John Stuart Mill 1849–1873*, 239.
[45] "Whewell on Moral Philosophy," 179.

dogs, and hogs." Mill replies that it is "to most persons" in the slave states of America not a tolerable doctrine that we may sacrifice any portion of the happiness of white men or women for the sake of a greater amount of happiness to black men or women. It would have been intolerable five centuries ago "to most persons" among the feudal nobility, to hear it asserted that the greatest pleasure or pain of a hundred serfs ought not to give way to the smallest of a noble person. "According to the standard of Dr. Whewell," Mill asserts, "the slavemasters and the nobles were right."[46]

Mill points out that witchcraft, magic, astrology, oracles, ghosts, gods, and demons were once universally believed in. His point is that in morals as in science and metaphysics, universal belief is not conclusive evidence of truth. But he questions whether there is any universal agreement in ethics, whether there is a single virtue held to be a virtue by all nations, in the same sense, and with the same reservations. What passes for the universal voice of mankind "is merely the voice of the majority, or, failing that, of any large number having a strong feeling on the subject.... With Dr. Whewell, a strong feeling, shared by most of those whom he thinks worth counting, is always an *ultima ratio* from which there is no appeal. He forgets that as much might have been pleaded, and in many cases might still be pleaded, in defence of the absurdest superstitions."[47]

From Mill's point of view, based upon his belief that morality is progressive, these arguments against the authority of God, of Nature, or of a moral sense are conclusive. But would they be to someone who believed him- or herself to have knowledge of God's will, to someone who saw certain behavior as unnatural and therefore wrong, or to someone who had considered moral judgments that could not be shaken by any empirical evidence? Ethical theories are debated against a background

[46] Ibid., 186.
[47] Ibid., 194.

of metaphysical and methodological presuppositions. To refute some ethical theories, it is necessary to refute the background assumptions about God, Nature, and moral psychology. That is beyond the scope of interpreting and defending Mill's position, but I think that this chapter has shown that Mill has powerful arguments against his opponents.

3

QUALITIES OF PLEASURE

MILL'S claim that some pleasures are superior to others on grounds of difference in quality is one of the most controversial claims in his utilitarian ethics. Many critics have asserted that he abandoned hedonism in supposing that there are qualitative differences among pleasures. Some defenders of Mill have used passages from other writings to analyze the distinction as merely one of quantity. Mill's presentation leaves a number of questions unanswered. I claim, however, that Mill is correct in analyzing pleasures and pains as differing in quality as well as quantity, and that this is a consistent hedonist position. I deny, however, that those experienced in the pleasures that employ our distinctively human faculties always prefer them to those involving only animal faculties.

In this chapter I first summarize the section of Chapter 2 of *Utilitarianism* in which Mill introduces the notion of qualitative differences in pleasures and point out the probable influence of Francis Hutcheson. Next I seek to give the most charitable interpretation to what Mill says, so as to make the theory as plausible as possible, but I do point out ambiguities and objections. Then I present other criticisms and discuss the extent to which they can be dismissed or answered.

Mill introduces the notion of qualitative differences between pleasures as an answer to the objection that hedonism, the theory of life on which Mill's utilitarianism is founded, is a doctrine worthy only of swine. Mill's reply is that if human beings were capable of no pleasures except those of which swine are capable, the rule of life that is good enough for the one would be good enough for the other. But human beings have faculties more elevated than the animal appetites, and when once made conscious of them, do not regard anything as happiness that does not include their gratification. The higher faculties that he names are the intellect, the feelings and imagination, and the moral sentiments.[1] He claims that it is quite compatible with the principle of utility to recognize the fact that some kinds of pleasure are more desirable and more valuable than others. Mill explains what he means as follows: "If I am asked, what I mean by difference of quality in pleasures, or what makes one pleasure more valuable than another, merely as a pleasure, except its being greater in amount, there is but one possible answer. Of two pleasures, if there be one to which all or almost all who have experience of both give a decided preference, irrespective of any feeling of moral obligation to prefer it, that is the more desirable pleasure. If one of the two is, by those who are competently acquainted with both, placed so far above the other that they prefer it, even though knowing it to be attended with a greater amount of discontent, and would not resign it for any quantity of the other pleasure which their nature is capable of, we are justified in ascribing to the preferred enjoyment a superiority in quality, so far outweighing quantity as to render it, in comparison, of small account" (211 [II, 5]).

Mill claims that those who are equally acquainted with, and equally capable of appreciating and enjoying, both the pleasures of animal appetites and those of distinctly human faculties do give a preference to the "manner of existence which employs their higher faculties" (221 [II, 6]). Few humans would consent to be changed into any lower animal even for the promise of the fullest allowance of the beast's pleasure, and "no intelligent human being would consent to be a fool, no instructed person would be an ignoramus, no person of feeling and conscience would be selfish and base, even though they should be persuaded that the fool, the dunce, or the rascal is better

---

[1] John Stuart Mill, *Utilitarianism*, 211 (ch. 2, par. 4). Citations to this work throughout this chapter will be in parentheses in the text.

satisfied with his [or her] lot than they are with theirs" (211 [II, 6]). Mill explains that this is due to a sense of dignity, "which all human beings possess in one form or other ... and which is so essential a part of the happiness of those in whom it is strong, that nothing which conflicts with it could be, otherwise than momentarily, an object of desire to them" (212 [II, 6]). Mill says that those who think that this takes place at a sacrifice of happiness confuse happiness and contentment. A being with fewer capacities may be more easily contented, but is not thereby happier. "It is better to be a human being dissatisfied than a pig satisfied; better to be Socrates dissatisfied than a fool satisfied. And if the fool, or the pig, is of a different opinion, it is because they only know their own side of the question. The other party to the comparison knows both sides" (212 [II, 6]).

Mill admits that people do choose lower pleasures, but claims that this is quite compatible with the intrinsic superiority of the higher. People often, he says, from infirmity of character, choose the nearer good, though they know it to be the less valuable, but this occurs when the choice is between two bodily pleasures as well as when it is between bodily and mental. Some who begin with youthful enthusiasm for everything noble, as they advance in years, sink into indolence and selfishness. But Mill claims that before they devote themselves exclusively to the lower ones, they have become incapable of the other kind. "Capacity for the nobler feelings is in most natures a very tender plant, easily killed, not only by hostile influences, but by mere want of sustenance; ... they addict themselves to inferior pleasures, not because they deliberately prefer them, but because they are either the only ones to which they have access, or the only ones which they are any longer capable of enjoying. It may be questioned whether any one who has remained equally susceptible to both classes of pleasures, ever knowingly and calmly preferred the lower ..." (213 [II, 7]).

Mill says that on the question, which is the most worth having of two pleasures, or which of two modes of existence is the most grateful to the feelings, apart from its moral attributes and from their consequences, the judgment of those who are qualified by experience of both is the only procedure available. But he claims that there is no other tribunal for judgments of quantity between two pleasures or between two pains, or whether a particular pleasure is worth having at the cost of a particular pain (213 [II, 8]). In summary, the test of quality, and the rule for measuring it against quantity, is "the preference felt by those who, in their opportunities of experience, to which must be added their habits of self-consciousness and self-observation, are best furnished with the means of comparison" (214 [II, 10]).

It may be only of historical interest, but the wording of Mill's presentation of the distinction between pleasures on grounds of quality is so similar to that of Francis Hutcheson (1694–1746) that Mill must have been influenced by Hutcheson's account in *A System of Moral Philosophy* (1755). There Hutcheson distinguishes between pleasures of the same kind, whose values are "in a joint proportion of their intenseness and duration" and pleasures of different kinds, whose value includes that of "dignity."[2] Hutcheson says that we have a sense of dignity of some kinds of enjoyment that no intensity or duration of the lower kinds can equal, were they also as lasting as we could wish. Hutcheson asks whether all orders of beings are equally happy if each obtains the enjoyments respectively most relished. His answer is that at this rate the meanest brute may be as happy as the wisest human. Not all orders of beings have equal happiness even if each can gratify all the desires and senses it has. "What may make a brute as happy as that low order is capable of being, may be but despicable to an order endued with finer perceptive powers, and a nobler sort of desires. . . . The superior orders in this world probably experience all the sensations of the lower orders, and can judge of them. But the inferior do not experience the enjoyments of the superior. . . . Each one is

[2]   Francis Hutcheson, *A System of Moral Philosophy* (1755), bk. 1, sects. 475–6; selection reprinted in *British Moralists*, L. A. Selby-Bigge, ed., vol. 1, 421.

happy when its taste is gratified as it can then be. But we are immediately conscious that one gratification is more excellent than another, when we have experienced both."[3] Hutcheson says that the higher enjoyments, such as social affections, admiration of moral excellence, and pursuits of knowledge, do not impair sense or appetite. So persons who enjoy both in their due seasons are the best judges of all enjoyments.

Mill did not agree with Hutcheson's theory of a moral sense, and he probably would have given a different psychological account of pleasure and pain, but this passage from Hutcheson is too similar to Mill's to think that Mill did not reflect it in his own account.

There are several things to notice and to question about Mill's account.

One problem is Mill's apparent identification of the higher pleasures with the distinctively human and the "mental" pleasures, in contrast to animal appetites and "bodily" pleasures.[4] There are some examples in which the contrast is clear. Presumably nonhuman animals do not do mathematics, conjugate Greek, or even do philosophy, and these "mental pleasures" can be contrasted with such "bodily pleasures" as sunbathing; eating or drinking when hungry or thirsty; getting cool when hot or warm when cold; and sexual stimulation. But some higher animals are quite curious and seem to take pleasure in satisfying their curiosity. Some are quite good at solving problems and perhaps take pleasure in doing so. More obviously, many animals show social feelings toward other animals, or their human masters, and emotions such as fear of punishment and delight in reward. So the correlation between brutish pleasure

---

[3] Hutcheson, sec. 478; Selby-Bigge, 423.

[4] Rem B. Edwards in "Do Pleasures and Pains Differ Qualitatively?" *Journal of Value Inquiry* 9 (1975): 270–81, and in *Pleasures and Pains*, seeks to make sense of Mill's claim by maintaining that the "lower" pleasures are localized bodily pleasures and the "higher" pleasures are nonlocalized. I do not agree with this way of making the distinction or with this as an interpretation of Mill. Edwards does, however, agree with Mill in supporting qualitative differences in pleasures.

and bodily pleasures does not completely hold up. On the human side, the distinction between mental and bodily pleasures is difficult to maintain. Humans, when sunbathing, eating, drinking, and having sex, do not simply engage in appetite satiation; they involve their "higher faculties" while gratifying their "lower appetites." Many pleasures, such as appreciation of music and visual art, involve pleasure to the physical senses as well as intellectual and emotional response. So the distinction is one between poles of a spectrum with a great deal of overlap, rather than mutually exclusive categories. For the purpose of rebutting the criticism that hedonism is a doctrine worthy only of swine, the distinction is useful. It is not so useful, however, as a set of categories for hedonistic analysis, because it is important to remember that there is no precise correlation between mental and distinctively human pleasures or between bodily pleasures and animal appetites. And, whichever concept is applied to the two ends of the spectrum, there is a great overlap between the mental and the bodily and between the "animal" and the distinctively human.

Another important point is to note that Mill's position consists of three claims. One is that there are qualitative differences between pleasures as pleasures. Another is that some of these are superior to others on grounds of quality. A third is that the qualitatively superior are those that involve the distinctively human faculties. The first of these could be true while the second and third were false; that is, there could be qualitative differences between pleasures as pleasures, but these qualitative differences might not involve superiority and inferiority. The first and second could be true without the third; that is, there could be qualitative superiority and inferiority, but the superior might not be correlated with the distinctively human faculties.

The first of these claims is based on introspective psychology. Disputes resulting from introspection are notoriously difficult to settle, which is the reason that professional psychologists have turned to overt behavior to get testable results. But regarding the subject of qualitative versus quantitative differences in pleasures and pains, introspection is the only procedure that is available.

Let us consider some examples, to make more concrete Mill's abstract discussion. There are different experiences that are pleasurable. That is not in dispute. The question is whether the pleasure of these experiences is qualitatively different. Reflect upon how it feels to enjoy the beauty of a sunset, how it feels to doze off to sleep for an afternoon's nap, how it feels to a salesman to make a sale, how it feels to a ballplayer to score a goal, how it feels to a mathematics student to solve a mathematics problem. Each of these is a different kind of experience. Each state of consciousness has qualitatively different characteristics. But is there a qualitatively different pleasure in each, or at least in some in contrast to others?

One theory of pleasure, which can be called the "hedonic tone" theory, is that the pleasure feels the same in all cases, no matter how different the cases may be in other regards. When enjoying a sunset, one is having visual experiences that are different from any of the other cases. When scoring a goal, one is having kinesthetic experiences of bodily motion that do not characterize the others, and one is having beliefs of achievement that are different from the beliefs when one is solving a mathematics problem, and so on. The nonpleasure aspects of the experiences are of different kinds. But, according to this theory, the pleasure feels the same. It may come in intense brief surges, or it may come in mild continuous states, but it is the same feeling, differing only in intensity and duration. The sources of pleasure are diverse, and the accompanying feelings are diverse, but the pleasure feeling is identical in all cases, a distinct and qualitatively homogeneous feeling attached to the otherwise different experiences.

Another theory of pleasure, which can be called the "attitude"[5] theory, is the view that pleasure is not itself a

---

[5] For a recent discussion of these two theories, which I have labeled "hedonic tone" and "attitude" theories, without recognition of the third

sensation nor any other kind of feeling, but an attitude toward the feeling aspects of experience. If one likes a visual sensation (or other type of experience), manifested behaviorally by seeking its continuance and repetition, then it is a pleasurable one. Some would claim that when one tires of a certain type of experience, such as looking at a sunset or having one's back scratched, the visual or tactile sensations haven't changed, and there isn't a distinct pleasure sensation that has changed. It is just that one no longer likes it. The attitude theory can also be applied to pains, analyzing pains as experiences that one dislikes. It is also possible, however, that there is an asymmetry between pains and pleasures. The attitude theory may well be the best account of pleasures while pains are best regarded as sensations.

These two theories can be combined. It may be that some pleasures involve a sensation of pleasure while others involve only an attitude. Or it may be that some or all pleasures involve both. When the analysis is applied to pains, most philosophers would recognize that there are pain sensations and not merely attitudes of aversion to nonpain feelings. And the distinction between the two could be used to make Mill's distinction between qualitatively different pleasures: animal appetites involve bodily sensations[6] while the use of human faculties involves attitudes of liking and disliking based on a sense of dignity. But I do not think that this is Mill's position. For Mill, I think, there are qualitative differences among bodily pleasures as well as between bodily and mental pleasures, and these are

---

possibility discussed in the following text, see L. W. Sumner, "Welfare, Happiness, and Pleasure," *Utilitas* 4 (1992): 199–223, esp. 203–7.

[6] In *System of Logic* Mill says: "When sensations are called bodily feelings, it is only as being the class of feeling which are immediately occasioned by bodily states; whereas the other kinds of feelings, thoughts, for instance, or emotions, are immediately excited not by anything acting upon bodily organs, but by sensations, or by previous thoughts. This, however, is a distinction not in our feelings, but in the agency which produces our feelings: all of them when actually produced are states of mind" (*System of Logic*, 53).

differences in pleasure feelings, not just in preferences for the nonpleasure aspects of experience.

Consider two pleasurable tactile experiences, such as having one's back scratched and sunbathing on a warm summer day. Both are feelings on the surface of the skin, with different nonpleasure sensations. One involves a sensation of warmth; the other, a sensation of being scratched. I would claim, and I think it is Mill's position, that there are also different pleasure feelings, not a qualitatively identical pleasure feeling, whether sensate or attitudinal, arising from or attached to the tactile sensations. The phenomena may be even more pronounced regarding pains. There is a difference between a painful sting and a painful ache, which are introspectively different as pains, not just in the causes or accompanying nonpain sensations. On a recent trip to the dental hygienist, I was aware of the difference between the pain sensation when my gums were touched in a painful way and when a soft spot on a tooth was touched. One pain was "sharper" than the other. There were also differences in my dislike of the two, in that when there was pain in a tooth I feared that it would require more dental work, while the pain to the gums was judged to be just temporary. The pain to the tooth hurt less, but bothered me more. I would claim that there were pain sensations per se that could be distinguished from the dislike of them, and that there were differences both in sensations and in the attitude of dislike.

Likewise, there are differences in the felt pleasure or pain of emotional or intellectual pleasures or pains. The pleasure of hearing or telling a good joke is quite different from the pleasure of hearing that a friend has recovered from an illness, and the difference is not just the nonpleasure ingredients of the experience, nor the difference in intensity and duration of the attitude of liking the experience. Enjoying a good joke has its feeling of pleasure as well as any attitude toward the intellectual experience of cleverness that makes it funny, and it is different from the feeling of pleasure of relief at hearing of a friend's better health. I believe that Mill thinks that pleasures and pains have these phenomenologically different qualities in their pleasure aspect. And I think that attention to such examples shows that he is correct.

Mill says, in notes to his father's psychology, that the pleasure or pain may be detached from the sensation: "In the case of many pleasurable or painful sensations, it is open to question whether the pleasure or pain, especially the pleasure, is not something added to the sensation, and capable of being detached from it, rather than merely a particular aspect or quality of the sensation. It is often observable that a sensation is much less pleasurable at one time than at another, though to our consciousness it appears exactly the same sensation in all except the pleasure. This is emphatically the fact in cases of satiety, or of loss of taste for a sensation by loss of novelty. It is probable that in such cases the pleasure may depend on different nerves, or on a different action of the same nerves, from the remaining part of the sensation. However this may be, the pleasure or pain attending a sensation is . . . capable of being attended to by itself. . . . The pleasure or pain of the feeling are subjects of intellectual apprehension; they give the knowledge of themselves and of their varieties."[7]

It might be claimed that the attitude theory is the better account of what Mill has just described – that "a sensation is much less pleasurable at one time than at another, though to our consciousness it appears exactly the same sensation in all except the pleasure." The attitude theory would say that one has simply changed one's desire for the sensation; it isn't that the sensation at one time was accompanied by a distinct pleasure sensation and at another time it wasn't. But why has the desire changed? The account that Mill would give is that the accompanying pleasure sensation has changed. When Mill says that the pleasure or pain is subject to introspective apprehension, is one apprehending only one's likings and dislikings or

[7] James Mill, *Analysis of the Phenomena of the Human Mind*, 2nd ed., vol. 2, p. 185, n. 36.

is one apprehending also the pleasure or pain that one likes or dislikes?

Here we have something analogous to the question that Socrates asks of Euthyphro in Plato's dialogue of that name. When Euthyphro says that piety is what the gods love, Socrates asks if the gods love it because it is pious or is it pious because it is loved. The analogy here is that we can ask whether a pleasurable sensation is liked because it is pleasurable or is it pleasurable because it is liked. I think that Mill would say, and I think that he would be correct in saying, that it is liked because it is pleasurable. There is an introspectively available feeling, distinct from other aspects of an experience, that is the pleasure component, and that is liked. When the experience ceases to have that component, then I change my attitude toward it and become indifferent or averse to the experience.

Mill is an introspective psychologist, not a behaviorist. In his notes on his father's *Analysis of the Phenomena of the Human Mind*, John Stuart has no objection to his father's statement, concerning the difference between pleasures and pains and indifferent sensations, that a person knows the difference by feeling it.[8] There are behavioral results of pleasures and pains. James Mill says that an indifferent sensation is such that I care not whether it is long or short; a pain is such that I would put an end to it instantly if I could; a pleasure is of such a kind that I like it prolonged. But the state of being conscious of a pleasure, or of the revived idea of a pleasure, like other states, is known only by having it.[9] There were reasons that scientific psychology in the generation after Mill gave up introspection as the method of gaining evidence on which to build testable psychological theories. But introspection is Mill's method of identifying the ingredients of human consciousness, and it is indispensable.

When one introspects upon a state of pleasure or pain, one may find both a pleasure or pain sensation and also an attitude

[8] Ibid., 184.
[9] Ibid., 189.

toward the pleasure or pain. In the preceding example of pain at the dental hygienist's, the dull pain in a tooth bothered me more than the sharp pain in the gum. Being bothered is an attitude toward the pain, and it is a painful attitude. Thus the discomfort of the total experience was more painful because of my fear of further dental work than if I had not had such a thought. Some therapies for chronic pain involve attempts to get the patient to develop an attitude of acceptance toward the pain. The pain is still there, but the total state of consciousness is more bearable if the patient can have an attitude of acceptance. With an attitude of acceptance there is not the additional pain of feeling frustration or even panic by inability to relieve the pain.

If pleasures and pains differ qualitatively, as Mill claims, why do we call all of them "pleasures" and "pains"? Mill is not attempting to use these terms in accordance with the nuances of ordinary English usage. They are terms of introspective psychology to identify features of our consciousness. His claim is that when we introspect we find that pleasures and pains can be more or less intense, and that they can last for a longer or a shorter time, but that they also feel different from one another while still being enough alike to be called by the same name.

The pleasure of different experiences can differ qualitatively and still be pleasure because qualitatively different instances of pleasure can have "family resemblances" that make all of them instances of pleasure while still having differences. To think otherwise is to commit an "essentialist fallacy" of assuming that anything covered by one concept or referred to by one word must be identical in some respect. Although Mill had not read Ludwig Wittgenstein's analysis in terms of family resemblances[10] to explain linguistic common names, Mill's theory of classification included something like that notion.[11] With

[10] Ludwig Wittgenstein, *Philosophical Investigations*, translated by G. E. M. Anscombe, 3rd ed., 32e (sec. 67).

[11] Mill says that a name "not infrequently passes by successive links of resemblance from one object to another, until it becomes applied to things having nothing in common with the first things to which the

regard to simple feelings, Mill appeals to remembered resemblance to explain the signification of names: "the words sensation of white signify, that the sensation which I so denominate resembles other sensations which I remember to have had before, and to have called by that name."[12] Mill does not say that the qualitative resemblance must be identity, so long as it resembles other experiences of that sort more than it resembles any experiences of a different sort. In this example, it need not be a sensation of pure white; so long as it resembles other instances of white more than gray or yellow or some other color sensation, it counts as a sensation of white.

Applying this analysis to the term "pleasure," Mill would say that the word "pleasure" signifies that the sensation or feeling so denominated resembles other sensations or feelings that one remembers having had before and having called by that name. So long as it resembles other instances of pleasure more than some other state of consciousness, it counts as a sensation or feeling of pleasure. G. E. Moore explicitly holds a different theory of the meaning of common words in his critique of Mill.

---

name was given..." (*System of Logic*, 152). When this happens, Mill says that we have a muddle that needs clarification. But even when by successive extension there is not even gross resemblance, "still at every step in its progress we shall find such a resemblance" (Ibid., 153). In regard to most classes, it is possible to analyze the class into its defining characters. But he recognizes that a genus or family may include species that do not have all of the characters on which the classification is based. William Whewell had analyzed this as based on resemblance to a type, considered as eminently possessing the characters of the class. Mill objects to this as the standard analysis of classes, but recognizes that some classes are of this sort. "Our conception of the class continues to be grounded on the characters; and the class might be defined, those things which *either* possess that set of characters, *or* resemble the things that do so, more than they resemble anything else." He adds that this resemblance itself "is not, like resemblance between simple sensations, an ultimate fact" for the degree and nature of resemblance can be represented by an enumeration of characters (*System of Logic*, 721–2).

[12] *A System of Logic*, 136 (bk. 1, ch. 8, sec. 2).

He says, "'Pleasant' must, if words are to have any meaning at all, denote some one quality common to all the things that are pleasant; and, if so, then one thing can only be more pleasant than another, according as it has more or less of this one quality."[13] Moore's theory of the meaning of terms is unduly simplistic. As indicated in the examples discussed previously, pleasures do not have to be identical in their pleasure component to merit the name "pleasure."

I will not further try to defend Mill's theory of the signification of terms, but I do think that he is correct that there are differing kinds of pleasure referred to by the term, that these differ in their pleasure aspect, that this difference can be recognized introspectively, and thus that Mill is correct in saying that there are qualitative differences among pleasures.

Supposing that Mill is correct that there exist qualitative differences between pleasures, there remain the questions whether some of these are more valuable than others apart from quantity and, if so, whether the superiority in quality is correlated consistently with the use of "higher" faculties. These two questions can be discussed together, for Mill's method for testing and measuring qualitative superiority – the preference of competent judges – applies to both.

With regard to the first of the two questions, it is certainly the case that different people have different tastes, but it is not clear whether two people differ in their preference because the pleasure has qualitative superiority for one of them or because it has a quantitative superiority for that person. If another person enjoys playing video games and I don't, it may be that the other person gets intense and enduring enjoyment, while any enjoyment I get is mild and short-lived. It is difficult to know whether these interpersonal comparisons are based on quality or quantity.

---

[13] G. E. Moore, *Principia Ethica*, 77–8. For a critique of Moore, see Henry R. West, "Mill's Qualitative Hedonism," *Philosophy* 51 (1976): 101–5.

Within one individual's experience, there is preference change over time, in the short and the long run, but whether preference depends on quantity or quality is still difficult to discern. On one occasion I prefer the enjoyment of reading a book to the enjoyment of physical activity, and on another occasion I prefer the enjoyment of physical activity to that of reading. It is difficult to know whether the preference is one for quality or quantity. When I'm tired of reading and want exercise, I am no longer getting as much pleasure from the reading. Mill himself says that a happy life will consist of "many and *various* pleasures" (215 [II, 12], emphasis added), and that tranquility and excitement "are in mutual alliance, the prolongation of either being a preparation for, and exciting a wish for, the other" (215 [II, 13]). But these statements are compatible with the claim that the value of a pleasure is measured by its intensity and duration, if intensity is diminished by, or duration is cut short by, boredom or fatigue.

When a preference change is permanent, rather than temporary, and when there continues to be capacity for experience and enjoyment of both, it does seem more likely to be based on quality. If I at one time enjoyed reading comics and am still able to enjoy them when I read them but find the sports news or the editorials more interesting, that may be a sign that the quality of pleasure that I get from the comics is not now as pleasurable as the quality of pleasure that I get from following a sports team or passing judgment on the soundness of a political opinion. Part of the problem in deciding whether a preference is based on quality or quantity is that we may use quantitative language to describe qualitative preference. I may say that I enjoy the sports section more than the comics, which sounds like a quantitative judgment, when what I mean is that I prefer the kind of pleasure that I get from the sports section. But another complication, which will be discussed in the following text, is that there may be "second-order" pleasures (or pains), based on the kind of "first-order" pleasure being enjoyed. I may associate with other sports fans rather than comic strip readers and enjoy being knowledgeable about sports. Or I may enjoy the self-image of myself as someone who keeps up with political events and opinions in preference to the self-image of someone who indulges in mere amusement. This complexity of experience is important in assessing Mill's theory of the superiority of pleasures employing our higher faculties.

Another difficulty in assessing the qualitative superiority of pleasures is that intrinsic value is difficult to separate from instrumental and moral value. Mill's competent judges are to base the judgment of the qualitative superiority of a pleasure on it "merely as a pleasure," irrespective of any feeling of moral obligation to prefer it and independent of its consequences. This is a difficult requirement. For example, if one enjoys exercising for health, the pleasure is partially dependent upon the belief that it will be healthful. The activity is regarded as desirable both on account of the expected consequences and from the pleasure of the activity; so the total pleasure felt in exercising is partially dependent upon belief in the expected consequences. The value of the expected consequences can be separated from the intrinsic value of the pleasure of the activity in theory, but it is difficult in practice to separate pleasure felt from the value of the one from pleasure felt due to the value of the other. This is especially true of pleasures that are the result of psychological conditioning. Thus, in addition to having opportunities of experience and habits of self-consciousness and self-observation, Mill's competent judges must be good at analyzing the desirability of an activity or experience into its component values, separating the instrumental from the intrinsic and feelings of moral obligation from feelings of nonmoral gratification.

Turning to the question of the superiority of the distinctively human pleasures, which he calls the "higher" pleasures, Mill's position and his arguments for it are extremely ambiguous. Does Mill think that on every occasion in which there is a choice between a qualitatively higher pleasure and a qualitatively lower pleasure, a competent judge would prefer the higher pleasure? This would be a very implausible theory. For one thing, each kind of pleasure varies in magnitude. It would be absurd to think that the slightest distinctively human pleasure is found more gratifying to the feelings than the greatest pleasure from animal appetite.[14] There is textual evidence against this interpretation, for Mill says that "the test of quality, and the rule for measuring it against quantity" (214 [II, 10]) is the preference of competent judges, implying that at least in some cases quantity may outweigh quality. In any case, because it is absurd to think that the slightest superiority in quality would outweigh any amount of quantity of an alternative on every occasion, let us not attribute that view to Mill.[15]

In arguing for the superiority of the distinctively human pleasures, Mill first seems to be asking whether one would choose a "higher" pleasure on every occasion of choice. But the argument rests on a different question: whether one would be willing to resign it for any quantity of the other, whether one prefers a "manner of existence" that employs the higher faculties or would be willing to sink into a lower "grade of existence." This is a quite different issue. A person may prefer sunbathing to listening to music on some occasions and not on others. On some occasions, sunbathing may be a more pleasurable activity, but not on others. But if asked which one would a person be more willing to "resign" or do without for

[14] This seems to be the view that Jonathan Riley ascribes to Mill. He treats a difference in quality as an infinite difference in quantity. Jonathan Riley, "On Quantities and Qualities of Pleasure," *Utilitas* 5 (1993): 291–300. Riley's position is criticized by Geoffrey Scarre, "Donner and Riley on Qualitative Hedonism," *Utilitas* 9 (1997): 355–60, but Scarre does not interpret Mill as I do. Riley replies to Scarre in Jonathan Riley, "Is Qualitative Hedonism Inconsistent?" *Utilitas* 11 (1999): 347–58.

[15] Leslie Stephen correctly criticizes Mill on this point, if we were to interpret Mill in that way. "It is not true absolutely that 'intellectual' pleasures are simply 'better' than sensual. Each is better in certain circumstances. There are times when even a saint prefers a glass of water to religious musings." *The English Utilitarians*, vol. 3, 305. He also said that Mill claimed an imaginary consensus of all better minds. Stephen is more relativistic, saying that "value" must depend upon the person as well as the thing.

the remainder of one's life, one might well prefer to do without the enjoyment of sunbathing than to do without the enjoyment of music, even if on some occasions one prefers sunbathing.

When asking what one would prefer to do without, a great deal depends upon the scope of the question. To modify the preceding example, one could be asked about a preference to do without the enjoyment of music altogether or to do without the enjoyment of classical music, which is a question of narrower scope. One could be asked about a preference to do without the enjoyment of sunbathing, or nude sunbathing, or sunbathing on sand beaches. One could be asked about a preference to do without the enjoyment derived from the sense of sound, which is more general than music, or to do without the sense of warmth, which is more general than sunbathing.

When the question is what one would be willing to "resign," Mill's question can be reversed and put concerning the "bodily" pleasures with great force. Would you be willing to resign all the pleasures of eating, drinking, sexual gratification, and physical exercise and physical comfort for any amount of the pleasures of the intellect? In contemplating what is lost by a person who is paralyzed or has lost sight or hearing, some of the losses are instrumental. The person cannot go some places without assistance or cannot participate as freely in intellectual or social or aesthetic activities that require use of limbs or sight or hearing. But some of the loss is animal appetite for sensory stimulation. The loss of that is an impoverishment of enjoyment. A competent judge could easily say that no quantity of intellectual or emotional or imaginative pleasure could fully compensate for the loss. It is not, as with the thought experiment of being transformed into a beast or a fool or an evil person, the loss of one's distinctive personality. But it is a loss for which there may be no quantity of pleasure from other sources that would make it a preference.

Mill himself was probably an incompetent judge of the value of lower pleasures. According to his autobiography, in his childhood no holidays were allowed, lest the habit of work should

be broken and a taste for idleness acquired. He was never allowed to play with other children. He says that he could do no
feats of skill or physical strength and remained inexpert in anything requiring manual dexterity; the animal need of physical
activity was satisfied by walking and his "amusements, which
were mostly solitary, were in general of a quiet, if not a bookish
turn. . . ."[16] This is not the picture of someone who knows both
sides of the question.

My conclusion is that it is not a fair criterion of the superiority of pleasures one by one to ask what one would be willing to
resign or do without. The question may be useful in answering
the objection that hedonism is a doctrine worthy only of swine,
but it does not establish that distinctively human pleasures are
consistently preferred to animal appetite on grounds of quality.
There also are apparent counterexamples. Playing with children is an activity that gives humans a great deal of pleasure,
and I would judge that it is a qualitatively superior pleasure.
But it is not one that necessarily employs the higher faculties.
Animals play with their offspring and other young animals with
apparent enjoyment. I have seen a puppy come into the yard
of an old dog and rouse the old dog to play, with apparently
greater enjoyment than the old dog had experienced recently. I
have seen similar behavior among mature humans in response
to a child. This seems to be an enjoyment that humans share
with animals; that does not involve great intellect, imagination,
emotion, or moral sentiment, but that is sometimes preferred
by presumably competent judges.[17]

I believe that the real key to understanding Mill's position
is that the human psyche is complex. We not only have enjoyments and sufferings. We take pleasure or pain in what we
enjoy or suffer. At the same time that we are enjoying a pleasure such as sunbathing, we are also feeling pleasure or pain
at the thought that we are getting a tan or risking skin cancer;

[16] John Stuart Mill, *Autobiography*, in *Autobiography and Literary Essays*, 39.
[17] Daniel Holbrook, *Qualitative Utilitarianism*, 104.

that we are relaxing on vacation or wasting time that might be used more productively; that we are fit for our age and look good or that we are flabby and look out of shape; and so on. At the same time that we are enjoying the acquisition of knowledge by studying the philosophy of John Stuart Mill, we are feeling pleasure or pain at the thought that we are learning from one of the great intellects of all time or that we are studying a dead, white, European male whose philosophy has been studied again and again and may not have anything new to say in the twenty-first century; that we are exercising our minds or that we are in an ivory tower instead of addressing the great needs of world hunger and overpopulation; that we are working hard or that we could be sunbathing; and so on. Thus the self-image that goes with any pleasure or pain can be the source of a "second-order" pleasure or pain. I think that this is the role of Mill's sense of dignity. If one has a self-image that gives pleasure when one is engaged in exercise of the higher faculties, then, in addition to the "first-order" pleasure of exercising the mind, of aesthetic appreciation, of social feelings or moral sentiment, there is the "second-order" pleasure of thinking of oneself as having those thoughts or feelings. And if one is degrading oneself through overindulgence in "first-order" pleasures of eating, drinking, or sexual promiscuity, then there is "second-order" pain at the thought that one is doing so. When first- and second-order pleasures and pains are combined in a total experience, the quality (and the quantity) of the pleasure of the total experience is different from consideration of the quality (and quantity) of the first-order pleasure alone.

Mill's own psychological views support this analysis. In his notes to his father's psychology, he says that "... one idea seldom, perhaps never, entirely fills and engrosses the mind. We have almost always a considerable number of ideas in the mind at once...."[18] Mill also discusses situations where one

---

[18] James Mill, *Analysis of the Phenomena of the Human Mind*, 2nd ed., vol. 2, p. 69, n. 18.

desires to have a different set of desires from those that one has, for example where one wishes that one had stronger motives for a particular end. "The present [case that he is discussing] is one of the complex cases, in which we desire a different state of our own desires. By supposition we do not care enough for the immediate end. . . . But we are dissatisfied with this infirmity of our desires: we wish that we cared more for the end: we think that it would be better for us if this particular end, or our ends generally, had greater command over our thoughts and actions than they have."[19]

The foregoing explains, I think, another reason why the question of what one would "resign" in the way of pleasures is different from the question of which of two pleasures is superior when taken in isolation. One can engage in pleasures of eating without thereby becoming a swinish glutton. One can engage in pleasures of drinking without thereby becoming an alcoholic wino. The degrading self-image is not triggered by a temperate indulgence in pleasures of animal appetite, and therefore does not evoke second-order pains, whereas the idea of resigning all human pleasures for a beastly existence does do so. The self-image of a life including both sensate and "higher" pleasures, unless one has been conditioned by a puritanical or ascetic upbringing, is that of a person living a full rich life.

In summary, Mill thinks that an introspective analysis of pleasures and pains leads to the conclusion that pleasures and pains differ as pleasures and pains in their hedonically felt qualitative differences as well as in their intensity and duration. An explanation of this is that pleasures and pains have "family resemblances" that make them all appropriately classified as pleasures and pains, rather than something else, without their all being qualitatively identical.

Taste for one qualitatively different pleasure rather than another may in many cases depend upon its giving quantitatively

[19] Ibid., n. 66, beginning on p. 372; the quotation is from p. 375.

greater pleasure on that occasion, rather than on its qualitative superiority, but Mill is right that there may also be preference for one pleasure rather than another based on qualitative superiority. The fact that one sometimes prefers one kind of pleasure to another on qualitative grounds, however, does not imply that one always prefers that kind of pleasure on all occasions. And whether one would do so is not adequately answered by asking, as Mill does, whether one would choose a life without the superior pleasure for any quantity of the inferior. One gets different answers when one asks whether one would always prefer a certain kind of pleasure to another kind on every occasion and when one asks whether one would be willing to resign a certain kind of pleasure for any quantity of the other. The richest hedonic life in most cases consists of pleasures of various kinds.

Mill is also wrong to think that qualitative superiority is consistently correlated with the employment of higher distinctively human faculties, but he is correct that a sense of dignity influences the experience of pleasures. When pleasures are regarded as part of a pattern of life, a "manner of existence" that is in accord with or contrary to one's desired self-image, the complex experience, combining first-order pleasure or pain and second-order pleasure or pain, has a quality different from the first-order pleasure or pain alone and may make a difference in the preference of a competent judge regarding the hedonic desirability of that experience.

I turn now to some of Mill's critics whose charges I think can be answered, assuming the correctness of the interpretation or reconstruction that I have given so far.

One of the earliest and most persistent criticisms of Mill's distinction, both from those sympathetic to utilitarianism and from those hostile to it, is that in introducing qualitative differences in pleasures Mill is deserting his hedonism.[20] J. B.

---

[20] Ernest Albee, in *A History of English Utilitarianism*, 251–2, says of the qualitative-quantitative distinction: " ... nothing in Mill's ethical writings has been so thoroughly discussed.... [T]here is perfect agreement

Scheewind, in his survey of early criticisms of Mill's *Utilitarianism*, cites reviewers who made this claim when the essay first appeared.[21] The charge is illustrated in the only full-length book on Mill's utilitarianism published in the nineteenth century and less than a decade after the publication of *Utilitarianism*. In it John Grote contrasted the "old" with the "new" utilitarianism. He presents a dilemma. Either "quality" is "quantity" under a different name, or it is a nonhedonistic value. He claimed that Mill has deserted Bentham's rigor: "... quality is quantity estimated in a different manner, namely, not by definite analysis, which was Bentham's method, but by human experience and testimony without such analysis."[22] On the other hand, if quality is really different, the "worthiness" of pleasures is not simply that of being pleased or of enjoyment, but on the basis of considerations of right, duty, virtue. "If you determine your preferableness only by actual experience, you have but quantity after all.... [B]ut that it is of a different kind, or that its quality is really different, we must be conscious of something of a reason why it is greater than the other: and here it is that we have the consideration alien to utilitarianism, the appeal from sense to reason...."[23] Henry Sidgwick, sympathetic with utilitarianism, says, "The distinctions of quality that Mill and others urge may still be admitted as grounds of preference, but only in so far as they can be resolved into distinctions

at the present day among competent critics, of whatever ethical convictions, as to the inconsistency of this view with his general hedonistic position...."

21 J. B. Schneewind, "Concerning Some Criticisms of Mill's *Utilitarianism*, 1861–76," in *James and John Stuart Mill: Papers of the Centenary Conference*, John M. Robson and Michael Laine, eds., 35–54, citations from pp. 46–7.
22 John Grote, *An Examination of the Utilitarian Philosophy*, edited by Joseph Bickersteth Mayor, 47. Chapter 3 is "On Quality of Pleasure," 45–57. Posing such a dilemma is common among critics, for example, W. R. Sorley, *The Ethics of Naturalism*, 2nd ed., 60–3.
23 Grote, 51–2.

of quantity."[24] Otherwise, Sidgwick asserts, "... when one kind of pleasure is judged to be qualitatively superior to another, although less pleasant, it is not really the feeling itself that is preferred, but something in the mental or physical conditions or relations under which it arises...."[25] F. H. Bradley, hostile to utilitarianism, argues a theme common to many critics, that qualitative distinctions make it impossible to make a judgment between different pleasures: "Given a certain small quantity of higher pleasure in collision with a certain large quantity of lower, how do you decide between them? To work the sum you must reduce the data to the same denomination. You must go to quantity or to nothing; you decline to go to quantity, and hence you can not get any result.... Higher, then, as we saw above, has no meaning at all, unless we go to something outside pleasure...."[26] Ernest Albee says that Mill's inconsistency may be expressed succinctly: "If all good things are good in proportion as they bring pleasure to oneself or others, one cannot add to this statement that pleasure itself, the assumed criterion, is more or less desirable in terms of something else (e.g., human dignity) which is not pleasure."[27]

In these critiques of Mill, as in so many since then, the basic assumption is made that pleasure is a kind of sensation that feels the same, no matter its source; so only the intensity and duration of this one kind of sensation can be grounds for preference. This begs the question against Mill. If Mill is correct that there really are introspectively different feelings that are all varieties of pleasure and not of something else, then it is possible for these to be compared on the basis of their felt differences and for some to be preferable to others. Again, the pleasure is not qualitatively superior because it is preferred. It is preferred because

---

[24] Henry Sidgwick, *Methods of Ethics*, 121. See also Henry Sidgwick, *Outlines of the History of Ethics*, 247.

[25] Sidgwick, *Methods of Ethics*, 128.

[26] F. H. Bradley, *Ethical Studies*, 119. This view is echoed more recently, for example, in H. J. McCloskey, *John Stuart Mill: A Critical Study*, 66–8.

[27] Albee, 252.

it is qualitatively different, and this difference is found to be more desirable. Furthermore, this difference is not an appeal from sense to reason nor an appeal to nonhedonic values such as nobility.

T. H. Green comes close to my analysis of Mill but rejects it. He says that everyone recognizes that pleasures admit of distinction in quality according to the conditions under which they arise, for example, the satisfaction of bodily wants in contrast to pleasures of sight and hearing. And he says that the "sense of dignity" may be some special pleasure. But then, he says, there is additional quantity, analyzable on Benthamite terms.[28] My reply is that the pleasure or pain arising from a sense of dignity need not be a mere quantitative addition. It may also be a qualitatively distinct pleasure, just as the satisfaction of bodily wants are contrasted with the pleasures of sight and hearing, and it may be found preferable for that qualitatively distinct feeling.

James Seth, in an article published in 1908, says of the qualitative/quantitative distinction that a difference in degree "as is often the case in psychology" becomes a real difference in kind, a difference in degree so great as to assume the character of incommensurability.[29] My interpretation of Mill does not develop qualitative differences from extreme quantitative differences, and it does not involve incommensurability. Qualitative differences in pleasures and pains are commensurable through felt preference, based on one's own or others' experience of the qualitatively different pleasures or pains. Mill's

[28] T. H. Green, *Prolegomena to Ethics*, 169–74.
[29] James Seth, "The Alleged Fallacies in Mill's 'Utilitarianism,'" *Philosophical Review* 17 (1908): 488. Jonathan Riley's interpretation of qualitatively different pleasures as infinite quantitatively different pleasures does not lead to incommensurability, for any higher pleasure always has more value than a lower pleasure, and pleasures of a single quality can be compared on ordinary quantitative grounds. Riley, "On Quantities and Qualities of Pleasure," 291–2. I claim that there is commensurability through the evidence of competent preference without the assertion that there is a reduction to quantity and certainly not a reduction to a distinction of infinite quantity.

ambiguous question of what one would do without in exchange for any quantity of the "lower" pleasures should not be taken to imply that they are incommensurable.

The effort to interpret difference in quality as a difference in quantity so great as to create a qualitatively different psychological effect has been echoed by other writers. Ernest Sosa refers to Mill's remark in Chapter 5 of *Utilitarianism* when discussing the difference between the sentiment of justice and the sentiment of the more common cases of utility "that the difference in degree (as is often the case in psychology) becomes a real difference in kind" (251 [V, 25]). Sosa applies this to the distinction between the lower and the higher pleasures.[30] My interpretation, again, is that this is not the case with higher and lower pleasures. It is not that intellectual pleasures are so intense that they become qualitatively different. They may be mild in intensity but still different in kind.

Mill's appeal to the qualitative differences in pleasures has been widely discussed in philosophical periodicals as well as in every book dealing with Mill's ethics. I have referred to only a sample of the commentary. In my interpretation, Mill is correct to analyze pleasures and pains as differing qualitatively as well as quantitatively, and the fact that humans are capable of qualitatively different kinds of pleasures than nonhumans is an answer to the charge that hedonism is a doctrine worthy only of swine. But I have rejected Mill's claim that distinctively human pleasures are consistently preferred by those who are experienced in both human pleasures and the pleasures of animal appetite. The latter are also important ingredients of a rich life for a rational animal.

---

[30] Ernest Sosa, "Mill's *Utilitarianism*" in *Mill's* Utilitarianism: *Text and Criticism*, James M. Smith and Ernest Sosa, eds., 154–72. Pages 161–72 deal with quantity versus quality. See also Rex Martin, "A Defence of Mill's Qualitative Hedonism," *Philosophy* 47 (1972): 140–51, for a critique of Sosa's interpretation. Wendy Donner has an extended discussion and critique of Sosa in Wendy Donner, *The Liberal Self*, 46–9.

4

WAS MILL AN ACT- OR RULE-UTILITARIAN?

IN the twentieth century a distinction has been made between forms of utilitarianism in which the rightness or wrongness of actions is a matter of the consequences of each particular action, case by case, and forms of utilitarianism in which the rightness or wrongness of actions is a matter of whether they are in accord with or in violation of a rule, with the rule justified by the consequences of its acceptance or general practice in the society. Richard Brandt, in his book *Ethical Theory*,[1] published in 1959, introduced the terms "act-utilitarianism" and "rule-utilitarianism" to mark the distinction.[2] These terms have since come to be used generically to cover a family of alternative theories.

Perhaps the most important division in types of rule-utilitarian theories is between "utilitarian generalization" and a "moral code" rule-utilitarianism, based on recognized rules enforced by sanctions. Utilitarian generalization starts with the particular case and generates rules by asking, "What would happen if everyone did the same?" requiring that an agent act in accord with what would have best consequences as a general practice rather than what would have best consequences in the individual case.[3] Moral code theories can be divided into those

[1]   Richard B. Brandt, *Ethical Theory*, ch. 15.
[2]   Since then the distinction between act and rule theories has also been applied to include nonhedonistic consequentialist theories using the terms "act-consequentialism" and "rule-consequentialism."
[3]   One of the problems for utilitarian generalization is the relevant description of the act to be generalized. David Lyons has argued that on one criterion of relevance, utilitarian generalization would permit

that take only existing moral codes into account and those that propose that one act in accordance with an ideal moral code.

In a letter to John Venn, Mill rejects utilitarian generalization *in theory*: "I agree with you that the right way of testing actions by their consequences is to test them by the natural consequences of the particular action, and not by those which would follow if every one did the same. But for the most part, the consideration of what would happen if every one did the same, is the only means we have of discovering the tendency of the act in the particular case."[4] Although I think that Mill sometimes wants the tendency of a particular act in particular circumstances to be calculated, this does not make him an exclusive "act-utilitarian," as will be seen in the following discussion.

Even before Brandt's introduction of the terminology that has come into general use, the distinction between the two possible theories had been recognized and discussed,[5] and

and require the same acts as act-utilitarianism. See David Lyons, *Forms and Limits of Utilitarianism*, ch 3. Lyons's thesis depends upon a controversial notion of "contributory causation." See Henry Robison West, "Act-Utilitarianism and Rule-Utilitarianism," ch. 8; Donald Regan, *Utilitarianism and Co-operation*, 13ff.

4   Letter to John Venn, April 14, 1872, *The Later Letters of John Stuart Mill 1849–1873*, 1881. Roger Crisp thinks that this letter shows that Mill is an act-utilitarian. See Roger Crisp, *Routledge Philosophy Guidebook to Mill on Utilitarianism*, 117. But that Mill does not hold the position of utilitarianism generalization does not make him an act-utilitarian. There are other options.

5   Some of the most frequently cited discussions are R. F. Harrod, "Utilitarianism Revised," *Mind* 45 (1936): 137–56; S. E. Toulmin, *An Examination of the Place of Reason in Ethics*, ch. 11; Jonathan Harrison, "Utilitarianism, Universalisation, and Our Duty to Be Just," *Proceedings of the Aristotelian Society* N. S. 53 (1952–3): 105–34; P. H. Nowell-Smith, *Ethics*, ch. 15 and 16; A. K. Stout, "But Suppose Everyone Did the Same," *Australasian Journal of Philosophy* 32 (1954): 1–29; John Rawls, "Two Concepts of Rules," *The Philosophical Review* 64 (1955): 3–32; J. J. C. Smart, "Extreme and Restricted Utilitarianism," *Philosophical Quarterly* 4 (1956): 344–54; H. J. McCloskey, "An Examination of Restricted Utilitarianism," *The Philosophical Review* 66 (1957): 466–85.

J. O. Urmson argued for the rule-utilitarian interpretation of Mill,[6] an interpretation that was challenged with qualifications but not refuted by J. D. Mabbott.[7] Since then there have been a number of studies, some of which will be discussed in the following text, to point out that Mill's system is complex, incorporating not only rules but also rights and supererogation within the utilitarian framework.[8]

[6] J. O. Urmson, "The Interpretation of the Philosophy of J. S. Mill," *Philosophical Quarterly* 3 (1953): 33–40.

[7] J. D. Mabbott, "Interpretations of Mill's *Utilitarianism*," *Philosophical Quarterly* 6 (1956): 115–20. See also John M. Baker, "Utilitarianism and Secondary Principles," *Philosophical Quarterly* 21 (1971): 69–71; Brian Cupples, "A Defence of the Received Interpretation of J. S. Mill," *Australasian Journal of Philosophy* 50 (1972): 131–7; D. G. Brown, "Mill's Act-Utilitarianism," *Philosophical Quarterly* 24 (1974): 67–8; T. S. Chamblin and A. D. M. Walker, "Tendencies, Frequencies and Classical Utilitarianism," *Analysis* 35 (1974): 8–12; Jonathan Harrison, "The Expedient, the Right and the Just in Mill's *Utilitarianism*," *Canadian Journal of Philosophy*, supp. vol. 1 (1974): 93–107.

[8] The most extended study is Fred R. Berger, *Happiness, Justice, and Freedom: The Moral and Political Philosophy of John Stuart Mill*, ch. 3, "The Greatest Happiness Principle and Moral Rules." This chapter cites nearly all of the relevant passages in Mill for whether he was an act-utilitarian or a rule-utilitarian, concluding that he held a "strategic" conception of rules as a means for achieving an act-utilitarian result. My interpretation differs from this. Other important works on the topic are D. G. Brown, "What Is Mill's Principle of Utility?" *Canadian Journal of Philosophy* 3 (1972): 133–58; D. G. Brown, "Mill's Act-Utilitarianism"; Roger Hancock, "Mill, Saints and Heroes," *Mill News Letter* 10 (1975): 13–15; David Lyons, "Mill's Theory of Morality," *Nous* 10 (1976): 101–20, reprinted in David Lyons, *Rights, Welfare, and Mill's Moral Theory*, 47–65; David Lyons, "Human Rights and the General Welfare," *Philosophy and Public Affairs* 6 (1976–7): 113–29; David Lyons, "Mill's Theory of Justice," in *Values and Morals: Essays in Honor of William Frankena, Charles Stevenson, and Richard Brandt*, A. I. Goldman and J. Kim, eds., 1–20, reprinted in *Rights, Welfare, and Mill's Moral Theory*, 67–88; David Lyons, "Benevolence and Justice in Mill," in *The Limits of Utilitarianism*, Harlan B. Miller and William H. Williams, eds., 42–70, reprinted in *Rights, Welfare, and Mill's Moral Theory*, 109–46; D. P. Dryer, "Justice, Liberty and the Principle of Utility in Mill," in *New Essays on John Stuart Mill and Utilitarianism*, 63–73; David Copp, "The Iterated-Utilitarianism of

Was Mill an Act- or Rule-Utilitarian?

In this chapter I discuss the evidence bearing on whether Mill is an act-utilitarian or a rule-utilitarian, and I conclude that he is neither, if these are interpreted as exclusive and complete utilitarian moral theories. On the other hand, if these are interpreted as forms of utilitarian moral reasoning, he is both and much more. In some areas of morality, he wants rule-utilitarian criteria to be employed, thinking of morality as parallel to legality but with less formal sanctions. In other areas, he wants act-utilitarian criteria to be employed, and there are degrees of flexibility between the two. It is impossible to impose a unified act theory or a unified rule theory on Mill. For the promotion of greatest happiness, different procedures are appropriate for different areas of morality, for example, whether sanctions should be by law or by public opinion or by conscience. In some areas, habit formation and "character development" are needed. In some areas rules are needed; in others, less formal "precepts"; and in others the good judgment of the agent regarding the particular situation. For some conduct praise is appropriate but blame inappropriate. Unusual circumstances and even relevantly unique circumstances must be taken into account. I claim that all of this is consistent with the ultimate goal of promoting greatest happiness. Moral science is to determine which kinds of criteria are appropriate for what area of conduct. This interpretation is in general agreement with Lyons and Sumner, cited in the preceding footnote. I provide more detailed analysis and documentation from own Mill's writings.

A distinction can be made between the criteria for right action and the criteria for making correct decisions. These could differ.

J. S. Mill," in *New Essays on John Stuart Mill and Utilitarianism*, 75–98; L. W. Sumner, "The Good and the Right," in *New Essays on John Stuart Mill and Utilitarianism*, 99–114; F. R. Berger, "John Stuart Mill on Justice and Fairness," in *New Essays on John Stuart Mill and Utilitarianism*, 115–36; Gerald F. Gaus, "Mill's Theory of Moral Rules," *Australasian Journal of Philosophy* 58 (1980): 265–79; Rem B. Edwards, "The Principle of Utility and Mill's Minimizing Utilitarianism," *Journal of Value Inquiry* 20 (1986): 125–36.

It could be that the act-utilitarian formula works for identifying right actions but that more flexible procedures are more likely to produce those right actions identified by the act-utilitarian formula. Thus it could be that maximizing utility in each particular case is the criterion of right action but that this right action is more likely to be achieved by acting in accordance with justified rules rather than by attempting to calculate the utility of the particular action. Thus, Mill could be interpreted as an act-utilitarian in so far as the criterion of right action is concerned, but he could be seen as holding a "multilevel" view for decision procedures that agents should adopt.[9] My interpretation is not just that Mill has a multilevel view for decision making. I shall interpret him as having a multilevel view for right action as well.

In his essay Mill's first formulation of the creed of utilitarianism is: "that actions are right in proportion as they tend to promote happiness, wrong as they tend to produce the reverse of happiness."[10] This initial formulation should not be taken out of context as Mill's definitive statement of his utilitarian doctrine. Mill commonly states a thesis in a simple formula and then adds complications.[11]

---

[9] This is the view of Roger Crisp, *Routledge Philosophy Guidebook to Mill on Utilitarianism*, 113.

[10] John Stuart Mill, *Utilitarianism*, 210 (ch. 2, par. 2). Citations to this work will be in parentheses in the text.

[11] In *On Liberty*, Mill states in Chapter 1 that the object of the essay is to assert "one very simple principle," that "the only purpose for which power can be rightfully exercised over any member of a civilized community, against his [or her] will, is to prevent harm to others." But by the time that Mill reaches Chapter 4 of *On Liberty*, he has introduced complications and qualifications: it is not simply to prevent harm to others for which power can rightfully be exercised. There is a distinction between interests that ought to be considered rights and other interests that may be prejudicially affected. It is only "certain" interests, which ought to be considered as rights, that are to be protected by society "at all costs"; when conduct harms other interests, it is a question of whether the general welfare will or will not be promoted by interfering with it. Furthermore, those who receive the protection of

At first sight the utilitarian formula quoted previously looks like an act-utilitarian formula. It looks as if, in deciding what is morally right, one takes a particular action; calculates the tendency it has to promote happiness and its tendency to produce the reverse of happiness; subtracts the smaller tendency from the larger tendency and thus gets the preponderant "proportion" as the net tendency, then compares this with a similar calculation for all alternative actions, and so arrives at what is right or wrong in the situation. One may not be able to carry out the calculation before each action, but to the extent that one has the information that the calculation would give, one has the information that determines right or wrong action. This is approximately the way that Bentham says that one should proceed with his calculus.[12]

Even this formula, however, rules out one form of act-utilitarianism. One form of act-utilitarianism can be stated as the theory that an act is right if its consequences would *in fact* be as good as any alternative act, even if the agent could not know that. J. J. C. Smart makes the distinction with the following terminology: "Let us use the word 'rational' as a term of commendation for that action which is, on the evidence available to the agent, *likely* to produce the best results, and to reserve the word 'right' as a term of commendation for the action which does *in fact* produce the best results."[13] Utilitarianism formulated this way has been labeled "actual consequence utilitarianism."[14]

society owe a return for the benefit; so society is justified in enforcing their fair share of the burdens. These complications are not inconsistent with the initial statement in Chapter 1 of *On Liberty*, but they show that Mill has a tendency first to state his thesis in an overly simple formula and then to add qualifications and complications in later chapters. He does this in *Utilitarianism*.

12 Jeremy Bentham, *An Introduction to the Principles of Morals and Legislation*, 40 (ch. 4, especially pars. 6 and 7).

13 J. J. C. Smart, "An Outline of a System of Utilitarian Ethics," 46–7.

14 See, for example, Marcus G. Singer, "Actual Consequence Utilitarianism," *Mind* 86 (1977), 67–77. There is a considerable literature debating this formulation. Some contributions are Bart Gruzalski,

Mill, however, is not an actual consequence act-utilitarian. He uses the word "tendency" in his formulation to point to the fact that one does not have complete foresight, but only a degree of foreseeability, of an action's consequences.[15] In his early essay on "Sedgwick's Discourse," he made a distinction between the accidental and the natural consequences of an action. In reply to the objection that for a utilitarian it is necessary to foresee all the consequences of each individual action, Mill writes, "Some of the consequences of an action are accidental; others are its natural result, according to the known laws of the universe. The former, for the most part, cannot be foreseen; but the whole course of human life is founded on the fact that the latter can."[16] Thus, if Mill is an act-utilitarian, he is not an actual consequence act-utilitarian. His defense of the ability to foresee the consequences of individual actions, even if only imperfectly, does, however, support the act-utilitarian interpretation of Mill.

"Foreseeable Consequence Utilitarianism," *Australasian Journal of Philosophy* 59 (1981): 163–76; Brian Ellis, "Retrospective and Prospective Utilitarianism," *Nous* 15 (1981): 325–39; Peter Galle, "Gruzalski and Ellis on Utilitarianism," *Australasian Journal of Philosophy* 59 (1981): 332–7; Marcus Singer, "Incoherence, Inconsistency and Moral Theory: More on Actual Consequence Utilitarianism," *The Southern Journal of Philosophy* 20 (1982): 375–91; Mark Strasser, "Actual versus Probable Utilitarianism," *The Southern Journal of Philosophy* 27 (1989): 585–97.

[15] For use of the term "tendency," see John Stuart Mill, *A System of Logic*, 444–5, 869, and 898. Mill seems to use the term to refer to a set of cause-effect relations that may be counteracted by other cause-effect relations in operation in given circumstances. This gives us less than complete foresight, but enough for guidance: " . . . we must remember that a degree of knowledge far short of the power of actual prediction, is often of much practical value. There may be great power of influencing phenomena, with a very imperfect knowledge of the causes by which they are in any given instance determined. It is enough that we know that certain means have a *tendency* to produce a given effect, and others have a tendency to frustrate it" (*System of Logic*, 869 [bk. 6, ch. 5, sec. 4]).

[16] John Stuart Mill, "Sedgwick's Discourse," 63.

A sort of act-utilitarian interpretation is supported by a number of other things that Mill says. In answer to the objection that there is not time, previous to action, for calculating and weighing the effects of any line of conduct on the general happiness, he answers that during the whole past duration of the human species, mankind have been learning the tendencies of actions by experience. Mankind "must by this time have acquired positive beliefs as to the effects of some actions on their happiness; and the beliefs which have thus come down are the rules of morality for the multitude, and for the philosopher until he has succeeded in finding better" (224 [II, 24]). This point is also made in "Sedgwick's Discourse." Mill says that there would be great uncertainty about the consequences of actions if each individual had only his or her own experience to guide him or her. But we are not so situated. "Everyone directs himself [or herself] in morality, as in all his [or her] conduct, not by his [or her] own unaided foresight, but by the accumulated wisdom of all former ages, embodied in traditional aphorisms."[17] He says, however, that mankind still has much to learn as to the effects of actions on the general happiness; so these "corollaries" from the principle of utility admit of indefinite improvement. But, he says in *Utilitarianism*, "to consider the rules of morality as improvable, is one thing; to pass over the intermediate generalizations entirely, and endeavour to test each individual action directly by the first principle, is another" (224 [II, 24]). He compares having rules of morality to having a road laid down to a goal, and to the Nautical Almanack as an application of navigational guidance based on astronomy.

This passage looks as if the rules of morality are mere "rules of thumb," to be followed to save time and effort of calculation but not to be taken as authoritative in case a calculation should prove them to be mistaken or inapplicable to the particular case. This is what John Rawls calls the "summary" conception of rules, such that "rules are pictured as summaries of past

---

[17] Ibid., 65–6.

decisions arrived at by the *direct* application of the utilitarian principle to particular cases."[18] Rawls comments that "there goes with this conception the notion of a particular exception which renders the rule suspect on a particular occasion."[19]

There are other passages, however, that point to a stronger conception of rules, and even in this passage there is a reference to moral sanctions that will be important in considering passages from Chapter 5. In this passage Mill says: "It is truly a whimsical supposition that if mankind were agreed in considering utility to be the test of morality, they would remain without any agreement as to what *is* useful, and would *take no measures for having their notions on the subject taught to the young, and enforced by law and opinion*" (224 [II, 24], emphasis added). If there are "measures" taken for teaching the rules, and rules are to be "enforced," there is a social dimension to the rules that makes them more than rules of thumb for the individual utilitarian agent's choice of action case by case. This is supported by what Mill says about sanctions in Chapter 5.

In Chapter 5, Mill introduces a criterion by which to distinguish moral duty from general expediency: "We do not call anything wrong, unless we mean to imply that a person ought to be punished in some way or other for doing it; if not by law, by the opinion of his fellow creatures; if not by opinion, by the reproaches of his conscience. This is the real turning point of the distinction between morality and simple expediency" (246 [V, 14]).[20] This looks at first sight as if morality is limited to a set of rules enforced by sanctions – legal, popular,

---

[18] Rawls, "Two Concepts of Rules," 19.

[19] Ibid., 24.

[20] David Lyons, "Mill's Theory of Morality," *Nous*: 105–19; *Rights, Welfare, and Mill's Moral Theory*, 51–3. Lyons points out that in this context Mill is giving an analysis of moral concepts applicable to any moral system, not specifically a utilitarian system. This is true, but Mill evidently thinks that it applies to his own moral view as well. What is distinctive about utilitarianism is that utilitarian criteria would be used to decide which kinds of acts merit punishment and of what sort.

or the reproaches of conscience. This passage need not, however, be taken as a clear rejection of act-utilitarianism, because a radical act-utilitarian could claim that any act that does not maximize utility merits punishment by the conscience of the agent. Such a radical theory is implausible, and it is not one that Mill endorses. If act-utilitarianism is interpreted as making morally wrong any act less than maximally efficient for the production of best consequences, then Mill is clearly not an act-utilitarian of that sort.[21]

Another argument against interpreting Mill as an act-utilitarian is what he says about "supererogation," an act that is morally praiseworthy without its omission being morally blameworthy. Mill clearly thinks that not every act that has less than best foreseeable consequences is a matter for moral condemnation. In his book on *Auguste Comte and Positivism*, Mill argues for a distinction between what is required as a duty and what is good to do but goes beyond the call of duty: "It is not good that persons should be bound, by other people's opinion, to do everything that they would deserve praise for doing. There is a standard of altruism to which all should be required to come up, and a degree beyond it which is not obligatory, but meritorious. It is incumbent on every one to restrain the pursuit of his [or her] personal objects within the limits consistent with the essential interests of others. What those limits are, it is the province of ethical science to determine; and to keep all individuals and aggregations of individuals within them, is the proper office of punishment and moral blame. If in addition

---

[21] To take into account this limitation of morality to those acts for which some form of punishment is justified, David Copp presents a "Conscience Theory" as an interpretation of Mill. This is that an agent's doing an act is wrong if, and only if, there is an alternative to the act that would have better consequences, and it would be "maximally expedient" that if the agent did the first act, the agent would feel regret for this. In other words, this is an act-utilitarianism restricted to acts for which the sanction of conscience is justified. Copp, "The Iterated-Utilitarianism of J. S. Mill," 84.

to fulfilling this obligation, persons make the good of others a direct object of disinterested exertions, postponing or sacrificing to it even innocent indulgences, they deserve gratitude and honour, and are fit subjects of moral praise.... [B]ut a necessary condition is its spontaneity.... Such spontaneity by no means excludes sympathetic encouragement; but the encouragement should take the form of making self-devotion pleasant, not that of making everything else painful."[22]

In my interpretation, Mill holds a view that is neither a pure form of act-utilitarianism nor a pure form of rule-utilitarianism, but which has elements of both act-utilitarian moral reasoning and practice and elements of rule-utilitarian reasoning and practice.[23] This is not merely the strategic use of rules to achieve the act having best consequences, but the recognition that some areas of social life require authoritative rules that are not to be violated for marginally better consequences and some areas in which there are no such rules but that are still subject to moral sanction.[24] Mill wrote notes on his father's psychology text and inserted with approval an extended quotation from another of his father's books, his *Fragment on Mackintosh*. There James Mill says: "In the performance of our duties two sets of cases may be distinguished. There is one set in which a direct estimate of the good of the particular act is inevitable; and the man [or

---

[22] *Auguste Comte and Positivism*, 337–8.
[23] I have changed my interpretation from an earlier act-utilitarian view. See Henry R. West, "Mill's Moral Conservatism," *Midwest Studies in Philosophy*, vol. 1: *Studies in the History of Philosophy* (1976), 71–80.
[24] Gerald Gaus has a fourfold division of the function of rules and of kinds of rules in Mill's utilitarianism in "Mill's Theory of Moral Rules," 270–6. These are (1) the "almanac function," as guides for the art of morality, based on the tendencies of actions; (2) the "security function" to give people security that others will behave in certain predictable ways; (3) a "moralizing function" to induce sentiments that support the greatest happiness; and (4) as an indicator of liability to sanctions. Gaus thinks that violation of a moral rule performing this fourth function is a necessary condition for sanctions. I hold that Mill does not restrict moral sanctions in that way.

woman] acts immorally without making it. There are other cases in which it is not necessary.

"The first are those, which have in them so much of singularity, as to prevent them coming within the limits of any established class. In such cases a man [or woman] has but one guide; he [or she] must consider the consequences, or act not as a moral, or rational agent at all.

"The second are cases of such ordinary and frequent occurrence as to be distinguished into classes."[25] These are classes such as "Just, Beneficent, Brave, Prudent, Temperate; to each of which classes belongs its appropriate rule that men [and women] should be just, that they should be beneficent, and so on...."[26] If we accept this as reflecting J. S. Mill's view, it is clear that he believed that there are duties based on rules and there are duties based on the particular circumstances of a situation.

J. S. Mill's position is still more complicated by the fact that some rules have correlative rights that are to be respected and that entitle the right holder to make valid claims even if recognition of those claims in a particular case does not maximize utility. This is stated explicitly in a letter to George Grote in 1862, shortly after the publication of *Utilitarianism*. There he says, "...rights and obligations must, as you say, be recognised; and people must, on the one hand, not be required to sacrifice even their own less good to another's greater, where no general rule has given the other the right to the sacrifice; while, when a right *has* been recognised, they must, in most cases, yield to that right even at the sacrifice, in the particular case, of their own greater good to another's less."[27]

---

[25] James Mill, *Analysis of the Phenomena of the Human Mind*, 2nd ed., vol. 2, 312–13.

[26] Ibid., 312.

[27] Mill, Letter to George Grote, January 10 1862, *The Later Letters of John Stuart Mill 1849–1873*, 762. Partially quoted in John Skorupski, *John Stuart Mill*, 318.

A further complication arises from the fact that some types of acts that might have best consequences on rare occasions cannot be done but from motives that are incompatible with overall behavior having best consequences. There are two reasons for this. First, states of character are confirmed patterns of behavior that do not have complete flexibility. The habit of honesty, which is useful as a virtue, cannot be maintained while telling lies on all the occasions when a lie would have marginally better consequences; or, to put the point another way, to be able to lie on every occasion when doing so would maximize utility is incompatible with the most useful degree of habitual honesty. Secondly, acts presuppose states of mind that may be in themselves states of enjoyment or of wretchedness. Such mental states are important in a utilitarian calculation, for we must remember that Mill considers the pleasures of a nobleness of character, of being a person of feeling and conscience rather than selfish and base, among the qualitatively higher pleasures. Furthermore, these states of mind are fruitful in other consequences besides any particular act: "No person can be a thief or a liar without being much else: and if our moral judgments and feelings with respect to a person convicted of either vice, were grounded solely upon the pernicious tendency of thieving and lying, they would be partial and incomplete...."[28] There is nothing inconsistent about this. The ultimate principle of utility for Mill is the promotion of greatest happiness. Whether to calculate the consequences of actions case by case, or to act in accordance with rules, or to respect rights, or to act virtuously with other ends in immediate view is a matter of choosing appropriate means for the achievement of the greatest happiness.[29] Each of these procedures may have

---

[28] "Remarks on Bentham's Philosophy," 7.

[29] Cf. Lyons, "Mill's Theory of Morality," *Nous* 10 (1976): 116–17; *Rights, Welfare, and Mill's Moral Theory*, 63: "Unlike recent utilitarian theories, Mill is not preoccupied with either acts or rules. Mill is committed fundamentally to the end of happiness, and thereby to *whatever* means best serve that end. All such means may properly be judged by reference

an appropriate place in an overall utilitarian moral system, and following one of these indirect procedures is the right act to perform.[30]

The preceding paragraphs have argued against interpreting Mill as an act-utilitarian. Is he then a rule-utilitarian? The strongest case for interpreting Mill as a pure rule-utilitarian is found at the end of Chapter 2 of *Utilitarianism*. There, in discussing the objection that a utilitarian will be apt to make his own particular case an exception to moral rules, Mill replies that there "is no ethical creed which does not temper the rigidity of its laws, by giving a certain latitude, under the moral responsibility of the agent, for accommodation to peculiarities of circumstances"; and that there "exists no moral system under which there do not arise unequivocal cases of conflicting obligation" (225 [II, 25]).

These seem to be three different instances in which a utilitarian might appeal directly to the principle of utility. One is the case in which particular circumstances make it legitimate to violate a moral rule. A second is the case of circumstances in which there are conflicting obligations. A third is when there is no moral rule governing a choice, but important utilities are at stake. Can all of these instances be reduced to an appeal to a rule? Mill seems to think so. He says, "We must remember that only in these cases of conflict between secondary principles is it requisite that first principles should be appealed to. There is no case of moral obligation in which some secondary principle is not involved; and if only one, there can seldom be any real doubt which one it is, in the mind of any person by whom the principle itself is recognised" (226 [II, 25]). In Chapter 5, Mill gives an example of an instance in which there is

---

to that end, without the appraisal of social rules being subordinated to judgments of particular acts (as it is under act-utilitarianism) or the converse (as under rule-utilitarianism)."

[30] I think that this is the interpretation given by Sumner in "The Good and the Right," 112–13. See also Skorupski, *John Stuart Mill*, ch. 9, sec. 11, "Indirect Utilitarianism."

a conflict between obligations: "... particular cases may occur in which some other social duty is so important, as to overrule any one of the general maxims of justice. Thus, to save a life, it may not only be allowable, but a duty, to steal, or take by force, the necessary food or medicine, or to kidnap, and compel to officiate, the only qualified medical practicioner" (259 [V, 37]). Here there is a clear case of conflict of secondary principles.

But might there not be cases in which there is no other secondary rule involved? Suppose there is only the conflict between a moral rule, such as the prohibition of lying, and the general principle of utility. An instance cited by Mill in which he thinks that the moral rule is not overridden is to avoid momentary embarrassment. But suppose the embarrassment would be more than momentary, or rather extreme, and it is someone else's embarrassment? Is this a secondary rule that might be formulated, "Prevent other people's distress when you can"? Is this a "corollary" of the principle of utility? If so, "Promote other people's happiness when you can" would also qualify as a corollary. In any case, although Mill does not give instances in *Utilitarianism* in which the sanctions of public opinion or conscience should be applied to an act that, in particular circumstances, has such significant consequences for better or for worse that its commission or omission would be deserving of sanctions independently of the requirements of a moral rule, his system does seem to imply such. For example, in carrying out the duty of beneficence or charity, an individual has to make judgments as to how to do this most effectively. If one gives from one's resources to those of one's own country or neighborhood, when it will relieve minor distress, rather than giving to those of another country or class where it would relieve great distress, that would seem to be an instance deserving of the reproaches of enlightened utilitarian public opinion or at least of one's conscience. And although one could formulate a precept, "In charitable giving, try to relieve the greatest suffering," it isn't clear that this is anything but an injunction to use act-utilitarian criteria in determining one's action. Mill refused to make public disclosure of his atheistic religious views because he believed that this would deprive him of an audience for his progressive political views. This was a moral, not a prudential decision, and it would appear that he was using act-utilitarian criteria in making this decision. This could perhaps be redescribed as conforming to a rule, but it need not be.

There are other decisions that seem to be moral ones, such that the decision would deserve the reproaches of one's conscience if it were made selfishly or frivolously. Examples might be the decision of a person about what profession or vocation to enter, or the decision of a couple whether to have a child or whether to have an additional child. These are momentous choices, worthy of moral assessment, but they seem too individual and personal to fall under moral rules.

In the early editions of his *System of Logic*, Mill made a distinction between the role of judge and the role of legislator (or administrator) and found areas of morality for both kinds of reasoning. I think that this is worthy of lengthy quotation: "... [Q]uestions of practical morality are partly similar to those which are to be decided by a judge, and partly to those which have to be solved by a legislator or administrator. In some things our conduct ought to conform itself to a prescribed rule; in others, it is to be guided by the best judgment which can be formed of the merits of the particular case.

"... [I]n a certain description of cases at least, morality consists in the simple observance of a rule. The cases in question are those in which, although any rule which can be formed is probably (as we remarked on maxims of policy) more or less imperfectly adapted to a portion of the cases which it comprises, there is still a necessity that some rule, of a nature simple enough to be easily understood and remembered, should not only be laid down for guidance, but universally observed, in order that the various persons concerned may know what they have to expect: the inconvenience of uncertainty on their part being a greater evil than that which may possibly arise, in a minority of cases, from the imperfect adaptation of the rule to those cases.

"Such, for example, is the rule of veracity; that of not infringing the legal rights of others; and so forth: concerning which it is obvious that although many cases exist in which a deviation from the rule would in the particular case produce more good than evil, it is necessary for general security, either that the rules should be inflexibly observed, or that the license of deviating from them, if such be ever permitted, should be confined to definite classes of cases, and of a very peculiar and extreme nature."[31]

In other cases, "in which there does not exist a necessity for a common rule, to be acknowledged and relied on as the basis of social life; where we are at liberty to inquire what is the most moral course under the particular circumstances of the case, without reference, or without exclusive reference, to the authorized expectations of other people";[32] there one takes the end, which on the utilitarian view would be the greatest happiness, and inquires what are the kinds of actions by which this end is capable of being realized.

This is a clear statement that Mill thinks that in some areas, where there are useful rules for coordinating social behavior, and the rules create "authorized expectations," a rule-utilitarian procedure is appropriate. But this is not the totality of morality. There are other areas in which no such rules exist (or, perhaps, need not exist), and in these areas an act-utilitarian or perhaps a procedure of utilitarian generalization is appropriate.[33]

---

[31] *A System of Logic: Ratiocinative and Inductive*, 1154–5 (bk. 6, ch. 11, sec. 6 in 1st [1843] and 2nd [1846] editions).

[32] Ibid., 1155.

[33] The distinction between the role of the judge and that of the legislator is found in all editions of *System of Logic*: There are "cases in which individuals are bound to conform their practice to a pre-established rule, while there are others in which it is part of their task to find or construct the rule by which they are to govern their conduct" (*System of*

I claim that the passages quoted in the preceding paragraphs show that in some cases following the rule is the right action, not simply an action following a correct decision procedure. And there are other cases in which there is a moral choice that is not governed by an existing rule. Now it might be thought that the indeterminacy of right action, according to my interpretation, takes away some of the attractiveness of utilitarianism. One of the attractions of the Benthamite calculus is that even if it can't be put into practice, it gives a theoretical formula for determining right action. But this may be merely an appearance of precision. According to Bentham, actions are right as they *appear* to *tend* to produce the best consequences. But, more important, a moral theory that takes into account the complexity of moral life is better than one that is definite at the price of oversimplification.

In Mill's view, there is a convergence between rule-utilitarian and act-utilitarian criteria. Mill points out that an action may have indirect consequences upon the character of the agent and upon the practice of the useful rule. These indirect consequences, when recognized, may make the overall consequences of exceptions to useful rules less likely to be of positive marginal value. In his early essay, "Remarks on Bentham's

Logic, 943–4 [bk. 6, ch. 11 in editions of 1843–56; ch. 12 in later editions; sec. 2]). The section quoted in this footnote was replaced in later editions with a more extended discussion of the necessity of an ultimate standard or first principle of morality and other branches of the art of life, asserting that it is the promotion of happiness. There is no reason to believe that Mill did not continue to believe what was said there. In the later version, he argues for *virtues* based on the ultimate standard of happiness even if happiness is sacrificed in the particular case: "There are many virtuous actions, and even virtuous modes of actions (though the cases are, I think, less frequent than is often supposed) by which happiness in the particular instance is sacrificed, more pain being produced than pleasure. But conduct of which this can be truly asserted, admits of justification only because it can be shown that on the whole more happiness will exist in the world, if feelings are cultivated which will make people, in certain cases, regardless of happiness" (Ibid., 952 [sec. 7]).

Philosophy," Mill has a criticism of Bentham for failing to take all consequences into account. He interprets Bentham as making his calculation "solely of the consequences which that very action, if practised generally, would itself lead." (This, incidentally, is to interpret Bentham as in some sense an advocate of utilitarian generalization.) But Mill adds that the act tends to perpetuate the state or character of mind in which it has originated. He criticizes Bentham for ignoring the consequences upon character.[34]

These considerations provide one way to interpret Mill's comments in *Utilitarianism* about abstinence from lying. In discussing the case in which telling a lie would be expedient for the purpose of getting over some momentary embarrassment, or attaining some object immediately useful to ourselves or others, Mill points to the side effects upon the character of the agent and upon the practice of a useful rule: "But inasmuch as the cultivation in ourselves of a sensitive feeling on the subject of veracity, is one of the most useful, and the enfeeblement of that feeling one of the most hurtful, things to which our conduct can be instrumental; and inasmuch as any, even unintentional, deviation from truth, does that much towards weakening the trustworthiness of human assertion, which is not only the principal support of all present social well-being, but the insufficiency of which does more than any one thing that can be named to keep back civilization, virtue, everything on which human happiness on the largest scale depends; we feel that the violation, for a present advantage, of a rule of such transcendent expediency, is not expedient, and that he [or she] who, for the sake of a convenience to himself [or herself] or to some other individual, does what depends on him [or her] to deprive mankind of the good, and inflict upon them the evil, involved in the greater or less reliance which they can place

---

[34] "Remarks on Bentham's Philosophy," 7–8. This influence of actions upon character is the "moralizing function" of rules recognized by Gaus.

in each other's word, acts the part of one of their worst enemies" (223 [II, 23]). It would seem that Mill thinks that when *all* consequences are taken into account, including those upon the character of the agent and upon the useful rule and socially recognized virtue of honesty, the particular act would *not* be beneficial.[35]

As critics of act-utilitarianism have pointed out, however, a single lie does not destroy the confidence that people place in veracity. That would require a collection of acts of lying. And no single-member act in that collection is necessary or sufficient for the existence of the collection. Mill addresses this issue with the controversial claim that a hundredth part of the consequences of any hundred acts should be assigned to each act. In his essay on Whewell, Mill says, "If a hundred infringements would produce all the mischief implied in the abrogation of the rule, a hundredth part of the mischief must be debited to each of the infringements, though we may not be able to trace it home individually. And this hundredth part will generally far outweigh any good expected to arise from the individual act."[36] This notion of "contributory causation" is a highly controversial claim, and I cannot here address the arguments for and against it.[37]

But more important is something else that Mill says in reply to Whewell: "If one person may break through the rule on his [or her] own judgment, the same liberty cannot be refused

---

[35] To the claim that the violation of the useful rule might remain rare and kept secret, Mill says that the feeling of security and certainty "is impaired, not only by every known actual violation of good rules, but by the belief that such violations ever occur." Letter to John Venn, April 14, 1872, *The Later Letters of John Stuart Mill 1849–1873*, 1881–2.

[36] "Whewell on Moral Philosophy," 182.

[37] This conception is developed in Henry Robison West, "Act-Utilitarianism and Rule-Utilitarianism." It is assumed in David Lyons, *Forms and Limits of Utilitarianism*, and criticized in J. Howard Sobel, "'Everyone,' Consequences, and Generalization Arguments," *Inquiry* 10 (1967): 373–404, and in Donald Regan, *Utilitarianism and Co-operation*.

to others."[38] Mill's conception of morality is sufficiently social that he would not permit agents to be moral "free-riders." An individual agent is not permitted to benefit from the security of laws and moral rules and not follow them him- or herself. Mill considers, as an example, the murder of someone whose cruel behavior tends to increase human unhappiness. The individual act has consequences that favor it, but the counterconsideration, on the principle of utility is: "that unless persons were punished for killing, and taught not to kill; that if it were thought allowable for any one to put to death at pleasure any human being whom he believes that the world would be well rid of, nobody's life would be safe."[39] An agent is not permitted to maximize utility by engaging in exceptions to useful moral rules unless the exception can be generalizable. Mill is not thinking of morality just from the first-person point of view, asking, "What ought I to do?" with the behavior of others treated as if it were merely among the circumstances of action. He is thinking of morality from the social point of view, asking, "What morality ought there to be?" And from this point of view he thinks that there ought to be rules taught and enforced by sanctions of law, public opinion, and conscience.[40] But, in addition, the principle of utility requires that people be sensitive

---

[38] "Whewell on Moral Philosophy," 182.

[39] Ibid., 181.

[40] David Lyons raises the question of a conflict between Mill's commitment to happiness when it comes into conflict with moral judgments based on what acts are deserving of sanctions. Lyons seems to see this as a conflict between Mill's *conception* of morality and his ultimate commitment to the end of happiness and thus a question of whether moral values are supposed to take precedence over all others. See Lyons, "Mill's Theory of Morality," *Nous* 10 (1976): 118–19; *Rights, Welfare, and Mill's Moral Theory*, 65. I see it as a question whether the particular moral rule requires inflexibility or how much inflexibility to be an effective moral rule. I think that Mill's "commitment" to happiness is the ultimate commitment, but that it cannot be achieved without social morality, which in some cases prohibits agents from maximizing happiness in particular cases.

to the consequences of particular actions that are not covered by such rules.

Finally, Mill's theory of morality is not just a combination of act- and rule-utilitarian criteria. As I mentioned, he has a place for rights, which are correlative to especially stringent obligations to "assignable" people; he has a place for praise and condemnation of people's characters as well as their actions (elements of "virtue ethics"); and he has a place for supererogation. The structure of Mill's moral theory is truly complex, not the simple model of either act-utilitarianism or rule-utilitarianism, or a mixture of the moral reasoning of both.

In summary, Mill is neither a pure act-utilitarian nor a pure rule-utilitarian. It is not that he was unaware of the possible distinction. It is that he thought that both kinds of moral criteria, as well as additional aspects of the moral life, are useful in their places. And usefulness is, after all, the standard of a utilitarian.

5

SANCTIONS AND MORAL MOTIVATION

IN Chapter 3 of *Utilitarianism*, Mill is addressing the question
of what motives there are to be moral. He points out that
the question arises whenever a person is called upon to *adopt*
a standard. Customary morality, which education and opinion
have consecrated, presents itself as being *in itself* obligatory, and
when one is asked to believe that morality *derives* its obligation
from a more general principle around which custom has not
thrown the same halo, the assertion is a paradox. The specific
rules, such as not to rob or murder, betray or deceive, seem
to be more obligatory than simply a matter of promoting the
general happiness, which is proposed as their foundation. So
the question, "What motives are there to follow the utilitarian
morality?" will arise until the influences that form moral character have taken the same hold of the principle of utilitarianism
as they have taken of some of the rules of morality that could
be derived from that principle – until the feeling of unity with
our fellow creatures has become as deeply rooted in our character as the horror of crime is in an ordinarily well-brought-up
young person. In the meantime, until such a happy moment
arrives, the difficulty is not peculiar to the doctrine of utility, but
is inherent in every attempt to analyze morality and to reduce
it to principles.

Mill's claim in this chapter is that all the same motives that
now lead people to obey customary morality or to obey rules
based on any other system of morals can lead them to obey
utilitarian morality, and that there is an additional source of
motivation as well.

Mill, following Bentham, uses the word "sanctions" to refer to the sources of motivation, in this context motives to be moral. Mill classifies them as "external" and "internal." Under the former heading are hope of favor and fear of displeasure from our fellow creatures and from the Ruler of the Universe (if one has a belief in the divine). These are the motives that Bentham analyzed as the political, the moral or popular, and the religious sanctions. Bentham made a distinction between the enforcement of morality by law and public policy, carried out by judges or others specifically designated for that office (the political), and the enforcement of morality by popular opinion (the moral or popular). In each case these are "external" sanctions. Even if there were no other motives to be moral, these would operate, and these sanctions are consistent with utilitarianism. It is useful to have laws prohibiting theft and murder and other crimes, although the utilitarian would want to have these subjected to critical analysis to see if they are the best possible laws and public policies. So utilitarians do not differ from others in seeking to have the political sanction enforce some forms of behavior. Other people as well as oneself desire their own happiness and commend conduct by which they think that their happiness is promoted. So hope of favor and fear of displeasure of others will conduce to behavior that promotes the happiness of others. And if people believe in the goodness of God, those who think that conduciveness to the general happiness is the criterion of good must believe that this is what God approves. Thus utilitarianism has available to it these external sanctions. Mill points out that we also have sympathy with and affections for other people and may have love or awe of God as well as hope or fear of favor or disfavor.

But it is the "internal" sanction that really interests Mill. This is the feeling of pain, attendant on the violation of duty, which is the essence of conscience. Mill thinks that conscience is *acquired* – "derived from sympathy, from love, and still more from fear; from all the forms of religious feeling; from the recollections of childhood and of all our past life; from self-esteem, desire of the esteem of others, and occasionally even self-abasement."[1] Thus, Mill thinks that conscience is an internalization of the external sanctions complicated by various other associated feelings. He says that this complicated character of its origin gives it a sort of mystical character that leads people to believe that it cannot possibly attach itself to any other objects than those that are found in our present experience to excite it. But Mill sees no reason why conscience may not be cultivated to as great an intensity in connection with the utilitarian as with any other rule of morals. Also, Mill thinks that his claim does not depend upon whether the feeling of duty is innate or acquired. If innate, it is still an open question as to what objects this feeling naturally attaches itself, and Mill sees no reason why it should not be in regard to the pleasures and pains of others.

If, as Mill believes, moral feelings are acquired, the feelings might be analyzed away as arbitrary conditioning, if there were not a natural basis for the feelings. Mill believes that for a utilitarian conscience there is such a basis. It is the desire to be in unity with our fellow creatures, which he believes to be a universally powerful principle in human nature and to become stronger with the influences of advancing civilization. Cooperating with others requires that collective interest is the aim of actions; one's own ends are at least temporarily identified with those of others, and this leads one to identify one's *feelings* more and more with the good of others, and to demonstrate these feelings to them. And even if one does not have such feelings, one has an interest in others having them in order to support their share of cooperation. Mill thus thinks that these feelings can be reinforced by external sanctions, and that as civilization goes on and improvements in political life remove inequalities

---

[1] John Stuart Mill, *Utilitarianism*, 228 (ch. 3, par. 4). Citations to this work in this chapter will be in parentheses in the text.

of legal privilege between individuals or classes, there is an increasing tendency for each individual to feel a unity with all the rest. Even in the present imperfect state of society, where such social feelings are inferior to selfish ones, those who have such social feelings do not regard them as a superstition of education or a law despotically imposed by the power of society, but as an attribute that it would not be well for them to be without. This conviction Mill calls the "ultimate sanction" of the utilitarian morality.

In Chapter 3, then, Mill is not attempting to answer the question, "Why ought I to be moral?" or "Why ought I to be moral if I accept the utilitarian principle that happiness and unhappiness are the only (positive and negative) ends of life?" In this chapter Mill is doing moral psychology. He is taking a third-person point of view. He is first attempting to show what motivates anyone to be moral, regardless of the content of the moral principles. He then argues that there is an additional source of motivation for utilitarian morality.

Mill's psychological theory is "associationist." He follows his father James Mill (and Bentham) in believing that from a small number of primitive sources of motivation, the extremely complex set of motivations of a mature person are developed by association with pleasure and/or pain. This is not the place to give a full exposition of this theory, but it is appropriate to call attention to its effort to explain moral actions and dispositions to act. The chief locus of Mill's discussion is in his notes to his father's *Analysis of the Phenomena of the Human Mind*.[2] J. S. Mill's notes are as extensive as the original text. In these notes, Mill attempts to express any disagreement with his father's analysis; so when Mill has no comment upon the text, the text as well as Mill's notes may be taken as J. S. Mill's view. In his book James Mill gives an associationist account of much motivation, including moral motivation. He thinks that there is a universal

---

[2]   James Mill, *Analysis of the Phenomena of the Human Mind*, 2nd ed.

feeling of sympathy for the happiness or suffering of other individuals:

"There is nothing which more instantly associates with itself the ideas of our own Pleasures, and Pains, than the idea of the Pleasures and Pains of our Fellow-creatures. . . .

"The idea of a man enjoying a train of pleasures, or happiness, is felt by every body to be a pleasurable idea. The idea of a man under a train of sufferings or pains, is equally felt to be a painful idea. . . ."[3]

And from this one can come to form a general feeling for mankind:

"Now, as our complex Idea of Mankind, is made up of the aggregate of the ideas of Individuals, including the interesting trains called Love of their Pleasures, Hatred of their Pains; Love of their Kindness, Aversion to their Unkindness: the generation of the affection, called Love of Mankind, is, for our present purpose, sufficiently shewn."[4]

John Stuart comments on this section of the *Analysis of the Phenomena of the Human Mind* with approval. He says that it explains how we acquire attachments to persons who are the causes or habitual concomitants of pleasurable sensations in us, or of relief from pains; in other words, those persons become in themselves pleasant to us by association; and through the multitude and variety of the pleasurable ideas associated with them, the derived pleasures become pleasures of greater constancy and even intensity, and altogether more valuable to us than any of the primitive pleasures of our constitution. These considerations show: "how it is possible that the moral sentiments, the feelings of duty, and of moral approbation and disapprobation, may be no original elements of our nature, and

---

[3] Ibid., n. 217. J. S. Mill thinks that his father's exposition is unclear. He says that if it is meant that in such cases the pleasure or pain is consciously referred to self, this is a mistake. The idea of pleasure is recalled in association with the other person as feeling the pleasure or pain, not with one's self as feeling it.

[4] Ibid., 230.

may yet be capable of being not only more intense and powerful than any of the elements out of which they may have been formed, but may also, in their maturity, be perfectly disinterested: nothing more being necessary for this, than that the acquired pleasure and pain should have become as independent of the native elements from which they are formed, as the love of wealth and of power not only often but generally become, of the bodily pleasure, and relief from bodily pains, for the sake of which, and of which alone, power and wealth must have been originally valued. No one thinks it necessary to suppose an original and inherent love of money or of power; yet these are the objects of two of the strongest, most general, and most persistent passions of human nature; passions which often have quite as little reference to pleasure or pain, beyond the mere consciousness of possession, and in that sense of the word quite disinterested, as the moral feelings of the most virtuous human being."[5]

Although Mill and his father follow Bentham in holding a psychological theory that can be called psychological hedonism, the younger Mill's theory is different from that held by Bentham and the elder Mill. One version of psychological hedonism is that one always acts to maximize net pleasure (or minimize net pain) in the future, interpreting "net" pleasure or pain as the result, using an accounting metaphor, when the value of pains has been "subtracted" from the value of pleasures, or vice versa. This seems to have been Bentham's view: "... [O]n the occasion of every act he exercises, every human being is led to pursue that line of conduct which, according to his view of the case, taken by him at the moment, will be in the highest degree contributory to his own greatest happiness...."[6] James Mill seems to have also held this view.[7] I think that this

---

5   Ibid., 230, n. 45 by J. S. Mill found on 233–4.

6   Quoted by Henry Sidgwick, *Practical Ethics*, 246, from Introduction to Bentham's *Constitutional Code*, vol. 9 of Bentham's *Works*, J. Bowring, ed., 2.

7   James Mill, *Analysis of the Phenomena of the Human Mind*, 193.

view is obviously false. I often postpone a painful task or succumb to a pleasure of the moment knowing full well that my behavior will not promote my greatest happiness and that I shall later regret it.

John Stuart Mill, however, held a more complex version of psychological hedonism. It differed from Bentham's in two respects.

First, the pleasure or pain motivating an action may not be pleasure or pain in prospect: "... [T]hat all our acts are determined by pains and pleasures *in prospect*, pains and pleasures to which we look forward as the *consequences* of our acts ... as a universal truth, can in no way be maintained. The pain or pleasure which determines conduct is as frequently one which *precedes* the moment of action as one which follows it. A man [or woman] ... recoils from the very thought of committing the act.... His [or her] conduct is determined by pain; but by a pain which precedes the act, not by one which is expected to follow it."[8] Mill may have oversimplified Bentham's position in his criticism. Bentham says that two senses of the term "motive" need to be distinguished. One is a pleasure or pain that prompts to action, which is previous to the act. But, Bentham says, in every case the agent looks to the consequences of the act in order to have the idea of pleasure or pain regarding the act.[9] Mill seems to think that the antecedent pleasure or pain can, by association, attach to the thought of the act without considering the consequences. In any case, we are interested here in Mill's theory, not Bentham's.

Second, through the process of association and habit formation, a course of action that was originally willed because it was associated with pleasure or the avoidance of pain may be willed out of habit: "a motive does not mean always, or solely, the anticipation of a pleasure or pain.... As we proceed in the

---

[8] John Stuart Mill, "Remarks on Bentham's Philosophy," 12.
[9] Jeremy Bentham, *An Introduction to the Principles of Morals and Legislation*, ch. 10, sec. 6.

formation of habits, and become accustomed to will a particular act or a particular course of conduct because it is pleasurable, we at last continue to will it without any reference to its being pleasurable."[10] At this stage we have a "person of confirmed virtue, or any other person whose purposes are fixed, [who] carries out his [or her] purposes without any thought of the pleasure he [or she] has in contemplating them or expects to derive from their fulfilment; and persists in acting on them, even though these pleasures are much diminished ... or are outweighed by the pains which the pursuit of the purposes may bring upon him [or her]" (238 [IV, 11]).

Mill's theory may still be regarded as a complex theory of psychological hedonism, for, according to Mill, all habits are de-rived from desires and aversions, and desires and aversions for objects other than pleasure and pain were ultimately derived, by association, from the desire for pleasure and the aversion to pain. Examples that Mill discusses in Chapter 4 of *Utilitarianism* are the desire for money or for virtue. Another example dis-cussed in the *Analysis of the Phenomena of the Human Mind* is the desire for power.

It is important to see the difference between Mill's theory and Bentham's (or James Mill's) in order to understand Mill's account of unselfish action. Mill is a psychological hedonist, but not a psychological egoist. Bentham and James Mill were not psychological egoists, in the sense of being selfish, for they believed that the source of an agent's pleasure could be the pleasure of another person. But Mill can more easily account for the hero and the martyr who voluntarily do without happi-ness for the sake of something that they prize more than their individual happiness (217 [II, 15]). One can come to associate one's own happiness with the happiness of others, coming to desire the happiness of others as a part of one's own happiness, and one can also develop a confirmed character of acting to promote the interest of others. Not all actions that are *originally*

[10] John Stuart Mill, *A System of Logic*, 842 (bk. 6, ch. 2, sec. 4).

motivated by one's own pleasure and avoidance of pain need to be motivated, after becoming matters of confirmed character, by one's own pleasure and avoidance of pain.

Even when actions are motivated by the maximizing of the pleasure and minimizing of pain of the agent, actions may still be distinguished with regard to the source of pleasure and pain. As previously noted, Bentham and James Mill did not ascribe all action to "self-interest," if that is interpreted to exclude the interests of others. Bentham gives a list of the kinds of pleasures and pains that include the pleasures of sense, of wealth, of skill, of amity, of a good name, of power, of piety, of benevolence, of malevolence, of memory, of imagination, of expectation, pleasures dependent upon association, and pleasures of relief. There is a nearly comparable list of kinds of pain.[11] When a pleasure is derived from some of these sources, although the agent feels or expects to feel pleasure in the act, the pleasure is derived from the condition of someone or something else. For example, the pleasures of amity and piety are derived from having, or believing oneself to have, the goodwill of other people or the Supreme Being, according to Bentham's analysis, and pleasures of benevolence are derived from the very feeling of goodwill toward others, from sympathy with the happiness of others, from social affections. When this degree of variety in sources of pleasures is recognized, it can be seen that even if a narrow conception of psychological hedonism were true, there could still be a great difference between a person who derived pleasure almost exclusively from sources that took little thought for the welfare of others and a person who derived extensive pleasure from benevolence, or pain from sympathy with the suffering of others. The latter sort of person, although literally self-interested in being motivated by personal pleasures and pains, is not selfish in the usual sense of the word. It is belief that *other* people are prospering that is the source of the

---

[11] Jeremy Bentham, *An Introduction to the Principles of Morals and Legislation*, ch. 5, secs. 2 and 3.

person's own pleasure and that *other* people are suffering that is the source of the person's own pain.

Bentham has a catalog of motives corresponding to that of pleasures and pains. To the pleasures of wealth corresponds the sort of motive that may be termed pecuniary interest; to the pleasures of a good name, the love of reputation; to the pleasures of sympathy, goodwill; and so on. These several motives, according to Bentham, are all prospects of pleasures and pains in the agent, but they have differing regard for the interests of the other members of the community; so they may be classified as either "social," "dis-social," or "self-regarding." In the social category Bentham places goodwill, love of reputation, desire of amity, and the motive of religion; in the dis-social category he places ill will; in the self-regarding category are physical desire, pecuniary interest, love of power, and self-preservation.

With respect to the motives that he terms social, that of goodwill Bentham calls "pure-social"; the others are "semi-social," in that they are self-regarding at the same time. Because goodwill is the motive that most often coincides with general happiness, it might seem that Bentham would favor a social order structured so as to produce actions motivated by goodwill. But this does not follow. Bentham has little confidence in the strength of this motive when it comes into conflict with other motives: "In *every* human breast (rare and short-lived ebullitions, the result of some extraordinarily strong stimulus or excitement, excepted) self-regarding interest is predominant over social interest; each person's own individual interest over the interests of all other persons taken together."[12] So, far more important than goodwill in bringing about moral behavior are sanctions. On Bentham's account sanctions make no appeal to the motive of goodwill. They appeal only to self-regarding motives or to the semisocial, which are self-regarding at the same time that they are other-regarding. Thus for Bentham the task of

---

[12] Quoted from Bentham's *Book of Fallacies* in J. S. Mill's "Remarks on Bentham's Philosophy," 14.

the benevolent person is not to promote institutions that promote benevolence but to promote institutions that create an identity of interest between an agent and others. That is the best way to ensure that people, including oneself, do acts promoting greatest happiness: "Towards the advancement of the public interest, all that the most public-spirited (which is as much as to say the most virtuous) of men can do, is to do what depends upon himself towards bringing the public interest, that is, his own personal share in the public interest, to a state as nearly approaching to coincidence, and on as few occasions amounting to a state of repugnance, as possible, with his private interests."[13]

Mill has far more confidence than Bentham in the role of moral feelings as motives and of social feelings as a foundation for moral feelings. Mill criticizes Bentham for omitting conscience or the feeling of duty from his list of motives: "... [O]ne would never imagine from reading him that any human being ever did an act merely because it is right, or abstained from it merely because it is wrong."[14] Mill thinks that in Bentham's mind this motive was probably blended with that of benevolence or sympathy, but Mill says that Bentham should have recollected that those who have a standard of right and wrong other than the greatest happiness often have very strong feelings of moral obligation.

In his own account of sanctions, Mill distinguishes between the "external" – hope of favor and fear of displeasure from our fellow creatures or from the Ruler of the Universe, "along with whatever we may have of sympathy or affection for them or of love and awe of Him, inclining us to do his will independently of selfish consequences" (228 [III, 3]) – and the "internal" sanction. The external sanctions apparently include Bentham's semisocial and social motives of reputation, religion, and sympathy or goodwill. But Mill emphasizes the importance of the

---

[13] Ibid.
[14] Ibid., 13.

"internal" sanction of duty – a pain attendant on violation of duty that, "in properly-cultivated moral nature, rises, in the more serious cases, into shrinking from it as an impossibility" (228 [III, 4]). Mill believes that this feeling is acquired, not innate, and "susceptible, by a sufficient use of the external sanction and of the force of early impressions, of being cultivated in almost any direction" (230 [III, 8]), but he also argues that once the general happiness is recognized as the ethical standard, the "social feelings of mankind; the desire to be in unity with our fellow creatures" (231 [III, 9]) provides a powerful natural sentiment for utilitarian morality. As indicated previously, Mill believes that this sentiment will develop to the extent that civilization and good social institutions develop.

Mill is also critical of Bentham's political theory for failing to take into account the effects of institutions upon motivation and character. Mill says that any act has a tendency to perpetuate the state or character of mind from which it originated. He says that it seemed never to have occurred to Bentham "to regard political institutions in a higher light, as the principal means of the social education of a people."[15]

We can now summarize the contrast between Bentham and Mill by itemizing three points of difference. First, Mill and Bentham differ in their psychological hedonism. Bentham thinks that every act is motivated by the prospect of a future pleasure or pain and that every act is aimed at maximizing net pleasure or minimizing net pain. Mill thinks pleasures or pains, in addition to being motives in prospect, may be antecedent or concurrent impulses to action or inaction, such that an agent, after a certain amount of conditioning or association, finds antecedent pleasure or pain in the thought of certain kinds of acts, and this pleasure or pain can be motivating. Even more important, agents can develop habitual dispositions to act in certain ways – committed purposes in life or confirmed character traits – such that they act out of habit without any desire or

[15] Ibid., 16.

forethought necessary at all. Second, Bentham does not ever recognize a motive of conscience or feeling of duty and, although he recognizes motives of sympathy or goodwill and other social motives, he thinks that these will usually give way to self-regarding motives in case of conflict. In contrast, Mill recognizes the motive of conscience or feeling of duty as an extremely powerful one, and he has far more confidence in the power of the social motives as constraints upon selfish behavior. Third, both Bentham and Mill recognize a need to establish a harmony of interests between self and others, but Mill thinks that this harmony of interests reinforces a motive of conscience directed toward the utilitarian end of the greatest happiness. In Mill's view, it is essential that people have their social motives and the dispositions that arise from them strengthened through institutional design and education. Consequently, Mill had admiration for forms of association of laborers with capitalists in profit-sharing arrangements and of laborers with other laborers. Mill thinks that that such associations would result in an increase in the productivity of labor, but, more importantly, they would result in the "moral revolution in society" that would accompany them: the healing of the standing feud between capital and labor, and "the conversion of each human being's daily occupation into a school of the social sympathies...."[16]

Mill's more complex psychological theory of motivation is more plausible than that shared by Bentham and James Mill. Actions are not always motivated by the prospect of future pleasures and pains, and conditioning can determine patterns of behavior that are habitual and dispositions amounting to traits of character. Mill is also correct to recognize a motive to do what is considered duty in those whose moral training has been normal, and there is no reason that this cannot be subjected to utilitarian criticism so that it attaches to those types of action that tend to promote the greatest happiness. Finally, Mill sees the importance of social arrangements in promoting

[16] John Stuart Mill, *Principles of Political Economy*, 792 (bk. 4, ch. 7, sec. 2).

an identity of interests between oneself and others and has hopes that this will increase with continuing interdependence in modern civilization. On this last point, his optimism may have been unfounded. To the extent that people live in prosperous and peaceful coexistence, they have less motivation to cheat and to coerce others. But conflicts in the effort to control scarce resources, both between individuals in a competitive society and between societies on a global scale, lead me to think that advancing technological "civilization" gives as many opportunities for conflicts of interest as it gives for identity of interests.

In the remainder of this chapter, I take up two controversies in moral psychology that are not addressed in Chapter 3 of *Utilitarianism*. One is the question of whether there can be moral judgments that are independent of at least some motivation on act accordingly. This controversy uses the terms "externalism" and "internalism," but it is not the same as Mill's distinction between external and internal sanctions. The other is the question of whether reason can motivate, which is related to the question of whether human agents have free will. My discussion of Mill's stand on free will, given primarily in writings other than *Utilitarianism*, is of interest in itself.

In some recent writing on moral motivation, a distinction has been drawn been "externalism" and "internalism,"[17] which is not the same as the distinction that Mill makes between "external" sanctions and "internal" sanctions. As William Frankena introduces the distinction between externalism and internalism, it is a question of whether moral judgments can be logically independent of motivation: "Many moral philosophers have said or implied that it is in some sense logically possible for an agent to have or see that he has an obligation even if

---

[17] W. D. Falk, "'Ought' and Motivation," *Proceedings of the Aristotelian Society*, N. S. 48 (1947–8), reprinted in *Readings in Ethical Theory*, Wilfred Sellars and John Hospers, eds., 492–510; William K. Frankena, "Obligation and Motivation in Recent Moral Philosophy," *Essays in Moral Philosophy*, A. I. Melden, ed., 40–81.

he has no motivation, actual or dispositional, for doing the action in question; many others have said or implied that this is paradoxical and not logically possible. The former are convinced that no reference to the existence of motives in the agent involved need be made in the analysis of a moral judgment; the latter are equally convinced that such a reference is necessary here."[18] The former view is "externalism"; the latter is "internalism."

Mill's distinction between external and internal sanctions is one of moral psychology, not of the analysis of moral judgments, but there is, no doubt, some relation. For Mill, a person who had adequately developed the internal sanction to do what is judged to be a duty, and not to do what is judged to be wrong, would, as a matter of fact, feel *some* motivation to act in accordance with a moral judgment. The motivation might be overridden by a self-interested motive, but it would still be there. Likewise, in a society with consistent rewards for duty and punishments for wrongdoing, a normal person would develop motives to do what is believed to be obligatory on the basis of past experience of external sanctions. But it would be an empirical question whether everyone capable of making moral judgments would always have an internal sanction or association with external sanctions adequate to create a pleasure or pain constituting a desire to act in accordance with the person's moral judgment in every case. There would seem to be, on Mill's account, no *logical* relation between judgments of obligation and motivation. Thus, Mill's abstract view would be externalism. But he clearly would view such persons, who had no motivation for what is judged obligatory, as being improperly educated; and he would regard societies that permit that to happen to be deficient societies.

Another issue in moral psychology is whether desires and only desires can be the seat of moral motivation or whether reasons alone can also suffice to motivate people to act morally.

[18] Frankena, 40.

One interpretation of Immanuel Kant's ethics is that in order for an act to have moral worth it must be free, and it is only when motivated by reason, not by inclinations due to heredity or environment, that an act is free and of moral worth.[19] This is not the place to go into Kant's theory, but it is an appropriate place to discuss Mill's theory of free will. As indicated previously, Mill analyzes moral motivation without appeal to reason, distinct from natural or acquired desires.

In *An Examination of Sir William Hamilton's Philosophy* Mill gives his most comprehensive statement regarding freedom of the will and its significance for moral accountability and justice. He holds the view that all events, including human actions, have causal determinants. He calls this view the doctrine of "necessity," although he believes that the term has misleading connotations. He depicts his opponents, holding the "traditional" doctrine of "free will," as believing that actions based on free will are unmotivated, that an action of free will is one going contrary to one's strongest motivation.

First, Mill argues against any evidence of the existence of free will that is based on consciousness. Second, he analyzes our consciousness of moral accountability and argues that the traditional doctrine of free will would not support it, even with a theory of retribution. Third, he claims that even under the "utmost possible exaggeration" of the doctrine of necessity, the distinction between moral good and evil would exist and punishment would be justified. Finally, he clarifies the distinction between necessity and fatalism.

Mill's argument against the claim that we are immediately conscious of our free will is based on the distinction between a present fact and a possibility or future fact: "To be conscious of free-will, must mean, to be conscious, before I have decided, that I am able to decide either way. . . . But what I am *able*

---

[19] See Laurence Thomas, "Moral Psychology," in *Encyclopedia of Ethics*, 2nd ed., 1145.

to do, is not a subject of consciousness. Consciousness is not prophetic; we are conscious of what is, not of what will or can be."[20] Mill says that what I am conscious of is a belief that after choosing one course of action, I could have chosen another *if I had liked it better*. It is not that I could have chosen one course while I preferred the other, all things considered. I often elect to do one thing when I should have preferred another "in itself," apart from its consequences or from the moral law that it violates, and this preference for the thing in itself, abstracted from its accompaniments, is often loosely described as preference for the thing. It is this imprecise mode of speech, Mill asserts, that makes it not seem absurd to say that I act in opposition to my preference: "that my conscience prevails over my desires" as if conscience were not itself a desire, "the desire to do right."[21] Mill uses murder as an example: "I am told, that if I elect to murder, I am conscious that I could have elected to abstain: but am I conscious that I could have abstained if my aversion to the crime, and my dread of its consequences, had been weaker than the temptation? ... When we think of ourselves hypothetically as having acted otherwise than we did, we always suppose a difference in the antecedents: we picture ourselves as having known something that we did not know, or not known something that we did know; which is a difference in external inducements; or as having desired something, or disliked something, more or less than we did; which is a difference in internal inducements."[22]

Mill also gives an analysis of the feeling of making an effort to resist a desire. He says that the author that he is quoting thinks that the effort is all on one side, representing the conflict as taking place "between me and some foreign power, which I conquer, or by which I am overcome. But it is obvious that 'I' am both parties in the contest; the conflict is

[20] *An Examination of Sir William Hamilton's Philosophy*, 451.
[21] Ibid.
[22] Ibid.

between me and myself; between (for instance) me desiring a pleasure, and me dreading self-reproach. What causes Me, or if you please, my Will, to be identified with one side rather than the other, is that one of the Me's represents a more permanent state of my feelings than the other does. After the temptation has been yielded to, the desiring 'I' will come to an end, but the conscience-stricken 'I' may endure to the end of life."[23] Mill concludes that the difference between bad and good persons is not that the latter act in opposition to their strongest desires; it is that their desire to do right, and their aversion to doing wrong, are strong enough to overcome any other desires that may conflict with them. And this is the object of moral education: weakening those desires and aversions likely to lead to evil and exalting the desire of right conduct and aversion to wrong, plus developing a clear intellectual standard of right and wrong so that moral desire and aversion may act in the proper place.

Having rejected a direct consciousness of free will, Mill discusses whether opposition to our strongest preference is implied in what is called our consciousness of moral responsibility. On the basis of this analysis he concludes that such free will would be incompatible with moral responsibility.

Mill says that the feeling of moral responsibility is the feeling of liability to punishment, but this is of two kinds. First, it may be simply the expectation that if we act in a certain manner, punishment will *actually* be inflicted upon us. Or it may mean knowing that we shall *deserve* that infliction. Mill claims that the first is based on a belief that could come only from teaching or reasoning from experience, not from pure consciousness, and its evidence is not dependent on any theory of spontaneous volition. So the issue between Mill and his opponents is not expectation of punishment but consciousness that we deserve punishment; but, he points out, this feeling that we deserve to be punished is seldom found in any strength in the absence of

[23] Ibid., 452.

such expectations. For evidence of this he cites despots who seem to have no sense of accountability, and he points to class and caste societies where it is felt only toward equals. Mill says that in analyzing the consciousness that we deserve to be punished, it matters not in this discussion whether we are utilitarians or anti-utilitarians. It is sufficient if we believe that there is a difference between right and wrong.

Mill claims that insofar as the traditional doctrine of free will is true, punishment would not be justified: "Punishment proceeds on the assumption that the will is governed by motives. If punishment has no power of acting on the will, it would be illegitimate, however natural might be the inclination to inflict it. Just so far as the will is supposed free, that is, capable of acting *against* motives, punishment is disappointed of its object, and deprived of its justification."[24] Thus the metaphysical doctrine of free will, when its implications are acknowledged, works against any consciousness that one deserves punishment.

In the argument just given, Mill is assuming that punishment is forward-looking, aimed at changing the motives of the agent punished or the motives of other agents through the example. Another supposed justification of punishment is retribution: to make the criminal suffer for past crime, rather than to change future behavior of the agent or of others by example. Mill rejects the retributive justification for punishment, "which makes it intrinsically fitting that whenever there has been guilt, pain should be inflicted by way of retribution."[25] But he says that retribution isn't supported by the free-will doctrine either. "Suppose it true that the will of a malefactor, when he [or she] committed an offence, was free, or in other words, that he [or she] acted badly, not because he [or she] was of a bad disposition, but from no cause in particular: it is not easy to deduce from this the conclusion that it is just to punish him [or her].

[24] Ibid., 458.
[25] Ibid., 462.

That his [or her] acts were beyond the command of motives might be a good reason for keeping out of his [or her] way, or placing him [or her] under bodily restraint; but no reason for inflicting pain upon him [or her]."[26] Mill is pointing out that the traditional doctrine of free will, which disassociates actions from character as so far formed, makes behavior either random and unpredictable or like that of an insane person who acts out of control. In either case, retributive punishment is unjustified.

Mill gives a psychological account of how retributive sentiments are formed. In childhood the ideas of wrongdoing and punishment become associated, usually without any reason given for the connection. "This is quite enough to make the spontaneous feelings of mankind regard punishment and a wrongdoer as naturally fitted to each other; as a conjunction appropriate in itself, independently of any consequences."[27]

Mill has so far given a critical analysis of the free-will doctrine. But he has to answer those who say that on the theory of necessity, punishment is unjust because a person cannot help acting as he or she does, and it cannot be just to be punished for what one cannot help. This is the objection of the Owenites. Actions, the Owenites said, are the result of character, and a person is not the author of his or her own character. In reply to this Mill attempts to provide an account of the justification of punishment compatible with the doctrine of necessity. Mill's first reply is the rhetorical question: Is it inappropriate to punish "if the expectation of punishment enables him [or her] to help it, and is the only means by which he [or she] can be enabled to help it?"[28]

Mill says that there are two ends that, on the necessitarian theory, justify punishment: the benefit of the offenders themselves and the protection of others. The first is therapeutic,

[26] Ibid., 463.
[27] Ibid., 463–4.
[28] Ibid., 457.

"no more unjust than to administer medicine."[29] The justification is that "by counterbalancing the influence of present temptations, or acquired bad habits, it restores the mind to that normal preponderance of the love of right."[30] In its other aspect, as used to protect the just rights of others against unjust aggression by the offender, it is likewise just. "If it is possible to have just rights, (which is the same thing as to have rights at all) it cannot be unjust to defend them. Free-will or no free-will, it is just to punish so far as is necessary for this purpose, as it is just to put a wild beast to death (without unnecessary suffering) for the same object."[31]

Furthermore, Mill says, a person holding the necessitarians' view won't *feel* that punishment for wrong actions is unjust. He or she won't feel that, because an act is a consequence of motives, it therefore was not his or her fault. First, it is one's own defect for which the expectation of punishment is the appropriate cure. Second, the word "fault" is the name for a defect displayed – insufficient love of good and aversion to evil.

Finally, Mill distinguishes his theory from "Asiatic fatalism" and from "modified fatalism." The former is that certain things are going to occur regardless of attempts to avoid them, as with the story of Oedipus. The second is that "our actions are determined by our will, our will by our desires, and our desires by the joint influence of the motives presented to us and of our individual character; but that, our character having been made for us and not by us, we are not responsible for it, nor for the actions it leads to, and should in vain attempt to alter them."[32] It is the last phrase to which Mill objects. Not only our conduct but our character is in part amenable to our will. We can improve our character. We shall not indeed do so unless

[29] Ibid., 458.
[30] Ibid.
[31] Ibid., 460.
[32] Ibid., 465.

we desire our improvement and desire it more than we dislike the means that must be employed for the purpose. But it is a fact that we may dislike our current dispositions to behavior, our bad habits, and, if so, we may take steps to change them. To take the attitude that we are helpless against our own moral defects is, in Mill's view, faulty psychology.

MILL'S "PROOF" OF THE PRINCIPLE
OF UTILITY

THE "Principle of Utility" is that happiness is desirable, and the only thing desirable, as an end; all other things being only desirable as means to that end.[1] In Chapter 4 of *Utilitarianism*, Mill addresses himself to the question: "Of What Sort of Proof the Principle of Utility Is Susceptible." In Chapter 1, Mill has explained that "this cannot be proof in the ordinary and popular meaning of the term. Questions of ultimate ends are not amenable to direct proof. Whatever can be proved to be good, must be so by being shown to be a means to something admitted to be good without proof."[2] If "it is asserted that there is a comprehensive formula, including all things which are in themselves good," the formula "is not subject of what is commonly understood by proof..." (208 [I, 5]). But he then goes on to say, "We are not, however, to infer that its acceptance or rejection must depend on blind impulse or arbitrary choice.... The subject is within the cognizance of the rational faculty; and neither does that faculty deal with it solely in the way of intuition. Considerations may be capable of determining the intellect either to give or withhold its assent to the doctrine, and this is equivalent to proof" (208 [I, 5]).

The twelve paragraphs of Chapter 4 present an argument that, if successful, is one of the most important arguments in

---

[1] D. G. Brown, "What Is Mill's Principle of Utility?" *Canadian Journal of Philosophy* 3 (1973): 1–12, reprinted in *Mill's Utilitarianism: Critical Essays*, David Lyons, ed., 9–24. There has been controversy about what to count as Mill's "Principle." Brown's article is persuasive.

[2] John Stuart Mill, *Utilitarianism*, 207–8 (ch. 1, par. 5). Citations to this work in this chapter will be in parentheses in the text.

all of moral philosophy, for it would establish hedonism, in the broad meaning that Mill attaches to pleasure, as the valuational foundation for all of life and for morality as a part of that.

Unfortunately, few commentators on Mill have had their intellects convinced, and perhaps even fewer have agreed on the correct interpretation of the argument. J. B. Schneewind says of it: "A greater mare's nest has seldom been constructed. It is now generally agreed that Mill is not, in this chapter, betraying his own belief that proof of a first moral principle is impossible, but there is not a general agreement as to what he is doing."[3] Writing in 1965, Schneewind said that in the last fifteen years there had been more essays dealing with the topic of "Mill's Proof" than with any other single topic in the history of ethical thought.

Opponents of hedonism have been brutal in attacking the argument. As early as 1870, in the first full-length book on Mill's *Utilitarianism*, John Grote accused Mill of ambiguity in sliding from using "desirable" to refer to what is *actually desired* to using it to refer to what is *ideally desirable* – the *summum bonum*. The latter, he claimed, cannot be established by observation. Grote's editor, Joseph Mayor, also called attention to what he claimed is a false analogy between visible and audible, which mean "capable of being seen and heard," and desirable, which "does not mean capable of being desired, but deserving to be desired."[4] Mayor also charged Mill with the "fallacy of composition," using the word "all" at one time distributively and at another time collectively.[5] These charges, that Mill commits

---

[3]   J. B. Schneewind, Introduction to *Mill's Ethical Writings*, 31.

[4]   John Grote, *An Examination of the Utilitarian Philosophy*, Joseph Bickersteth Mayor, ed., n. 65.

[5]   Mayor interprets Mill's argument as asserting that each human being A, B, C, etc., naturally desires his own happiness; A, B, C, etc., make up all human beings, and the happiness of A, B, C, etc., makes up the happiness of all human beings; therefore every human being naturally desires the happiness of all human beings. As will be shown in the

the "fallacy of equivocation" and the "fallacy of composition" continue to be made by twentieth-century commentators.[6] In addition, G. E. Moore is famous for accusing Mill of committing the "naturalistic fallacy" of asserting that "good" means "desired."[7]

These accusations have led to a popular view that Mill's Chapter 4 is a complete failure. Typical is a statement such as George Sabine's in *A History of Political Thought*: "The desire for one's own greatest pleasure is the individual's only motive, and the greatest happiness of everyone is at once the standard of social good and the object of all moral action. Mill united these propositions by an argument so patently fallacious that it became a standard exhibit in textbooks of logic."[8]

In light of these attacks on Mill's logic, it is worthwhile to examine in detail the logic of his argument. Furthermore, Mill says that the evidence and his argument from it is "equivalent to proof," and at the end of Chapter 4, he even says that if the doctrine he has argued for is true – that nothing is a good to human beings but insofar as it is either pleasurable, or a means of attaining pleasure or averting pain – "the principle of utility is *proved*" (239 [IV, 12], emphasis added). In what

---

following text, this is not Mill's argument. Note that Mayor has used the word "desires," the psychological term, not "is a good to," the value term that Mill uses. F. H. Bradley, engaging in the same misinterpretation, makes a parody of it: "If many pigs are fed at one trough, each desires his own food, and somehow as a consequence does seem to desire the food of all; and by parity of reasoning it should follow that each pig, desiring his own pleasure, desires the pleasure of all." F. H. Bradley, *Ethical Studies*, 113. Others, recognizing that Mill moves from what is "a good" to one person to what is "a good" to the aggregate of all persons, have similarly accused him of the fallacy of composition. There is an extended study of this charge in Necip Fikri Alican, *Mill's Principle of Utility: A Defence of John Stuart Mill's Notorious Proof*, ch. 4.

6   For example, H. J. McCloskey, *John Stuart Mill: A Critical Study*, 62.

7   George Edward Moore, *Principia Ethica*, 66.

8   George H. Sabine, *A History of Political Theory*, 707.

follows, I present the structure of the argument in deductive form. In that way we can determine the nature of the premises he introduces, locate the gaps that prevent it from being a valid deduction, and see if plausible assumptions can be formulated or interpretations offered that will support the premises and bridge the gaps. I shall present what I believe to be a reasonable interpretation of what Mill had in mind, and I shall claim that the assumptions necessary to make the argument sound are – though controversial – at least plausible.

The conclusion that Mill is seeking is stated in paragraph two: "The utilitarian doctrine is that happiness is desirable, and the only thing desirable, as an end, all other things being only desirable as a means to that end" (234 [IV, 2]). The connection between this idea and morality is mentioned at the end of paragraph nine, where he says that the promotion of happiness is the test by which to judge all human conduct, "from whence it necessarily follows that it must be the criterion of morality, since a part is included in the whole" (237 [IV, 9]). Mill has a complex view of the way the ultimate standard of the promotion of happiness is to be applied in morality, as is discussed in the chapters of this work that deal with rules, rights, and justice. And morality is only one of the "three departments" of what he calls the "Art of Life." These views on testing conduct, and the place of morality within this framework, are found elsewhere in the essay and in *System of Logic.*[9] They are not part of the proof and are discussed elsewhere. The proof is aimed only at the conclusion that happiness is desirable and the only thing desirable as an end.

The structure of the argument is very simple. In paragraph three Mill argues that happiness is desirable. In the remainder of the chapter he argues that happiness is the only thing desirable. The outline of the argument can be given in Mill's own words.

[9]   John Stuart Mill, *A System of Logic*, ch. 12, sec. 6.

The argument that happiness is *a* good is so obvious to Mill that he presents it in one paragraph:

(1) "The sole evidence it is possible to produce that anything is desirable is that people do actually desire it" (para. 3).

(2) "Each person, so far as he [or she] believes it to be attainable, desires his [or her] own happiness" (para. 3).

(Therefore,)

(3) "Happiness is a good" (para. 3).

Although he substitutes the expression "is a good" for the earlier expression "is desirable," I presume that this is only for stylistic reasons, and I think that he would regard these two expressions as interchangeable in this context.[10]

The argument to show that happiness is the only thing desirable as an end is likewise based on the evidence of actual desire:[11]

(4) "Human nature is so constituted as to desire nothing which is not either a part of happiness or a means to happiness" (para. 9, but argued through paras. 5–10).

(Therefore,)

(5) "Nothing is a good to human beings but in so far as it is either pleasurable or a means of attaining pleasure or averting pain" (para. 11).

Here his use of "pleasure" and "pleasurable" instead of "happiness" is, once again, merely stylistic. Throughout the essay he says that by "happiness" he means pleasure and freedom from pain.

This is the simple outline of the argument. It is complicated by the fact that each individual's desire is for that individual's *own* happiness, whereas the utilitarian doctrine that Mill is

---

[10] In her essay, "Mill's Theory of Value," *Theoria* 36 (1970): 100–15, Dorothy Mitchell makes a distinction between "desirable" and "good" based on an analysis of the use of "desirable" in contexts of ordinary language. I think that she is correct that they are not synonyms in English, but I think, nevertheless, that Mill is using them as such in this essay.

[11] Necip Fikri Alican gives a different outline of this "second part" of Mill's proof. See Necip Fikri Alican, *Mill's Principle of Utility*, 158–9.

seeking to establish is that the *general* happiness is the foundation of morality.[12] In paragraph three, this distinction is explicit. Having said that each person desires his or her own happiness, Mill says that we have all the proof it is possible to require "that happiness is a good, that each person's happiness is a good to that person, and the general happiness, therefore, a good to the aggregate of all persons."

These propositions we may state as separate theses:

(3A) "Each person's happiness is a good to that person" (para. 3).

(3B) "[T]he general happiness, therefore, [is] a good to the aggregate of all persons."

This distinction also can be introduced into the second part of the argument. Without doubt the psychological premise (4) means:

(4*) Each person desires nothing that is not either a part of his [or her] happiness or a means of his [or her] happiness.[13]

And parallel to (3A) and (3B), the distinction between each person and the aggregate of all persons can be introduced. This would give:

(5A) Nothing is a good to each person but insofar as it is either a part of his [or her] happiness or a means of his [or her] happiness.

(5B) Nothing is a good to the aggregate of all persons, therefore, but insofar as it is either a part of the general happiness or a means of the general happiness.

---

[12] For a discussion of this point, see H. R. West, "Reconstructing Mill's 'Proof' of the Principle of Utility," *Mind* 81 (1972): 256–7.

[13] This part of Mill's psychological doctrine is stated explicitly in his essay on "Whewell's Moral Philosophy." He quotes Whewell as saying that "we cannot desire anything else unless by identifying it with our happiness." To this Mill says that he should have nothing to object, "if by identification was meant that what we desire unselfishly must first, by a mental process, become an actual part of what we seek as our own happiness; that the good of others becomes our pleasure because we have learnt to find pleasure in it; this is, we think, the true philosophical account of the matter" ["Whewell's Moral Philosophy,"184].

From (3B) and (5B), we can then deduce an interpretation of the "utilitarian doctrine" as follows:

(6) "[The general] happiness [or a part of the general happiness] is desirable, and the only thing desirable, as an end, all other things being only desirable as means to that end" (para. 2).

Examining the argument, it can be seen that (1) is a methodological premise; (2) and (4) are factual premises; (3) or (3A) and (5) or (5A) are supported by (2) and (4), respectively; and (3B) and (5B) putatively follow from (3A) and (5A), respectively. The premise (2) is probably uncontroversial. One's own happiness, even interpreted as "an existence made up of few and transitory pains, many and various pleasures" (215 [II, 11]), is at least one thing desired as an end by each person, so far as he [or she] believes it to be attainable. Even the ascetic desires this, either believing it to be attainable only in some afterlife or believing it to be incompatible with the satisfaction of other desires. The controversial premises are (1) and (4), and the controversial steps are from the fact of happiness being desired to its being normatively desirable, and from each person's happiness being desirable to that person to the conclusion that the general happiness is desirable to the aggregate of all people. There seem, then, to be three central issues: (A) Mill's methodology, which is to argue for what is desirable on the evidence of what is in fact desired; (B) his psychological hedonism, that one desires one's own happiness as an end and nothing as an end that is not a part of one's happiness; and (C) the argument that if each person's happiness is a good and inclusive of the only good for that person, as an end, the general happiness is a good, and encompasses the only good, as an end, to the aggregate of all persons. I shall take these issues up in turn.

First, is actual desire the sole evidence it is possible to produce that anything is desirable? It is hardly necessary to point out that Mill did not say that "desirable" or "good" *means* "desired," as G. E. Moore says he does. He is not committing a naturalistic or definist fallacy.[14] But Mill opens himself to this charge by his language in a footnote in Chapter 5, where he says, "...for what is the principle of utility, if it be not that 'happiness' and 'desirable' are synonymous terms" (257n [V, 36]).[15] This is a puzzling use of "synonymous," but it would be absurd to think that Mill's appeal to psychological evidence, "practised self-consciousness and self-observation, assisted by the observation of others" (237 [IV, 10]), is to support the claim that "happiness is desirable" is a tautology. Mill apparently simply means that the two terms are applicable to the same phenomena, one descriptively, the other normatively. Mill is quite explicit in demarcating factual from normative propositions.[16]

It is also incredible to think, as Joseph Mayor argues, that Mill was misled by the similarity of the verbal endings of "visible" and "audible" into thinking that "desirable" means "able to be desired."[17] The significance of the analogy that he is making between "visible" and "desirable" is announced in the first paragraph of the chapter: The first premises of our knowledge do not admit of proof by reasoning, but are subject to a direct appeal to the senses; the first premises of conduct are subject to a direct appeal to our desiring faculty (234 [IV, 1]). If "desirable" meant "able to be desired," it would be a matter of knowledge.

[14] Moore's interpretation of Mill as committing the "naturalistic fallacy" is analyzed and refuted by E. W. Hall, "The 'Proof' of Utility in Bentham and Mill," *Ethics* 60 (1949–50): 1–18.

[15] R. F. Atkinson calls attention to the problem in that passage in "J. S. Mill's 'Proof' of the Principle of Utility," *Philosophy* 32 (1957): 164.

[16] This is found in *System of Logic* where he says that a first principle of an art (including the art of life, which embodies the first principles of all conduct) enunciates an object aimed at and affirms it to be a desirable object. It does not assert that anything is, but enjoins that something should be. "A proposition of which the predicate is expressed by the words *ought* or *should be*, is generically different from one which is expressed by *is*, or *will be*" (*A System of Logic* 949 [bk. 6, ch. 12, sec. 6]).

[17] This claim is found in many criticisms but also in some that think that Mill was not misled but was intentionally using "desirable" in the sense of "capable of being desired." An example is Grenville Wall, "Mill on Happiness as an End," *Philosophy* 57 (1982): 537–41.

But Mill does not regard what is desirable as a matter of fact. The analogy is that as judgments of matters of fact are based on the evidence of the senses and corrected by further evidence of the senses, so judgments of what is desirable are based on what is desired and corrected by further evidence of what is desired. The only evidence on which a recommendation of an ultimate end of conduct can be based is what is found to be appealing to the desiring faculty.

The argument does, however, also include an appeal to desire by what is a pragmatic argument: "If the end which the utilitarian doctrine proposes to itself were not, in theory and in practice, acknowledged to be an end, nothing could ever convince any person that it was so" (234 [IV, 3]). Nothing about the logic of recommending an end of conduct prevents any end whatsoever from being recommended, but only one based on actual desires will be convincing. This is one respect in which the "proof" is not a proof in the ordinary sense. There is no logical necessity about accepting desire as the sole evidence for desirability. It is logically possible that ends of conduct that are not in fact desired may be recommended without contradiction. The force of the appeal to what is desired is only to convince, not logically to rule out all other possibilities. But, unless there is a plausible alternative, it will carry weight.

The import of premise (1), then, is primarily negative. It denies the existence of an intellectual intuition of the normative ends of conduct. That is, Mill is denying that we intuit what is intrinsically a good in some directly cognitive way. And he is also denying that there is any overarching physical or metaphysical structure on the basis of which normative ends of conduct can be determined.

The only way to argue a negative claim such as this conclusively would be to take each putative alternative and examine it critically to try to show that it can be reduced to desire or else to absurdity. To some extent this is what Mill does in his efforts to show that such values as virtue are desired as parts of happiness. Virtue would be a candidate for something that is intuited to be good as an end. By accounting for the desire for virtue as due to psychological association of virtue and vice with pleasure and pain, Mill is indirectly accounting for any claim that virtue is intuited to be good as an end.

In *Utilitarianism* Mill does not address alternatives such as the position in Aristotle's *Nicomachean Ethics* that rational activity is the fundamental end of conduct based on the place of humans at the pinnacle a natural hierarchy in which rationality distinguishes humans from lower animals.[18] But in other writings he had argued against nature or God's will as foundations for ethics, as indicated in Chapter 2. Mill would probably argue that Aristotle's teleological view of nature is plausible only if one believes in a creator God; and his arguments against the benevolence of such a God, if there is such a God, would be arguments against basing the normative end of conduct upon the hierarchy of nature or, for that matter, the direction of evolution. And, as indicated in Chapter 2, he thinks that a purposive Nature, with or without a God, is far from benign.

Furthermore, Aristotle's strongest arguments against hedonism in the final book of *Nicomachean Ethics* are based on the evidence of desire. Aristotle gives as an argument against hedonism that "no one would choose to live with the intellect of a child throughout his life, however much he were to be pleased at the things that children are pleased at, nor to get enjoyment by doing some disgraceful deed, though he were never to feel any pain in consequence.[19] And there are many things we should be keen about even if they brought no pleasure, e.g., seeing, remembering, knowing, possessing the virtues. If pleasures necessarily accompany these, that makes no odds; we should choose these even if no pleasure resulted."[20] This is

[18] Aristotle, *Nicomachean Ethics*, translated by W. D. Ross, bk. 1, sec. 7.
[19] Mill may have had these passages in mind when arguing for the distinction between superior and inferior qualities of pleasure (footnote added).
[20] Aristotle, *Nicomachean Ethics*, bk. 10, sec. 3.

Aristotle's statement of the opponents of hedonism. His own conclusion is equivocal. He says that "whether we choose life for the sake of pleasure or pleasure for the sake of life is a question we may dismiss for the present. For they seem to be bound up together and not to admit of separation, since without activity pleasure does not arise, and every activity is completed by the attendant pleasure."[21] This is very close to Mill's claim that things other than happiness that are desired as ends are desired as parts of happiness. Furthermore, Aristotle supports Mill's use of desire as at least one criterion of what is good: "Those who object that that at which all things aim is not necessarily good are, we may surmise, talking nonsense.... [A]nd the man who attacks this belief will hardly have anything more credible to maintain instead. If it is senseless creatures that desire the things in question, there might be something in what they say; but if intelligent creatures do so as well, what sense can there be in this view?"[22]

Those who reject Mill's appeal to actual desires as the criteria for the ends of conduct have the burden of proof to give an alternative. As indicated in Chapter 2, Mill gives arguments against the most common alternatives – intuition, Nature, the will of God. I too am unconvinced by any of these alternatives. I believe that Mill's skepticism of alternatives is justified. However, the desires that we do have provide practical ends that will be pursued unless frustrated by the pursuit of the ends of other desires. These desires provide an arena in which practical reason can seek to bring order out of disorder by analyzing desires to determine which, if any, are illusory; which, if any, are fundamental; and what, if anything, is the common object of them all. It is this last question that Mill's psychological hedonism claims to answer.

Mill does not use the term "psychological hedonism," and the term itself is ambiguous. It may mean that one always acts

[21] Ibid., sec. 4.
[22] Ibid., sec. 2.

to maximize immediate momentary pleasure (or to minimize immediate momentary pain), or it may mean that one always acts to maximize net pleasure in the long run (or minimize net pain). Or these alternatives could be combined to say that one always acts either to maximize immediate momentary pleasure or net pleasure in the long run (or minimize pain, immediately or in the long run). Mill, however, holds a still different version, which is more plausible. It is that all motivation is ultimately from pleasure and pain, but through the process of association and habit formation, pleasure is not always the conscious object of desire and not all motives are the anticipation of pleasure or of pain: "... [A] motive does not mean always, or solely, the anticipation of a pleasure or of a pain. ... As we proceed in the formation of habits, and become accustomed to will a particular act or a particular course of conduct because it is pleasurable, we at last continue to will it without any reference to its being pleasurable."[23] This can still be called "psychological hedonism," I think, because Mill believes that all habits are derived from desires, and desires for and aversions from objects other than pleasure and pain are ultimately derived, by association, from the desire for pleasure and the aversion to pain. It is important to keep these distinctions in mind in examining the controversy surrounding what I have called Mill's psychological hedonism.

The argument for his psychological hedonism – Proposition (4) – has two parts. One is in paragraph eleven, which classifies as mere habit those ends of conduct that are sought neither as means of happiness nor as a part of happiness. Here Mill claims that such acts of will have become ends of conduct derivatively. "Will is the child of desire, and passes out of the dominion of its parent only to come under that of habit. That which is the result of habit affords no presumption of being intrinsically good" (238 [IV, 11]). An example of this habit formation would be obsessive or addictive behavior that is even contrary to conscious desire, or any pattern of behavior that has

---

[23] *A System of Logic*, 842 (bk. 6, ch. 2, sec. 4).

become habitual and is done without thought or deliberation. Mill's claim, then, leaves him with everything that affords any presumption of being intrinsically good as being also an object of conscious desire.

Mill may here underplay the role of genetics in human behavior. There may be much human motivation that is the product of natural selection, having survival value or having once had survival value and now producing behavior without ever going through the process of being an object of conscious desire. There is a fine line in the nervous system between what is autonomous (and genetic) and what is not autonomous. Some emotional reactions to situations may be genetically based. But isn't Mill right that such behavior has to be evaluated critically before providing any presumption of its being intrinsically good (or bad)? If the behavior is a means to survival, then it derives its value from the value of life, whose continuation it supports. And the value of life, or of the quality of life that makes life of value, is what is at issue here.

The other part of Mill's argument, found in paragraphs four through ten, is to claim that every object of conscious desire is associated with pleasure or the absence of pain, either as a means or an end. Many desires are acquired, such as the desire for virtue or for the possession of money, and have come to be desired through the mechanism of their association with pleasure or the absence of pain. Whether acquired or not, however, the ultimate ends of the desires can be regarded as experiences or states of affairs with a pleasure component: They are pleasures or "parts of happiness" (236 [IV, 6]). Although they may fall under various other descriptions, it is the fact that they are ingredients of happiness that provides a common denominator and supports a unified account of desire.

It is tempting to read into Mill the claim that it is the agreeable quality of the state of consciousness desired that is the real object of desire. Just as the sense-data theorist claims that one sees only sense data, although it is palpable that he sees things that, in common languages, are decidedly distinguished from sense data (i.e., from whatever common-language words are sense-data words – "sights," "sounds," "appearances," or whatever), so Mill might be thought to hold that one desires only the pleasure component of desired experiences, although it is palpable that people "do desire things, which, in common language, are decidedly distinguished from happiness" (234–5 [IV, 4]). J. S. Mill's father, James Mill, apparently did hold such a view: "... [W]e have a desire for water to drink, for fire to warm us, and so on." But, "... it is not the water we desire, but the pleasure of drinking; not the fire we desire, but the pleasure of warmth."[24] This is impossible to reconcile with J. S. Mill's talk of the objects of desire including "music," "health," "virtue," "power," "fame," "possession of money." These, in J. S. Mill's view, have come to be desired through association with pleasure, or their absence with pain, but once this has occurred the pleasure or pain may be felt not at the *prospect* of obtaining pleasure when the object of desire is attained, but pleasure may be felt *antecedently* at the prospect of obtaining the object of desire. In an early work, "Remarks on Bentham's Philosophy," Mill criticizes Bentham in this regard: "... [T]hat all our acts are determined by pains and pleasures *in prospect*, pains and pleasures to which we look forward as the *consequences* of our acts ... as a universal truth, can in no way be maintained. The pain or pleasure that determines conduct is as frequently one which *precedes* the moment of action as one which follows it. A man [or woman] ... recoils from the very thought of committing the act.... His [or her] conduct is determined by pain; but by a pain which precedes the act, not by one which is expected to follow it."[25] This is an important point in Mill's psychology, explaining how one can desire as an end things other than one's own experiences. I can desire that my children be happy, by the antecedent pleasure at the thought of their happiness,

---

[24] James Mill, *Analysis of the Phenomena of the Human Mind*, 2nd ed., ch. 19. J. S. Mill, in a note, criticizes this view.
[25] "Remarks on Bentham's Philosophy," 12.

not just by the thought that I shall be happy on finding out that they are happy. I can desire as an end that someone else recover from an illness by the antecedent pain felt on thinking about the illness, not just by the anticipation of later pain if the person does not recover. I can have desires for objective states of affairs through the mechanism of feeling pleasure or pain at the thought of the state of affairs.

Returning to Mill's examples, the desire for music, health, etc., has as its object music, etc., not just pleasure, although at the same time it may be for the pleasure of music, or there may be pleasure at the anticipation of music or of the pleasure of music. Furthermore, Mill does not need to make the strong claim that desire is only for the pleasure of music. He only needs to claim that, as a psychological fact, music, health, etc., would not be desired if no pleasure or freedom from pain or past association with these were connected with music, health, etc. Desire is evidence of desirability, but it does not confer desirability. This is obvious in the case of things desired as means. On reflection, it is also obvious in the case of things desired as ends. The possession of money is desired as an end by the miser. This desire does not make the possession of money as an end a normative object of action for a reasonable person. The evidence of desire must be analyzed; it is only by analysis of the fact that the miser desires the possession of money as part of his [or her] happiness – that he [or she] would be made happy by its possession or unhappy by its loss – that the evidence of desire fits into a comprehensive theory. It is this comprehensive theory that identifies the pleasure inherent in desirable things as what makes them desirable. The pleasure inherent in them does not itself have to be discriminated as the sole *object* of desire.[26]

Some commentators also have thought that Mill reduces the relation between desire and pleasure to a trivial one in the

---

[26] Wendy Donner has a detailed discussion of whether pleasure must be a phenomenally distinguishable element of the complex experience. See Wendy Donner, *The Liberal Self*, 19–23.

passage where he says that: "desiring a thing and finding it pleasant, aversion to it and thinking of it as painful, are phenomena entirely inseparable, or rather two parts of the same phenomenon – in strictness of language, two different modes of naming the same psychological fact; that to think of an object as desirable (unless for the sake of its consequences), and to think of it as pleasant, are one and the same thing; and that to desire anything, except in proportion as the idea of it is pleasant, is a physical and metaphysical impossibility" (237–8 [IV, 10]).

This statement is certainly puzzling to the twenty-first-century reader, but in context Mill is asking the reader to engage in "practiced self-consciousness and self-observation" (237 [IV, 10]). If the terms were reducible to one another independent of observation, it is hard to see why he would invite one to attempt what appears to be an empirical confirmation. A clue to interpretation is that "metaphysical" means approximately "psychological" for him.[27] In his notes to his father's *Analysis of the Phenomena of the Human Mind*, Mill takes issue with his father's statement, "The term 'Idea of a pleasure' expresses precisely the same thing as the term, 'Desire.' It does so by the very import of the words."[28] J. S. Mill says that desire "is more

---

[27] For example, he says that "the peculiar character of what we term *moral* feelings is not a question of ethics but of metaphysics," "Whewell's Moral Philosophy," 185. This interpretation of the term "metaphysical" is argued forcefully in M. Mandelbaum, "On Interpreting Mill's *Utilitarianism*," *Journal of the History of Philosophy* 6 (1968): 39.

[28] James Mill, *Analysis of the Phenomena of the Human Mind*, 2nd ed., 191. The passage continues: "The idea of a pleasure, is the idea of something as good to have. But what is a desire, other than the idea of something as good to have; good to have, being really nothing but desirable to have? The terms, therefore, 'idea of pleasure,' and 'desire,' are but two names; the thing named, the state of consciousness, is one and the same" (191–2). James Mill follows this by the comment that "aversion" and "desire" are ambiguous and are applied to the ideas of the causes of our pleasurable and painful sensations, as well as to the ideas of those sensations. We have an aversion to a food or to a drug. "The food is a substance of a certain colour, and consistence; so is the drug. There is nothing in these qualities which is offensive to us; only the taste"

than the idea of pleasure desired, being, in truth, the initiatory state of Will. In what we call Desire there is, I think, always included a positive stimulation to action. . . . "[29] According to J. S. Mill, then, a distinction is to be made between desiring a thing and thinking of it as pleasant. Desire is psychologically more complex and conceivably could have an object not thought of as pleasurable. It is obvious that it may have a more inclusive object, as is the case in desiring the means to an end when the means are unpleasant. In any case, the question is a psychological not a linguistic one.

Part of Mill's argument is that the nonhedonistic things desired as ends, such as virtue, are desired as "parts" of happiness. This requires further analysis and comment.

What can be meant by saying that something is desired as "part" of my happiness? Mill says, "The ingredients of happiness are very various, and each of them is desirable in itself, and not merely when considered as swelling an aggregate" (235 [IV, 5]). The ingredients or parts are not to be looked at merely as a means to a collective something termed happiness. ". . . [B]esides being means, they are part of the end" (235 [IV, 5]). He discusses the way in which the desire for money, originally desired as a means to other ends, may become desired as an end. The same, he claims, may be said for the majority of the great objects of human life, such as the desire for power or for fame. "What was once desired as an instrument for the attainment of happiness, has come to be desired for its own sake. In being desired for its own sake it is, however, desired as *part* of happiness. The person is made, or thinks he would be made, happy by its mere possession; and is made unhappy by failure to obtain it. The desire of it is not a different thing from

---

(192). James Mill also qualifies his statement by saying that desire is used to mark the idea of a pleasurable sensation when the future is associated with it. "The idea of a pleasurable sensation, to come, is what is commonly meant by Desire" (193).

[29] James Mill, *Analysis of the Phenomena of the Human Mind*, vol. 2, 194, n. 37.

the desire of happiness, any more than the love of music, or the desire of health. They are included in happiness. They are some of the elements of which the desire of happiness is made up. Happiness is not an abstract idea, but a concrete whole; and these are some of its parts. And the utilitarian standard sanctions and approves their being so. Life would be a poor thing, very ill provided with sources of happiness, if there were not this provision of nature, by which things originally indifferent, but conducive to, and otherwise associated with, the satisfaction of our primitive desires, become in themselves sources of pleasure more valuable than the primitive pleasures, both in permanency, in the space of human existence that they are capable of covering, and even in intensity" (236 [IV, 6]).

Although Mill expresses an evaluative judgment in the last sentence, asserting that some of the experiences that have come to be desired through association with primitive pleasures are more pleasurable than the primitive pleasures – they are "higher" pleasures, as he has argued in Chapter 2 – the argument rests on a psychological, not an ethical, claim. Mill is not at this point of his argument claiming that the desire for money as an end in itself makes it supremely desirable as an end in itself. It may very well be that coming to associate pleasure with possession of money, to the point that money has come to be desired as an end, is unfortunate, preventing one from finding happiness in other things that would give more pleasure. Mill's claim is that, as a psychological fact, one would not desire money as an end in itself unless it had been, or continues to be, associated with pleasure or the avoidance of pain.

There are really two dimensions to Mill's claim, and distinguishing them from one another will help to clarify his argument. One is a theory of how we come to desire things such as virtue as ends in themselves. It is a claim about the past as to how we have come to desire them. The other is an analysis of what it is that makes the thing to be currently desired and would make it no longer desired if it did not have a pleasure component.

The first of these dimensions comes from the general theory of associationist psychology, according to which an infant starts out with primitive sensations, some of which are pleasurable and some of which are painful, and develops "ideas" that are copies of the sensations or copies of the materials presented to the mind through the sensory experiences. Through resemblance or contiguity in space or succession in time, complex ideas are formed from the simple ideas of sensation, and through the faculties of memory, imagination, abstraction, classification, induction leading to beliefs concerning causal connections, and so on, the rich psychological life of a mature human being develops. Through association with pleasures or pains, ideas, states of belief, and activities that are originally indifferent – neither pleasurable nor painful – come to be pleasurable or painful. In his text, Mill uses music and health as examples of sources of sensations that are primitively pleasurable, although musical appreciation no doubt requires education to be developed to the fullest. It is easy to see how an individual, through association of health with agreeable feelings and sickness with disagreeable feelings, can come to desire health as an end and to choose appropriate means to stay healthy without thinking of health as itself a means to pleasure and avoidance of pain.

Associationist psychology would likewise account for the desire for power and fame as due to the experience of the feeling of power being conjoined with pleasure, and powerlessness conjoined with pain. After frequent associations, power comes to be sought for its own sake, and means are chosen to its attainment without paying attention to the pleasure associated with it or the pain associated with its absence. Thus, one part of Mill's argument, based on this psychological theory, is that one would never have desired power and fame as ends unless there had been a history in the individual's life of association of power or fame with pleasure and pain. If pleasure and pain are the *causes* of one's coming to desire power and fame as ends, then they are necessary conditions for such desires. It is therefore psychologically impossible to desire something as an end unless it has first been associated with pleasure or avoidance of pain. This theory was probably persuasive to Mill.[30] And it is at least the partial story, if not the whole story, of how we come to develop our ends in life. But it is not the only argument and perhaps not the most important for establishing Mill's conclusion. Pleasure and pain could be the psychological *means* by which goals in life are developed, but it does not follow that one therefore desires nothing that is not either a means of happiness or a part of happiness. That requires an introspective examination of current desires, not a story as to how those desires came to be developed.

The second part of Mill's argument is to engage in "practised self-consciousness and self-observation, assisted by observation of others" (237 [IV, 10]). Mill is claiming that anything that is desired as an end will be found to have a pleasure component or an avoidance of pain component, and that on self-observation, it will be found that we find our happiness there. A survey of some things that I desire may satisfy me that this is so. Many things will turn out not to be desired as ends, but clearly as means. I desire to lose weight, to be a good tennis player, to have time to listen to music. These are things that I seek to achieve, but they are obviously means to my happiness and not desired except as they are expected to increase my happiness or decrease my unhappiness.

To test Mill's claim, suppose that we take some end that is believed to be desired as an end independent of pleasure and pain. Aristotle gives as an argument against hedonism that we would desire "seeing, remembering, knowing, possessing the virtues" even if they brought no pleasure. The self-examination required here is difficult. Because these all *do* bring pleasure or avoidance of pain, it is extremely difficult to be sure that we

---

[30] For Mill's acceptance of the associationist theory, the chief source is James Mill, *Analysis of the Phenomena of the Human Mind*, 2nd ed. Mill's notes, with abstracts to identify their contexts, are reprinted in John Stuart Mill, *Miscellaneous Writings*, vol. 31 of *Collected Works of John Stuart Mill*, 93–253.

do not desire them independently. Let us take the activity of seeing. Not only does sight give us the pleasure of seeing the beauty of a blue sky or of a flower in bloom, it gives us the power of recognizing the faces of the people that we love, and its absence would make us dependent upon others for reading books and for much of our physical mobility. Let us try the thought experiment of supposing that seeing is painful. There would be trade-offs in pleasure and pain. It would be painful to use our sight to see the beauty of a blue sky in order to enjoy the pleasure of the beauty. Depending upon the pain, we might prefer to forgo the pleasure. Knowing is clearly a source of pleasure and avoidance of pain, and it isn't obvious that knowing is desired apart from that. Does one desire to have completely useless knowledge apart from past association with pleasure? Do I desire to know the number of molecules in this room? If so, isn't it because it will give me the pleasure of amazement or the pleasure of showing off my knowledge to someone? Possessing the virtues is a source not only of the respect of others but of self-esteem, which is pleasurable, and lack of self-esteem if I don't possess them. Can I separate these and say that I would desire to possess the virtues if doing so didn't give me self-esteem? So it isn't clear that seeing, remembering, knowing, and even possessing the virtues are desired independently of the pleasure or avoidance of pain that they bring.

But suppose that someone says that he or she would desire to know or to possess a virtue such as honesty even if painful. James Griffin gives the example of Freud refusing to take painkilling drugs in order to think clearly at the very end of his life: "I prefer," he said, "to think in torment than not to be able to think clearly."[31] This would seem to be an example refuting Mill's position. How might Mill reply to it? First, Mill might reply that this a case of habit. Freud has found his happiness tied

---

[31] James Griffin, *Well-Being*, 8, quoting Ernest Jones, *The Life and Work of Sigmund Freud*, 655–6.

up with his intellectual activities and achievements through a lifetime and now has developed an unbreakable pattern of behavior frustrating his desire to have relief from physical pain. He can't choose otherwise. But let us suppose that Freud is expressing a genuine desire to think clearly as an end in itself. A hedonistic account can easily be given of how he came to have this desire. Freud has come to associate pleasure with his intellectual activities and achievements. But is thinking clearly *now* something that is "part of his happiness," when it is at the expense of physical pain? It could be. Thinking clearly is part of Freud's sense of self-esteem. Self-esteem is part of his happiness and loss of it part of his unhappiness. This may be such that the pain of the thought of not thinking clearly is greater than the pain at the thought of physical pain.

The self-examination here described can be extended to one's desires for the well-being of one's children or friends. What do I most want for my children? I want them to be happy. I want them to find their happiness in intellectual and socially conscious activities. I want them to be in loving relationships and to possess the virtues. But I want them to find their happiness in these relationships and virtues, not to be in tormenting relationships or to suffer torment in the practice of the virtues.

Others may differ from my and Mill's self-examination. But I am persuaded that it is meaningful to assert that when desires for ends are distinguished from things sought merely on the basis of habit, they are desired as "parts of happiness." And my self-examination agrees with Mill that it is relationship to happiness and unhappiness that makes these things desired or undesired as ends.

Mill's substantive claim, then, is that desire and pleasure (or aversion and pain) are psychologically inseparable. If this is true, two things follow: first, Proposition (4) is established – each person desires nothing that is not either a part of his [or her] happiness or a means of his [or her] happiness; second, because attainment of pleasure and avoidance of pain are the common denominators of desire, the evidence of desire supports the theory that it is the pleasure and pain aspects of the objects of desire and aversion that make them desirable and undesirable and that should serve as the criteria of good and bad consequences in a normative theory of conduct.

An adequate defense of Mill's position would require a more thorough analysis of desire and of pleasure and pain, happiness and unhappiness. I believe, however, that the interpretation given shows that the position does not completely lack plausibility and that it might be supported by such a refined analysis.

I turn now to the move from Proposition (3A) to Proposition (3B). If the intellect is convinced that a person's happiness is good and the sole good to that person, does it follow that it will be convinced that the general happiness is a good and the sole good to the aggregate of all persons? Mill presumably thinks that this is obvious, simply asserting it without argument. He apparently thinks that he has practically established (3B) when he has established (3A), and (5B) when he has established (5A). I think that Mill has been misinterpreted in this argument because commentators have thought that the conclusion is a much stronger claim than it is. He is making a very weak claim, which is seen when we notice what he means by "the general happiness."

According to Mill "the general happiness" is a mere sum of instances of individual happiness. There are still two ways of understanding the argument. One is that "to that person" represents the point of view of the agent when he is making prudential decisions; "to the aggregate" represents the point of view of the benevolent person when he is acting morally. Some things can be said in support of this interpretation, but I do not think that it is the correct one. I think rather that Mill believes that his analysis of desire shows that happiness is the *kind* of thing that constitutes intrinsic welfare, wherever it occurs. All instances of happiness will be parts of the personal welfare of someone, that is, "a good *to someone*," but being instances of happiness, they have a common denominator that makes them the same

140

kind of thing wherever they occur – whether in different experiences of a given individual or in the experiences of different individuals.

Moreover, Mill assumes that the value of different instances of happiness can be thought of as summed up to generate a larger good. These assumptions are explicit in a letter that Mill wrote regarding the move from (3A) to (3B): "As to the sentence you quote from my *Utilitarianism*, when I said the general happiness is a good to the aggregate of all persons I did not mean that every human being's happiness is a good to every other human being, though I think in a good state of society and education it would be so. I merely meant in this particular sentence to argue that since A's happiness is a good, B's a good, C's a good, etc., the sum of all these goods must be a good."[32] His assumptions are even more explicit in a footnote to Chapter V of *Utilitarianism*. There, answering the objection that the principle of utility presupposes the anterior principle that everybody has an equal right to happiness, Mill says: "It may be more correctly described as supposing that equal amounts of happiness are equally desirable, whether felt by the same or by different persons. This, however, is not a presupposition; not a premise needful to support the principle of utility, but the very principle itself.... If there is any anterior principle implied, it can be no other than this, that the truths of arithmetic are applicable to the valuation of happiness, as of all other measurable quantities" (257–8 [V, 36]). It seems clear, then, that the "to each person" in (3A) and (5A) does not represent a "point of view," but simply the location or embodiment of welfare that cannot exist without location or embodiment, and the "to the aggregate of all persons" in (3B) and (5B) refers to the location or embodiment of welfare in a group of individuals, not a point of view. A good to the aggregate of A, B, C, etc., is interpreted by Mill to be a sum of good or goods to A, plus good or goods

---

[32] Letter to Henry Jones, June 13, 1868, *The Later Letters of John Stuart Mill 1849–1873*, vol. 16, 1414.

to B, plus good or goods to C, etc. He assumes both that happiness is arithmetical, capable of being summed up to find a total, "general" happiness, and that goods to different people are arithmetical, capable of being summed up to find a total good "to the aggregate of all persons."[33]

With these assumptions, (3B) does follow from (3A), for to say that the general happiness is a good to the aggregate of all persons is merely to say that A's happiness, plus B's happiness, plus C's happiness, etc., constitutes a good to A, plus a good to B, plus a good to C, etc. And (5B) follows from (5A). If nothing is a good to each person but insofar as it is a part of his or her happiness (or a means to it), then nothing will be part of the sum of goods to A, plus goods to B, plus goods to C, etc., but insofar as it is a part of the happiness of A or part of the happiness of B, etc., or a means to these. This explains why Mill did not bother to state (5A) and (5B) explicitly and why he passed from (3A) to (3B) in one sentence. The evidence of desire shows that happiness is the *kind* of thing desirable as an end. It is not a different kind of thing when it is located in A's experience from what it is when it is located in B's experience. Thus, whether or not any single individual desires the general happiness, if each of its parts is shown to be desirable by the evidence of desire, because of the kind of thing each part is, then the sum of these parts will be desirable because it is simply a summation of instances of the same kind of thing.[34] Given

---

[33] These assumptions are, of course, controversial. For example, they are denied by John Marshall, "Egalitarianism and General Happiness," in *The Limits of Utilitarianism*, 35–41. Marshall says that it is false that happiness is additive in the required way, even if instances of it are commensurable. "My height may be not only commensurable with but exactly the same as that of Smith, but there is not even clear sense, certainly no truth, in saying that in the two of us there is twice as much height as there is in either of us considered alone; there is even less sense in the corresponding claim about happiness" (36). For discussion, see the following text.

[34] John Marshall in "The Proof of Utility and Equity in Mill's *Utilitarianism*," *Canadian Journal of Philosophy* 3 (1973–4): 13–26, points out (16)

this interpretation, the "utilitarian doctrine," represented by (6), is perhaps better stated by making clear that Mill believes happiness, wherever it occurs, is what is desirable as an end. This could be restated with the following reinterpretation:

(6) "Happiness is [the kind of thing which is] desirable, and the only [kind of] thing desirable, as an end, all other things being desirable only as means to that end."

From this, the connection with morality is said to follow:

(7) "The promotion of [happiness] is the test by which to judge of all conduct from whence it necessarily follows that it must be the criterion of morality, since a part is included in the whole."

If my previous elucidation of Mill's argument for happiness as the kind of thing that makes the objects of desires desirable was convincing, then this conclusion has plausibility. Desire does not confer desirability; it is evidence for what kind of thing constitutes welfare. Thus, that one desires only one's own happiness does not restrict the desirability of happiness to one's own happiness. If the desirability of happiness *as such* is *identified* (and not created) by one's own desire for it in one's own experience, its desirability – wherever it is located – can be admitted by the intellect.

That the value of different instances of happiness is arithmetical is certainly controversial, but not, I think, indefensible.

the ambiguity in the question, "What is desirable as an end?" It can be taken to ask "What kind of thing?" or "What specific thing?" The answer that happiness is the kind of thing does not raise the question "Whose?" whereas the second does. He interprets Mill as thinking more in terms of the first question in using the evidence of desire to show that an individual's happiness is (*prima facie*) desirable, but thinks that Mill is thinking of the latter in thinking that the general happiness is desirable. This leads Marshall to say that happiness that is in conflict with the general happiness is not intrinsically good. I am claiming that on Mill's view it is still intrinsically good, being the kind of thing to be promoted, even if it should not be promoted in a situation of conflict. I believe that Marshall is reading too much into Mill's proof to find a proof of equity as well as a proof of what kind of thing is good in itself.

Without an operational definition for measurement, it is difficult to know how happy two different individuals are,[35] but it seems plausible that if two people do happen to be equally happy, then twice as much happiness exists. Mill recognizes the difficulty in determining how happy a person is. He thinks that Bentham's measures of intensity and duration are inadequate to capture the complex hedonic dimensions of experience, asserting that the only test of the comparative pleasure of two experiences is the unbiased preference of those who have experienced both. This is not a direct measurement of felt experience, because the experiences are seldom if ever simultaneous, and contexts are never exactly the same. It is a judgment based on memory and introspective analysis. In making interpersonal comparisons, this method is even less reliable, because one can assume only a rough equality of sensibility between persons, or make a rough estimate of difference in case evidence based on behavior or physiology shows a basis for difference. Thus summations of instances of happiness will be imprecise, but we do make judgments that one course of action will make oneself or another person more or less happy. These are not meaningless judgments. Even if only rough estimates, they assume (and I think justifiably) that different instances of happiness are commensurable. And although we have no way of arriving at units of happiness by which to do the arithmetic, I think that it makes sense to say that there are mental states that constitute pleasure and pain of some degree. It isn't that the degrees of pleasure and pain do not exist just because we do not have procedures for measuring them. There is more or less happiness in the

---

[35] Bentham sought to achieve an operational definition of a unit of happiness by introspective discrimination of the faintest degree of intensity or duration that can be distinguished, saying, "Such a degree of intensity is in every day's experience." And for purposes of public policy, he sought to achieve an operational measure of pleasure and pain by the correlation between pleasure and pain and the bestowal or deprivation of money. But he recognized some of the difficulties. See David Baumgardt, *Bentham and the Ethics of Today with Manuscripts Hitherto Unpublished*, app. 4.

world when people are enjoying themselves and when they are suffering.

That the general happiness is simply the sum of the happiness of all individuals and that the good to the aggregate of all is simply the sum of the goods to each is, like Mill's methodological principle, primarily negative in its import. Mill is denying that there is any happiness or any value that cannot be analyzed without remainder as the happiness or the good of some individual or individuals (including nonhuman individuals). To prove this would require refutation not only of every claim to other individual values, as discussed previously, but also of every claim to anything good as an end for society that is not analyzable into the good of individuals. I have not defended this, but I find Mill's skepticism plausible.

If Mill's proof is plausible, as I have argued, it does not follow that anyone will act on it. One's intellect may be convinced without one thereby being moved to conduct his or her life in such a way as to maximize his or her own happiness or being moved to identify the general happiness with his or her own and become a practicing utilitarian. That, according to Mill, requires a good state of society and education. But convincing the intellect is an important step.

7

UTILITY AND JUSTICE

IN Chapter 5 of *Utilitarianism*, entitled "On the Connection between Justice and Utility," Mill acknowledges that one of the strongest objections to utilitarianism as a complete account of ethics is the apparent independence of the idea of justice from the idea of what produces the greatest happiness, even if adherence to principles of justice does, in the long run, have that effect. If considerations of justice are independent of considerations of utility, it is possible that the two could come into conflict, that an unjust social arrangement could produce more happiness than a just one. In that case even someone sympathetic to utilitarianism on other grounds might feel that justice should take precedence in some or all such cases and that utilitarianism is not a complete ethical system. It is often said that utilitarianism is only an "aggregative" doctrine, not a "distributive" one. Or it is said that utilitarianism does not take seriously the separateness of persons: it seeks to maximize happiness without regard to whose happiness it is.

Before turning to an interpretation of Chapter 5 of *Utilitarianism*, I want to discuss the intuition that justice and utility are in conflict, using an example of a conflict between equality of utility and greater total utility.

Suppose for the sake of argument that it is possible to make interpersonal comparisons between quantities of utility. This is a controversial assumption, and it need not be precise in order for utilitarian judgments to be made, but suppose, for the sake of illustration, that in a particular case precise judgments can be made. Suppose that some three particular persons, A, B, and C, who are equally deserving or equally undeserving, can be given the utility shares (a), (b), and (c), respectively, in accordance with either Scheme I or Scheme II:[1]

	Scheme I	Scheme II
(a)	3 units	2 units
(b)	3 units	2 units
(c)	3 units	6 units

Scheme I seems intuitively more just (remembering that each person is equally deserving, whatever one's criteria for desert), yet Scheme II produces the greatest total welfare. If it is the doctrine of utilitarianism that Scheme II is more just simply because it has the greatest total welfare, this seems outrageously contrary to our commonsense idea of justice. If it is the doctrine of utilitarianism that Scheme II should be adopted, even though it is unjust, this makes utilitarianism a questionable moral doctrine. There are a number of assumptions in the example, however, that must be made explicit. That Scheme II is less just may not be so obvious upon examination of these assumptions.

The first assumption is that it is appropriate to raise the question as to which scheme is just, but there are many contexts in which doing this seems inappropriate. In some contexts, questions of justice and injustice simply do not arise, either because the difference in utility is not great enough to warrant use of the powerful normative terms "just" and "unjust," or because the basic requirements for anyone to complain of the injustice of the situation are not present; so it would be presumptuous to raise the question.

Suppose, for example, that A, B, and C are at a party and there is a choice between singing, which all like equally well (Scheme I), and dancing, which C likes twice as much as singing and three times as much as the others like dancing (Scheme II). I am inclined to say that it isn't worth dignifying the issue with

[1] Example found in Nicholas Rescher, *Distributive Justice*, 25.

the word "injustice" if the host insists on dancing. Or, we may want to say that because A and B are there as guests, they have no right to complain. A similar kind of phenomenon can make some inequalities irrelevant in situations where questions of justice do arise. If two equally qualified applicants seek a position, we may not consider it a matter of justice or injustice as to which one is employed, even if one would be happier in the job than the other or one would suffer greater disappointment in not getting the job. To take into consideration such matters may be regarded as a praiseworthy sign of sensitivity to human feelings, but not a question of justice. It may also be possible to call a decision just without calling a contrary decision unjust. If one of the two equally qualified candidates has overcome some handicap in becoming qualified for the position, we may wish to praise as just a decision to appoint that person, without calling a contrary decision unjust. So long as the most important criteria are observed, we may want to say that there has been no injustice, even if there are other criteria that could also be considered.

In some other contexts the question of justice or injustice arises only regarding procedure, not regarding the relative size of distributive shares. For example, if A, B, and C are playing roulette, they would not regard Scheme II as less just than Scheme I simply because of the inequality of shares and the fact that A, B, and C are all equally "deserving." They are neither deserving nor undeserving of any particular size distributive share, only deserving of a fair chance at winning. Assuming that there is an equal chance of getting the larger share, they would presumably opt for Scheme II as a pay-off schedule.

Now, to return to the illustration with the assumption that the context is one in which questions of justice and injustice are appropriate, it is still not obvious that Scheme II is less just. Three features of the example must be kept in mind in examining it.

A first point to observe is that the units are units of intrinsic value, such as happiness, not units of the means of happiness. If they were units of the means of happiness, such as, for example, income, it would not be obvious that Scheme II would result in greater happiness. Suppose that each unit were $10,000 of annual income. Three persons with annual income of $30,000 each might have a sum total of happiness (to the extent that happiness depends on income) greater than two with $20,000 and one with $60,000. This is due to the common applicability of what is known in economics as the Principle of Diminishing Marginal Utility. The marginal utility of something in classical economic theory is the ability of an additional unit to satisfy human wants. The Principle of Diminishing Marginal Utility reflects the phenomenon that as larger quantities of something are possessed, an additional unit has less ability to satisfy wants, because there are fewer wants left to be satisfied. In our example, the last $30,000 in annual income for person C in Scheme II may satisfy fewer wants than an additional $10,000 for each of persons A and B.

Another important fact, if we think of the distribution as means to happiness rather than happiness, is the instrumental value of these assets. If we think of the distribution as wealth or income, or even cultural advantages such as education and class status, disproportionate shares may lead to disproportionate power relations. If the richest person in the United States has wealth equal to the entire lowest 40 percent of the U.S. population (which was true when this was written), that individual has extraordinary power to control public policy affecting the welfare of that lowest 40 percent. That wealth, and income from it, can be used to control mass media and thus social and political attitudes; to influence elections and thus influence legislation affecting everyone; even to direct the services of philanthropic foundations by donations. It will also likely provide the next generation of that person's family members with education, personal contacts, and a capital base from which to put competitors at a disadvantage in a competitive society. Thus the distribution would not only be an inequality of condition, but an inequality of opportunity.[2] Thus, in interpreting the example, we must keep in mind that the shares are shares of happiness, not the means to happiness, and that there really is more happiness as a result of Scheme II.

A second point to keep in mind is that if A and B feel any resentment or envy or frustration over being relatively less well off, or any painful *sense* of injustice in the unequal shares, such feelings are already reflected in the numbers. If, for example, A and B each feel one unit of unhappiness over their inferior lives in Scheme II, the Scheme would be three, three, and six (a total of twelve) without that unhappiness. Otherwise, if the unhappiness has not already been subtracted, Scheme II should be one, one, six (a total of eight), and it would have a lower total than Scheme I.

A third, and most important, point is that even if these are shares of intrinsic value, not instrumental value, the distribution may have instrumental value, and that must be calculated and figured into the numbers. If A, B, and C work equally hard and do not receive equal happiness as a result, there may be a loss of incentive for further work with a loss in total utility in the long run. We shall see that this is the chief utilitarian argument for principles of justice that appear to be independent of the principle of utility. Principles requiring a certain pattern of distribution may be justified by the principle of utility, and thus subordinate to it, if in fact they produce the greatest total utility in the long run. The principles of justice may appear to be independent because in this particular case they directly require certain patterns of distribution, regardless of the total to be distributed, but they are not independent because they are justified by long-term aggregation.

These three characteristics of the illustration are difficult to discount in our intuitive reaction to it. Part of our feeling of the

---

[2]   See John Rawls, *A Theory of Justice*, 73: Fair equality of opportunity requires "preventing excessive accumulations of property and wealth and of maintaining equal opportunities of education for all."

"injustice" of Scheme II may be the feeling that if C has three times as much money as A or B, that money could be put to better use by distributing it more equitably. But such a reaction is one based on diminishing marginal utility of money as an instrumental value. Or, we may feel that if C has three times as much money, or wealth, or power, or authority, or any other advantage, it may be used to lower the future life prospects of A and B in a competitive society and thus not lead to greatest happiness in the long run. The feeling of wrongness of the inequality may thus be based on its consequences or costs in comparison with a more equal distribution and thus be subordinate to the maximization of intrinsic value, not independent of it. Part of the feeling of the injustice of Scheme II may be the sympathetic reaction that if I were A or B, I couldn't help resenting C's being better off, even if I ought to be benevolent and have only love for my neighbor. I may also make the judgment that a society in which there are such feelings can't be as good as one where all are equals in welfare, and where resentment and envy do not arise. Again, there are hidden utilities and disutilities, those of social harmony and resentment, entering into the intuition of justice and injustice, and these must be discounted or calculated into the numbers. And, finally, as mentioned, there is the problem of instrumental utilities of the distribution creeping in.

Supposing, now, that we have shorn the example of extraneous considerations. Would Scheme II be less just? I shall argue that under certain conditions it would not be. Then I shall argue that under other conditions, although it would be *justified* from an impartial point of view, it would be contrary to the standard concept of *justice*. This will lead to a discussion of the utility of the standard concept of justice.

Suppose that two parents have three children A, B, and C, and are faced with the choice (on their limited income) of giving all an equal education with an outcome according to Scheme I or of concentrating their resources upon the education of one with an outcome according to Scheme II. If they choose Scheme II, are they doing an injustice? To be sure that they don't play favorites, suppose that they choose which child is to benefit by some random method. It may seem unjust, in that C, who is no more deserving, is benefiting at the expense of A and B without their consent. But wouldn't they give their consent to enter the lottery if they were able? Assuming that we have the figures for utility correct, we can multiply the benefit times its probability to give an "expected" utility. Each child would have one-third chance of six units and two-thirds chance of two units, which gives an expected utility of three and a third for Scheme II, compared to three on Scheme I. The rational choice would be Scheme II; so the parents are acting in the interests of each child – the way a rational person would choose for himself or herself – in making the decision. Thus, Scheme II under these conditions is a just system.

Suppose, however, that the children have individual differences that make only one capable of benefiting from the concentration of resources. In that case the roulette analogy does not apply. The parents cannot use a random method of selection and choose as the child would have rationally chosen. But is it clear that Scheme II would then be unjust? Suppose that Scheme II is adopted. In that case A and B are worse off, by one unit, than they would be otherwise, in order that C should benefit. That seems unjust. But suppose that Scheme I is adopted. In that case C is worse off, by three units, than C would be otherwise. Isn't it a greater injustice to deprive C of three units of potential happiness for the total benefit of C's siblings of only two units than to deprive A and B of only one unit each for the benefit of C to the extent of three units? Why shouldn't the parents look at this as they would a decision within their own lives? If A, B, and C are not different individuals but different stages in my own life and I have a choice of three days (or three years) of enjoying myself according to Scheme I or Scheme II, the sensible thing to do, assuming that the numbers are correct measures of happiness, is to opt for Scheme II. I would feel that I had done no injustice to myself on the other two days (or years) if the enjoyment of all three added up to greater total enjoyment. This very analogy, however, leads to the fundamental objection to utilitarianism as a foundation for justice. Utilitarianism doesn't seem to recognize the different self-interests of different individuals. It treats different individuals as if they were different stages in the life of a single individual, where a greater benefit in one compensates for a greater loss in another. The critic says that utilitarianism does not take seriously the difference between persons.[3]

This does go against our commonsense intuitions concerning justice, namely, that different people have a right not to be treated as means to the greater benefit of others. But at the same time, if greater happiness results, why shouldn't they? Couldn't parents *justify* their decision to favor C at the expense of A and B on grounds that C would gain more than they would lose? As long as the welfare of all three individuals as a totality is kept in mind, this seems an adequate justification. It is inadequate only from a partial point of view, only when there is no genuine identity of interest. If A and B have an interest in C equal to their own, that is, if they are impartial, they will accept the justification that greater good results. But if A and B do not have an interest in C equal to their own, the "justification" that deprives them of a good for the greater good of another will be challenged. This justification is based upon a principle that does not assure them even minimal security in their own welfare. By this principle, a scheme of shares in which A and B suffer negative welfare for C's greater welfare (e.g., a Scheme III in which A, B, and C receive -1, -1, and 12, respectively) would be justified. This seems rational when A, B, and C are stages of one's life, but to accept this distribution seems heroic or saintly rather than the recognition of justice when A, B, and C are different persons. Thus, the preceding model of justification, which is appropriate for an impartial decision among competing

---

[3] This is one of the principal objections against utilitarianism given by John Rawls in *A Theory of Justice*, 27.

claims when there is a unifying identity of interest, does not appear to be an adequate analysis of the standard conception of justice where there is not a unifying identity of interest. As Mill shows in Chapter 5 of *Utilitarianism*, the "standard" conception of justice is not a single concept but a family of related concepts. Nevertheless, any one of these related concepts can come into conflict with the production of greatest total happiness on a given occasion.

If the standard conception of justice can come into conflict with the maximization of total welfare on a particular occasion, there are at least three ways to view this potential conflict. One is to see the standard principles of justice, to the extent that they conflict with total welfare, as claims based on self-interest and hence to be overridden from an impartial moral point of view. A second is to see the standard principles of justice as an independent set of moral considerations that at least sometimes, if not always, take precedence over or place restrictions upon considerations of total welfare in case of conflict. A third is to view the standard principles of justice as a set of principles that can take precedence over the criterion of total welfare in particular cases but that ultimately derive their moral authority from their contribution to the production of greatest total welfare in the long run. According to this third position, if there were to be only one distribution of welfare ever, the criterion of total welfare would be adequate when applied directly. But there is not only one distribution of welfare ever. Life is ongoing, and distributions of social benefits and burdens recur over and over through social, political, legal, and economic institutions. The principles of justice are a set of principles for criticizing social arrangements that determine distribution on a recurring basis. They must require not just the best result on one occasion but a structure that will produce the best result on a recurring basis. The structure that has this effect may be one that adjudicates self-interested claims on principles other than simply greatest total welfare case by case.

To return to our previous example, if life were a one-shot lottery, the greatest total welfare (taking into account diminishing marginal utility, envy, etc.) as a pay-off scheme might be acceptable as a rational wager for all concerned. But because life is a competitive struggle in which some have more talent than others, some have more wealth and power than others, etc., it is not a fair lottery with equal opportunity to win, and there is no relevantly informed impartial judge to make and enforce decisions that maximize total welfare, even if that were an acceptable criterion. In real life, considerations of justice function to allow claims to be made by or on behalf of self-interested parties, especially for the weaker party to invoke the morality of justice as a counter to the greater nonmoral power of adversaries, and to impose moral restrictions upon the exercise of that greater power. In a world in which there are self-interested parties competing to acquire the benefits and to avoid the burdens of society, a social structure that recognizes a set of principles giving parties legitimate claims to benefits and to avoidance of burdens offers the participants, especially weaker competitors, a system of security that in the long run has best consequences. This is a system of rights, enforced by legal or moral sanctions.

In a particular case a decision in accordance with the recognition of such rights may have consequences that are not as good as an impartial decision in the absence of such rights, but in the long run the best consequences are obtained by recognition and respect for such rights. And this requires that the rights be recognized and respected even in some cases where an alternative decision would produce greater total welfare.

The position at which we have now arrived is, I believe, the background for the position of Mill in Chapter 5 of *Utilitarianism*.[4] Justice, according to his analysis of the concept, coincides with those duties in virtue of which a correlative right

---

[4] John Stuart Mill, *Utilitarianism*, 203–60. Citations in this chapter will be in parentheses in text.

resides in some person or persons. Where injustice consists in treating a person worse than the person deserves, there is some assignable person who can claim the violation of a moral or legal right; where injustice consists in treating a person better than others, the wrong in this case is to competitors, who are also assignable persons, and are entitled to complain. In this respect justice is distinguishable from generosity and beneficence, in that although we ought to practice those virtues, no individual can claim them from a particular agent as a moral right. Or, if a moralist does attempt, as some have done, to claim that mankind have a *right* to all the good that we can do them, the moralist thereby includes generosity and beneficence within the category of justice, merging all morality into justice (247 [V, 15]).

As to an analysis of what is meant by the possession of a "right," Mill says that when we call anything a person's right, "we mean that he [or she] has a valid claim on society to protect him [or her] in the possession of it, either by the force of law or by that of education and opinion. If he [or she] has what we consider a sufficient claim, on whatever account, to have something guaranteed to him [or her] by society, we say that he [or she] has a right to it" (250 [V, 24]). Such valid claims, in a good society, according to Mill, would rest ultimately on general utility, justified by evidence that recognition and enforcement of such rights have better consequences than absence of that recognition and enforcement. Even in the present imperfect society many rights can be given such a justification, and those that can't be given such a justification can be criticized and reformed by appeal to general utility. General utility is the foundation for rights, but in particular cases rights generally take precedence over considerations of general utility.

Rights involve the most important and impressive kind of utility, namely security. All other earthly benefits, Mill says, are needed by one person, not needed by another, but security no human being can possibly do without. "[O]n it we depend for all our immunity from evil, and for the whole value of all and every good, beyond the passing moment; since nothing but the gratification of the instant could be of any worth to us, if we could be deprived of everything the next instant by whoever was momentarily stronger than ourselves" (251 [V, 25]). Thus it is appropriate on utilitarian grounds that claims to justice should take on "that character of absoluteness, that apparent infinity, and incommensurability with all other considerations . . . in binding force" (251 [V, 25]). But Mill reminds us that particular cases may occur, such as to save a life, in which some other social duty is so important as to overrule any one of the general maxims of justice. Thus, the priority of respect for rights at the expense of certain other utilities is defended on utilitarian grounds, but the possibility of overriding such rights on utilitarian grounds is also recognized. Furthermore, the substance of legitimate rights is decided, and the conflicts between these rights resolved, by appeal to what has best consequences.

In his discussion of justice in Chapter 5, Mill distinguishes between the powerful *sentiment* or *feeling* of justice or injustice and the *modes of conduct* designated as just or unjust. In analyzing the sentiment of justice, he concludes that the two essential ingredients are the desire to punish a person who has done harm, and the knowledge or belief that there is some definite individual or individuals to whom harm has been done (248 [V, 18]). He thinks that these are a spontaneous outgrowth of two natural sentiments that either are or resemble instincts: the impulse of self-defense and the feeling of sympathy. These we share with nonhuman animals, but with the difference that humans are capable of sympathizing, not only with those to whom we are intimately related but with all humans and even with all sentient beings. We also have intelligence to recognize the conduct that threatens the security of society generally is threatening to our own, and this can call forth the instinct or derived sentiment of self-defense. Thus the sentiment of justice is "the natural feeling of retaliation or vengeance, rendered by intellect and sympathy applicable to those injuries, that is, to those hurts, which wound us through, or in common with, society at large" (249 [V, 21]). Mill thinks that it is the enlarged sympathy that gives the sentiment its morality; it is the natural feeling that gives the sentiment its "peculiar impressiveness, and energy of self-assertion" (250 [V, 23]).

Mill may be correct in his analysis of the psychological origins of the sentiment of justice and injustice, but in modern society it is often more diffused than he states. The righteous indignation that arises when injustice occurs may be directed not at some individual agent of the injustice but at the "system," which permits or enforces the injustice. A law may be the agent of injustice, or economic arrangements may be the agent of injustice. Or it may be a tradition of racial prejudice or gender oppression. So the indignation may not be directed toward a "person" who has done harm, but toward something more impersonal – capitalism, or bigotry, or patriarchy, or paternalism, or immigration laws. Furthermore, the feeling may not be that it wounds or endangers *me* through, or in common with, society at large. It may be that sympathetically I feel that it hurts or endangers some segment of society to which I do not belong – some racial minority, or poor people, or people of a different gender or sexual orientation, or a religious group – even though I do not, and perhaps cannot, belong to that group of persons.

Leaving aside the *sentiment* of justice and injustice, Mill's analysis of a just or unjust *mode of conduct* goes through several steps. He finds it easier to analyze the negative – the unjust mode of conduct. He says that it may involve the violation of the *legal rights* of some persons, but because laws may be unjust it has to be extended to the violation of *moral rights*. More generally it is that persons not get what they *deserve*. It includes cases where an agent *breaks faith* with anyone by not keeping contracts or promises; and cases where decisions are partial, which is subordinate to desert or other rights. Finally, it may be a case of the violation of deserved *equality*. How these elements are combined into standards of justice in the areas of penal justice or fair distribution of benefits and burdens, however, is subject to great controversy. It becomes evident that there is not a single standard of justice to be contrasted with utility, and perhaps independent of it, but competing standards claiming the title of justice, and between them conflicting intuitions.

In the area of penal justice, Mill gives the following succinct statement of alternatives: "For instance, there are those who say, that it is unjust to punish any one for the sake of example to others; that punishment is just, only when intended for the good of the sufferer himself [or herself]. Others maintain the extreme reverse, contending that to punish persons who have attained years of discretion, for their own benefit, is despotism and injustice, since if the matter at issue is solely their own good, no one has a right to control their own judgment of it; but that they may justly be punished to prevent evil to others, this being an exercise of the legitimate right of self-defence. Mr. Owen,[5] again, affirms that it is unjust to punish at all; for the criminal did not make his [or her] own character; his [or her] education, and the circumstances which surround them, have made him [or her] a criminal, and for these he [or she] is not responsible" (252 [V, 28]). Mill says that all of these positions are based upon genuine conceptions of justice: the first, that it is unjust to single out individuals and make them a sacrifice, without their consent, for other people's benefit; the second, relying on the injustice of forcing persons to conform to another's notions of what constitutes their good, but recognizing the acknowledged justice of self-defense; the third, that it is unjust to punish persons for what they cannot help.

Mill recognizes that there have been efforts to reconcile the conflict between these principles. There is the doctrine of "free will" to meet Owen's objection, and there is the fiction of a social contract giving legislators the claim that those punished

---

[5]   Mill is here referring to Robert Owen (1771–1858), British social reformer (footnote added).

have given their consent to be punished for their own or others' good when they have violated the law. Mill rightly regards these as fictions, although he struggled with the question of how and to what extent an individual can be responsible for his or her own character.[6] In *System of Logic*, he also attempts to counter the conclusion driven by the theory of the Owenites. It is not just others who have formed our character. We are exactly as capable of making our own character, *if we will*, as others are of making it for us. "Yes (answers the Owenite), but these words, 'if we will,' surrender the whole point: since the will to alter our character is given us, not by any efforts of ours, but by circumstances which we cannot help; it comes to us either from external causes, or not at all."[7] To this Mill replies that our character has also been formed by experience – experience of the painful consequences of the character we previously had or by some strong feeling of admiration or aspiration. If we do *not* wish to alter our character, then there is no ground for feeling that we cannot do so. And if we *do* have the desire, we should know that this is one circumstance that molds our future character. The significance of this is that punishment can be one of those experiences of the painful consequences of the character we previously had that can lead us to wish to alter it. And because an individual's willing to alter his or her character can alter it, we are just in holding the individual responsible for his or her behavior. Whether this is called "behavior modification," to use a later term, or called "punishment," Mill's claim is that it is appropriate to hold individual agents subject to painful consequences of their behavior if it has good consequences to do so.

[6] See *Autobiography*, reprinted in *Autobiography and Literary Essays*, 175–7. Mill says that he felt that if his character and that of all others had been formed by antecedent circumstances then it was wholly out of our own power. He saw a solution to this in that though our own character is formed by circumstances, our own desires can do much to shape those circumstances.

[7] John Stuart Mill, *A System of Logic*, 841 (bk. 6, ch. 2, sec. 3).

There are also conflicting conceptions of justice in attempting to make punishment fit the crime. One is that the punishment should fit the crime, in its rigid form the retribution of an eye for an eye and a tooth for a tooth. According to this retributive theory, what amount of punishment is necessary to deter from the offense has nothing to do with the question of justice. An opposite view is that such a consideration is all in all: that it is not just to inflict on a fellow creature any amount of suffering beyond the least that will suffice to prevent the criminal from repeating, and others from imitating, similar misconduct (253 [V, 29]).

Mill's point in citing these conflicting theories of justice is to argue that one cannot appeal to a single principle of justice that conflicts with or may conflict with utility. There are multiple principles of justice that themselves conflict. One cannot say that utility is in conflict with justice per se. Utility may conflict with some one principle of justice but not with a competing principle of justice. In Mill's view, these conflicting principles require justification, and he believes that the appropriate method of justification is by appeal to the consequences of a system of justice based on each or on a combination of them with proper weight determined by consequences.

Turning to what is more narrowly called "distributive" justice, Mill gives two illustrations to show that there can be conflicting claims of justice in that area and that an appeal to consequences is the reasonable arbiter between them.

Should those with superior skill and talent receive more remuneration than others in a cooperative industrial enterprise? On the one hand society receives more from the skilled and efficient laborers; their services being more beneficial, it may be argued that society owes them a larger return for their services. Furthermore, a greater share of the product being actually their work, not to reward them proportionately may be regarded as a kind of robbery. Here Mill is appealing to still more fundamental principles of justice, such as the obligation to return good for good, or the obligation to respect as property that with which

161

laborers have mixed their labor. These in turn could be given a justification as having good consequences. In this particular case, one could also appeal to the utility of having those with skills and talents develop their skills and talents and utilize them for productive use, which is stimulated by a system of pecuniary incentives. On the other hand, Mill points out, it is argued that those who do the best they can deserve equally well, and ought not in justice to be put in a position of inferiority for no fault of their own; that superior abilities have already advantage more than enough, in the admiration they excite, the personal influence they command, and the self-satisfaction they enjoy in exercising them, without adding to these a superior share of the world's goods; and that society is bound in justice rather to make compensation to the less favored for this unmerited inequality of advantage than to aggravate it. Here Mill is appealing to the equalitarian tendencies in the concept of justice, which can be based in turn on the principle of diminishing marginal utility and on the envy that arises from invidious differences. These are grounds for equality or even compensatory justice to make up for natural or educational inequalities. Mill thinks that justice in this case has two sides to it, which it is impossible to bring into harmony on grounds of justice alone. Social utility alone can decide the preference. The question then becomes, which will have better consequences – to reward with pay equally or in accordance with product or effort (or need, which is a third criterion)? Traditional and capitalist pay schemes are almost all based on perceived merit or market value. Here I think that a utilitarian should be driven to a demand for radical change. One problem is that ideological prejudices influence the assessing of consequences. A capitalist economist, with faith in the efficiency of market distributions and blind to the lack of equal opportunity that comes from unequal distributions of initial wealth, will likely claim that the capitalist system and competitive pay schemes produce the best consequences. A socialist economist would argue otherwise.

A second example that Mill discusses is the justice of taxation. Should taxes be assessed equally or according to pecuniary means; and, if the latter, in simple proportion to wealth and income or graduated so that those with more resources pay at a higher rate as well? Mill points out that an argument can be made that it is just to take the same absolute sum from all, because the protection of law and government is (supposedly) afforded to and is equally required by all. Against this it is claimed that the state does more for the rich than the poor, protecting more property, but Mill denies this, pointing out that the rich would be far better able to protect themselves, in the absence of law or government, than the poor. (Mill obviously does not have a Marxist conception of the bourgeois state.) Mill thinks that the only resolution of the dispute is the utilitarian one – asking what scheme would have best consequences – and it is implicitly on this basis that higher taxes have been exacted from the rich.

These examples show that on utilitarian grounds some traditional principles of justice can be generated. The need for security of person and possessions leads to a system of laws and punishments to protect these vital assets, and security against misuse of legal power requires that there be due process and safeguards against arbitrary arrest and inordinate punishment. Punishing only the guilty and having the punishment fit the crime become principles of justice subordinate to utility. For persons to have a right to the product of their labor provides security in possession of the means of happiness, gives meaning to their work, and is an incentive for productive labor. On the other hand, to have a *prima facie* right to equality of distribution usually produces greater welfare because of the principle of diminishing marginal utility, because it reduces envy and it prevents abuse of power derived from concentrations of power. These are empirical claims, but they are generally recognized as having some validity. They are grounds for specific principles of justice, and if they are mistaken, or if their significance is exaggerated, the traditional claims of justice should be revised.

Questions as to which form of society is most just cannot be settled *a priori* by an analysis of the concept of justice nor by intuition as to which is most just. An empirical analysis of which form has best consequences is required, and the result of such an inquiry may dictate revisions in the substantive content of traditional rights or traditional principles of justice. Justice is conceptually tied to rights, which in turn are legitimate claims, but which claims should be recognized as legitimate is not a conceptual matter. It is a question of the greatest utility in the long run.

I end this chapter and the book by a consideration of how Mill might have responded to the most important recent work on justice – *A Theory of Justice* by John Rawls.[8] This is a monumental volume of more than six hundred pages, and its details cannot be discussed here. But it may be useful to sketch in outline its central points and to see how one holding Mill's theory might respond. According to my interpretation of Mill, there would not be as much discrepancy between Rawls and Mill regarding the substantive requirements of justice as might at first glance be supposed.

Rawls's procedure for identifying the principles of justice is to engage in an imaginative procedure such that the principles are to be chosen "behind a veil of ignorance," which imposes impartiality upon the choice. The members of society are to choose the principles without knowing their place in society (rich or poor, in position of authority or not, and so on) and without even knowing their distinctive personal values (whether religious or not, what their life ideals are, whether liberal or conservative, and so on). They would be rational, self-interested but without envy, and they would have any relevant general information. To enable their self-interest to operate, Rawls gives them the motivation to pursue certain goods that one would want, whatever other values one might have,

---

8   John Rawls, *A Theory of Justice*. References to this work in the remainder of this chapter will be in parentheses in the text.

which he calls "primary goods." These are more rather than less liberty and opportunity, wealth and income, power and authority, and the bases of self-respect. Under such conditions, Rawls argues, the principle(s) of justice chosen would not be the utilitarian principle, but would be two more specific principles: "the first requires equality in the assignment of basic rights and duties, while the second holds that social and economic inequalities, for example inequalities of wealth and authority, are just only if they result in compensating benefits for everyone, and in particular for the least advantaged members of society. These principles rule out justifying institutions on the grounds that the hardships of some are offset by a greater good in the aggregate. It may be expedient but it is not just" (14–15).

Rawls recognizes the independence between his procedure for how principles of justice are to be identified and the two principles that he claims would be chosen. So we can question whether Rawls's procedure is a better approach than a more direct utilitarian one, and we can ask how Rawls's two principles would differ from Mill's theory of justice, if we accept his procedure. Rawls recognizes that his procedure might lead to utilitarian principles of justice: "It is perfectly possible, from all that one knows at this point, that some form of the principle of utility would be adopted, and therefore that contract theory leads eventually to a deeper and more roundabout justification of utilitarianism" (29). There are two chief ways that Rawls avoids that conclusion. One is to argue that there are risks in utilitarian justice that one would not want to take. The other is to place such a degree of ignorance behind the veil of ignorance that one cannot know what the odds of those risks are, and therefore that one would adopt a "maximin" strategy to achieve the greatest welfare for the worst off, rather than a strategy to achieve the greatest overall welfare. I will not pursue the attempt to derive utilitarian justice from Rawls's procedure, although I think that the limits on knowledge, necessary to produce his "maximin" conclusions, are arbitrary.

The direct utilitarian approach would be to ask what principles of justice maximize overall utility in the long run. Mill's theory is that justice consists of the set of rights that society ought to protect for the greatest good of everyone. This is an empirical question, subject to debate on the basis of political and economic and legal theories. The same is true of the principles of justice chosen behind Rawls's veil of ignorance. The basic structure of society with its structure of rights is subject to debate based upon rationality and general knowledge. The difference is that for utilitarianism it is the greatest overall aggregate of welfare. Rawls, citing Mill, recognizes that commonsense precepts of justice, particularly those that concern the protection of liberties and rights or that express the claims of desert, are supported by utilitarian calculations. But, he argues, "there is no reason in principle why the greater gains of some should not compensate for the lesser losses of others; or more importantly, why the violation of the liberty of a few might not be made right by the greater good shared by many" (26). There is no reason "in principle," but if utilitarian calculations in the real world come out in agreement with Rawls, then there is substantive agreement between the theories. Rawls claims that there are commonsense convictions that the claims of liberty and right have a certain priority, if not absolute weight, over the desirability of increasing aggregate social welfare. He thinks that his procedure leads to this as a consequence of principles chosen in the "original position." "[U]tilitarianism seeks to account for them as a socially useful illusion" (28). For Mill, however, it is an empirical conclusion, not an illusion. Security is more basic for human happiness than marginally greater opportunity for other forms of welfare. The rights that Mill advocates are equal rights, not giving privilege to any class or race or religion. So it appears that there is a strong degree of similarity between Mill's justice and Rawls's first principle. Furthermore, when Rawls comes to argue for the priority of his first principle, it is on grounds of utilitarian calculations.

When Rawls comes to argue for the priority of his first principle, he too appeals to empirical facts, including the Principle of Diminishing Marginal Utility. On Rawls's theory, the priority of liberty does not operate under such hardships that basic wants of individuals cannot be fulfilled; it is not an absolute principle. He says that the basis for the priority of liberty is as follows: "as the conditions of civilization improve, the marginal significance for our good of further economic and social advantages diminishes relative to the interests of liberty, which become stronger as the conditions for the exercise of equal freedoms are more fully realized.... [A]s the general level of well-being rises (as indicated by the index of primary goods the less favored can expect) only the less urgent wants remain to be satisfied by further advances.... At the same time the obstacles to the exercise of the equal liberties decline and a growing insistence upon the right to pursue our spiritual and cultural interests asserts itself" (542–3). This is clearly an empirical generalization, appealing to the same kinds of facts as a utilitarian would appeal to in giving legitimacy to liberty rights. Rawls also makes empirical generalizations about the basis for self-esteem. "The basis for self-esteem in a just society is not then one's income share but the publicly affirmed distribution of fundamental rights and liberties" (544). Again, this is an empirical claim that a utilitarian would take into account in arguing for fundamental rights and liberties.

Rawls contrasts his approach with utilitarianism by saying that the latter adopts for society as a whole the principle of rational choice for one person. This leads to his use of administrative metaphors in characterizing utilitarianism. "The correct decision is essentially a question of efficient administration. This view of social cooperation is the consequence of extending to society the principle of choice for one man, and then, to make this extension work, conflating all persons into one through the imaginative acts of the impartial sympathetic spectator. Utilitarianism does not take seriously the distinction between persons"[9] (27). As indicated previously in discussing the example of the two schemes of equal distribution versus greater but unequal distribution, such a characterization would apply only if people were completely impartial and not self-interested. The aggregate utility that is the goal of utilitarianism is impartial, but the system of rights that constitute the utilitarian theory of justice, or at least my interpretation of Mill's theory, does not assume that people are not self-interested. Rights are protections of the security of self-interested individuals against other self-interested individuals.

Rawls's first principle guarantees equality of basic rights and liberties. His second principle is that inequalities of economic and social advantages must be for the benefit of everyone, or at least for the least advantaged. If inequalities are for the benefit of everyone, then obviously a utilitarian would accept that justification, assuming that all utilities including feelings of natural envy and long-term imbalances of power, etc., have been taken into account. When inequalities do not benefit the least advantaged segment of society, a utilitarian would have an argument against them, based on the diminishing marginal utility of economic goods and based on the conditions of self-esteem that were appealed to in the argument for equality of rights and liberties. Thus, again, there is a convergence between the substantive principles of justice that Rawls derives from his model and the principles that would follow from utilitarian calculation.

---

[9] Because Rawls makes all individuals alike under the conditions of the veil of ignorance, there is a sense in which his model does not take seriously the distinction between persons. Behind the veil, people know that there are differences between persons, but, like the impartiality of utilitarianism, they cannot give any special weight to any of those differences. The choice from behind the veil is not a contract between different individuals but a rational choice for one individual given constraints on information.

AN OVERALL VIEW OF MILL'S
UTILITARIANISM

T HE purpose of this appendix is to give an overall view of
Mill's essay entitled *Utilitarianism*. No attempt will be made
to engage in critical discussion of the issues that it raises. This
appendix is merely a summary of the structure and the main
points of the essay.

The essay has five chapters, the first of which, entitled "General Remarks," might be regarded as a preface. The second chapter, "What Utilitarianism Is," presents a succinct formulation of
the utilitarian "creed" and then attempts to answer objections
to it, objections supposedly based on mistaken interpretations
of its meaning. Chapter 3, "Of the Ultimate Sanction of the
Principle of Utility," is a discussion of the sources of motivation for conformity to a morality based on the general happiness. Chapter 4 is Mill's presentation "Of What Sort of Proof
the Principle of Utility Is Susceptible." The final and longest
chapter, which Mill had begun writing as a separate essay,[1]
is "On the Connexion between Justice and Utility." This last
chapter is in the form of an answer to another objection to
utilitarianism, but in this case the objection could be better
described as due to an inadequate and incomplete analysis of
the idea and sentiment of justice, rather than a mistaken interpretation of utility. Mill's project in the chapter is to show
that, when properly understood, justice is consistent with, subordinate to, and an important branch of utility, rather than
opposed to it.

---

[1] See "Textual Introduction" by J. M. Robson, in *Essays on Ethics, Religion
and Society*, cxxii–cxxiv.

Chapter 1, "General Remarks," is more than just a brief introduction to what is to follow. Mill comments upon the state of moral philosophy and identifies the major school of thought that he considers to be his antagonist. "From the dawn of philosophy," he says, "the question concerning the *summum bonum*, or, what is the same thing, concerning the foundation of morality," has been a problem in speculative thought, and "after more than two thousand years the same discussions continue, philosophers are still ranged under the same contending banners, and neither thinkers nor mankind at large seem nearer to being unanimous on the subject. . . ."[2]

Mill admits that there is a similar uncertainty regarding the first principles of all the sciences, but he contrasts the sciences, "where the particular truths precede the general theory," with a practical art, such as morals or legislation: "All action is for the sake of some end, and rules of action, it seems natural to suppose, take their character from the end to which they are subservient" (206 [I, 2]).

Mill says that the difficulty of providing a foundation for morality is not avoided by his opponents who claim that there is a natural faculty, or sense or instinct, informing us of right and wrong, for that faculty is supposed to supply us with general principles of moral judgments, not to discern what is right or wrong in the particular case at hand, as our other senses discern the sight and sound actually present. The moral sense is supposed to be a branch of our reason, not of our sensitive faculty. Mill contrasts this tradition, which he calls the intuitive school, according to which the principles of morals are evident *a priori*,[3] with his own tradition, which he calls the inductive,

---

[2]   *Utilitarianism*, 205 (ch. 1, par. 1). Citations to *Utilitarianism* are in parentheses in the text.

[3]   "*A priori*" is a term used by the German philosopher Immanuel Kant and others to label knowledge that is universal and necessary. The term would literally be translated "prior to," that is, prior to experience, but the claim is not that the knowledge is innate, preceding experience in time, so much as that its *validity* does not depend upon

according to which right and wrong, as well as truth and false-hood, are questions of observation and experience.

Mill asserts that the proponents of the intuitive school seldom attempt to list the *a priori* principles, still less to reduce them to one first principle or a determinate order of precedence among them, yet this ought, on their view, to be self-evident.

The nonexistence of an acknowledged first principle has made intuitive ethics not so much a guide as a consecration of whatever moral feelings people actually have, according to Mill. But he says that as people's feelings can't help but be influenced by what they suppose to be the effects of things on their happiness, the principle of utility – which Bentham called the greatest happiness principle – has had a large share in forming the moral doctrines even of those who reject its authority, and Mill asserts that all those *a priori* moralists who deem it necessary to argue at all find utilitarian arguments indispensable. He gives the example of Immanuel Kant. Mill claims that when Kant tries to deduce any actual duties from his *a priori* first principle – So act that the rule on which you act would admit of being adopted as a law by all rational beings[4] – Kant fails to show that there would be any contradiction to the adoption by all rational beings of the most outrageously immoral rules of

---

generalization from experience. It is knowledge that is intuitive or is acquired rationally. Thus the term is contrasted with "empirical." Knowledge that is empirical is sensory or based upon analysis and generalization from experience. The usual candidates for the claim to knowledge that is *a priori* are abstract mathematical and logical truths; fundamental principles about the world, such as that every event has a cause; some propositions about the nature or existence of God; and general principles of morality. One dispute between the rationalist tradition and the empirical tradition in modern philosophy is whether there is any *a priori* knowledge that is not merely "analytic," that is, true simply on the basis of the language or concepts used to express it.

4   Kant's formulation is actually not in terms of a "rule" but of a technical term usually translated "maxim," which is a principle of motivation and intention. Mill's interpretation of Kant is very questionable.

conduct. All he shows is that the *consequences* of their universal adoption would be such as no one would choose to incur (207 [I, 4]).

In the comments summarized in the preceding text, Mill has made a number of controversial assumptions, which are discussed critically in Chapter 2, "Mill's Criticism of Alternative Theories," of this book. He characterizes morals and legislation as practical arts, and he assumes what is today called a "teleological" view of morality. This is the view that there is some end or goal (in Greek, *telos*) of morality by which it is to be appraised, a view that is assumed when he identifies the question, "What is the foundation of morality?" with the question, "What is the *summum bonum*?" The latter might be translated, "What is the greatest or total good?" That Mill does not even consider these to be distinct questions is important, as is shown in Chapter 2. Another controversial assumption, which he attributes to his opponents as well, is that morality consists of rules. This is discussed at length in Chapter 4 of this book. Finally, his grouping of the contending schools into the intuitive and the inductive, without further classes or distinctions, is significant and is a topic in Chapter 2.

Having made some remarks about his opponents, Mill introduces the remainder of his essay, or at least Chapters 2 and 4, in two brief paragraphs at the end of Chapter 1. He says that he will attempt to contribute something toward the understanding and appreciation of the utilitarian or happiness theory and toward such proof as it is susceptible. The latter cannot be proof in the ordinary or popular meaning of the term, he says. Questions of ultimate ends are not amenable to direct proof, for whatever can be proved to be good must be so by being shown to be a means to something admitted to be good without proof. When it is asserted that there is a comprehensive formula, including all things that are in themselves good, the formula is not subject to what is commonly understood by proof, but its acceptance or rejection still need not be by blind impulse, arbitrary choice, or intuition. Considerations may be presented capable of determining the intellect to give or to withhold assent, "and this is equivalent to proof" (208 [I, 5]).

Preliminary to such considerations, the formula should be correctly understood. So before going into the philosophical grounds for the utilitarian standard, Mill will attempt to show more clearly what it is and to dispose of objections that are due to mistaken interpretations of its meaning. This is the subject of Chapter 2.

In Chapter 2, Mill first dismisses the misunderstanding that utility is opposed to the agreeable or the ornamental. The word "utilitarian" is popularly used that way; but as the name for a philosophical school of thought, a name that Mill claims credit for introducing, it recognizes value in the contribution of anything to pleasure in any of its forms, including the enjoyment of beauty or the pleasures of amusement. Mill then presents a formulation of the utilitarian "creed": "The creed which accepts as the foundation of morals, Utility, or the Greatest Happiness Principle, holds that actions are right in proportion as they tend to promote happiness, wrong as they tend to produce the reverse of happiness. By happiness is intended pleasure, and the absence of pain; by unhappiness, pain, and the privation of pleasure. To give a clear view of the moral standard set up by the theory, much more requires to be said; in particular, what things it includes in the ideas of pain and pleasure; and to what extent this is left an open question. But these supplementary explanations do not affect the theory of life on which this theory of morality is grounded – namely, that pleasure, and freedom from pain, are the only things desirable as ends; and that all desirable things (which are as numerous in the utilitarian as in any other scheme) are desirable either for the pleasure inherent in themselves, or as a means to the promotion of pleasure and the prevention of pain" (210 [II, 2]).

There are several things noteworthy in this formulation. One is the distinction between a theory of morality and a "theory of life" on which this theory of morality is grounded. The theory of life is apparently a theory of what things are desirable and undesirable as ends, and it is this hedonistic theory of value to which Mill will attempt to persuade the intellect to give assent in his "proof" in Chapter 4. The theory of morality that is founded on it is called, in *System of Logic* and elsewhere, only one branch of the "Art of Life."[5]

Morality is concerned with actions directed toward the end specified as desirable by the theory of life. But not all actions that tend to promote happiness or unhappiness are appropriately enforced as morally required or prohibited. Mill makes this explicit in Chapter 5. Here, however, he does not add that restriction, and that has caused some confusion in interpreting Mill's theory of morality, as is indicated in Chapter 4 of this book. But here Mill does say that actions are right or wrong as they *tend* to promote happiness or produce unhappiness, and the tendency of actions can be judged only by past experience of actions of that type. A particular action that could be foreseen to have bad consequences would be an action of a different type from one that could be foreseen to have good consequences. If an action of a type whose tendency is to have good consequences were, by unforeseeable accident, to produce bad consequences, Mill would presumably say that the agent had done the right thing, even if it turned out to be unfortunate.

Having noticed that Mill formulates his position in terms of the tendency of actions, there is no need to think that he is making any distinction when he speaks of the tendency of actions to *promote* happiness and to *produce* the reverse of happiness.

---

5   John Stuart Mill, *A System of Logic*, 949, and 943, n. c. In the editions of 1843 and 1846, Mill says "ethics, or morality, is properly a portion of the art corresponding to the sciences of human nature and society: the remainder consisting of prudence or policy, and the art of education" (943, n. c [ch. 11, sec. 1 of those editions]). In editions of 1851–72, a longer section was added in which he refers to "the Art of Life, in its three departments, Morality, Prudence or Policy, and Aesthetics; the Right, the Expedient, and the Beautiful or Noble, in human conduct and works" (949 [ch. 12, sec. 6 of those editions]).

I believe that this is merely a stylistic change to avoid repetition. It may be true that one can have greater certainty that pain will result from actions that tend to produce pain than one can have that pleasure will result from actions that tend to produce pleasure; that point might be made by saying that actions tend to produce pain but only to promote happiness. But I don't think that Mill is making that point in this context.

Having given a rough formulation of the theory of morality and the theory of life of utilitarianism, Mill proceeds in the remainder of Chapter 2 to defend both against various objections. Listing these is difficult, because he goes into further objections to the replies that he gives to one objection, but what follows is a possible enumeration of the objections and a brief statement of each of Mill's answers.

(1) A first objection is that to suppose that life has no higher end than pleasure is a doctrine worthy only of swine. Mill answers that human beings are capable of pleasures higher than those of swine, and that those who are equally capable of appreciating and enjoying pleasures of the higher and lower kinds prefer that which employs their higher faculties (210–13 [II, 3–8]).

(1a) In this context, Mill considers objections to the preceding claim, namely, that many who are capable of the higher pleasures occasionally, under the influence of temptation, postpone them to the lower, and that many who begin with youthful enthusiasm for everything noble sink into indolence and selfishness as they advance in years. Mill's reply to the first is that from infirmity of character one can make an election for a nearer good, knowing it to be less valuable; and to the latter, that capacity for the nobler feelings is in most natures "a very tender plant, easily killed, not only by hostile influences, but by mere want of sustenance; and in the majority of young persons it speedily dies away if the occupations to which their position in life has devoted them, and the society into which it has thrown them, are not favourable to keeping that higher capacity in exercise" (212–13 [II, 7]).

This distinction between pleasures of higher and lower kinds is one of the most controversial claims in Mill's essay. Many commentators have claimed that this distinction is a desertion of hedonism, bringing in a nonhedonistic criterion of superiority. Others have argued that Mill's method of measuring superiority of pleasures – the preference of those who are qualified by experience of both kinds – makes Mill a "preference" utilitarian rather than a "mental state" utilitarian. A discussion of Mill's "qualitative hedonism" is the subject of Chapter 3 of this book.

But Mill says that this distinction – that some pleasures are preferable in kind, apart from the question of intensity – is not necessary to answer the original objection. The superiority of "mental" over "bodily" pleasures can be established on the basis of their instrumental as well as their intrinsic value – the greater permanency, safety, uncostliness, etc., of the former (210–11 [II, 4]). And, he continues, because the utilitarian standard is not the agent's own greatest happiness but the greatest amount of happiness altogether, even if it can be doubted whether a noble character is always happier for its nobleness, there can be no doubt that it makes other people happier and that the world in general is a gainer by it (213–14 [II, 9]).

Having introduced the distinction between higher and lower pleasures, Mill revises his description of the "ultimate end," according to the greatest happiness principle, to call it: "an existence exempt as far as possible from pain, and as rich as possible in enjoyments, both in point of quantity and quality; the test of quality, and the rule for measuring it against quantity, being the preference felt by those who, in their opportunities of experience, to which must be added their habits of self-consciousness and self-observation, are best furnished with the means of comparison" (214 [II, 10]). And in this context he gives a further analysis of morality: "This, being, according to the utilitarian opinion, the end of human action, is necessarily also the standard of morality; which may accordingly be defined, the rules and precepts for human conduct, by the observance of which an existence such as has been described might be, to the greatest extent possible, secured for all mankind; and not to them only, but, so far as the nature of things admits, to the whole sentient creation" (214 [II, 10]).

(2) A second objection that Mill takes up is that happiness cannot be the rational purpose of human life because it is unattainable. To this Mill replies that if by happiness is meant a continuity of highly pleasurable excitement, it is indeed impossible. But what is meant by happiness is "not a life of rapture," but "moments of such, in an existence made up of few and transitory pains, many and various pleasures, with a decided predominance of the active over the passive, and having as a foundation of the whole, not to expect more from life than it is capable of bestowing" (215 [II, 12]). Mill thinks that such an existence is even now the lot of many, during considerable portions of their lives, and asserts that the "present wretched education, and wretched social arrangements, are the only real hindrance to its being attainable by almost all" (215 [II, 12]). Mill describes the importance of balance between tranquility and excitement in a happy life, and he blames selfishness and want of mental cultivation for making life unsatisfactory for those who are tolerably fortunate in their outward lot. He sees no reason why an amount of mental culture sufficient to give an intelligent interest in "the objects of nature, the achievements of art, the imaginations of poetry, the incidents of history, the ways of mankind past and present, and their prospects for the future" should not be the inheritance of everyone born in a civilized country. And he sees no reason that any human being should be a selfish egotist, devoid of feeling or care for others. As for outward conditions, he believes that poverty in any sense implying suffering can be completely eliminated by the wisdom of society and that disease can be indefinitely reduced. And this will reduce another source of unhappiness, the premature loss of loved ones (215–17 [II, 13–14]).

(3) Another objection is that people can do without happiness, and all noble human beings have regarded doing without

it as a necessary condition of all virtue. Mill agrees that it is noble to be capable of resigning one's own portion of happiness, or chances of it, but he argues that this self-sacrifice is not good in itself. It must be for some worthy end. When the renunciation contributes worthily to increase the amount of happiness or decrease the amount of pain in the world, then it is admirable. If it does not, then it is wasted (214, 217–18 [II, 11,15–17]). Mill says that between one's own happiness and that of others, utilitarianism requires the agent to be "as strictly impartial as a disinterested and benevolent spectator. In the golden rule of Jesus of Nazareth, we read the complete spirit of the ethics of utility. To do as one would be done by and to love one's neighbour as oneself, constitute the ideal perfection of utilitarian morality" (218 [II, 18]). The utilitarian will also support laws and social arrangements to harmonize the interests of every individual with that of all and seek through education and opinion to establish an "indissoluble association" between the happiness of each and the good of others (218 [II, 18]).

(4) Another objection, which follows from the point just made, is that it is expecting too much to require that people always act from the inducement of promoting the general interests of society. To answer this, Mill makes two points. The first is a distinction between the standard of right and wrong action, on the one hand, and, on the other hand, the various motives that may induce people to act the way that they do. One need not be acting from the motive of impartial benevolence in order for an action to be in accordance with the utilitarian standard: ". . . ninety-nine hundredths of all our actions are done from other motives, and rightly so done, if the rule of duty does not condemn them" (219 [II, 19]). The other point is that even when acting "from the motive of duty, and in direct obedience to principle," it is usually not necessary "that people should fix their minds upon so wide a generality as the world or society at large. The great majority of good acts are intended, not for the benefit of the world, but for that of individuals, of which the good of the world is made up . . ." (220 [II, 19]).

The first of these points, the separation of the rightness or wrongness of actions from the motives of the agents, is a difficult one. Motives are proper objects of appraisal, Mill says, but they have to do with the worth of the agent, rather than the correctness of the act: "He [or she] who saves a fellow creature from drowning does what is morally right, whether his [or her] motive be duty, or the hope of being paid for his [or her] trouble..." (219 [II, 19]). These are equally right actions, but the former shows the agent to be more morally admirable. In later editions (1864 on), Mill added a footnote to attempt to answer a challenge to this claim. The challenge went as follows: Suppose that a tyrant saved a man from drowning so that he could inflict upon him even more cruel tortures. Would it be right to speak of that rescue as a "morally right act"? In reply, Mill seems to make two different points in characterizing this act as different from the usual case of saving a person from drowning, although he does not clearly distinguish them. First, he calls attention to the act's place within a series of acts, or as part of a larger act, which makes it different from the usual case of saving a life. "The rescue of the man is, in the case supposed, only the necessary first step of an act far more atrocious..." (219, [II, 19], note added to editions from 1864 on). Second, he distinguishes between "the very different ideas of Motive and Intention," making the intention but not the motive an essential feature of the action. The intention is "what the agent *wills to do*"; the motive is "the feeling which makes him [or her] will so to do" (219 [II, 19], note continued on 220). Mill apparently thinks that the intention, as the end or aim of the action, is an essential feature of voluntary action and is important in identifying the *action's* tendency to produce good or bad consequences, whereas the motive, as what moves the agent to have that aim, is a feature of the *agent*, not the action, and has a tendency to produce good or bad consequences only indirectly by tending to produce actions of a right or wrong kind.

In speaking of an act as a necessary step in a larger act, Mill's analysis has significance beyond the distinction between motive and intention, namely, that an act in one context may be significantly different from the apparently similar act in another context. In the example this is due to the intentions of the agent, who plans to engage in subsequent acts of torture. In other contexts, the foreseeable consequences might be due to factors other than the intentions of the agent but still be grounds for significantly distinguishing the tendency of the act from an otherwise similar act done in normal circumstances. This point is discussed more fully in Chapter 4 of this work, in discussing the place of rules in Mill's ethics.

Related to this is the second part of Mill's reply to the objection that it is exacting too much to expect that people act to promote the general interests of society. In the case of abstinences – of things that people forbear to do, from moral considerations – Mill concedes that they are concerned with consequences for society at large. The passage is relevant to the issue of whether Mill is an "act" or a "rule" utilitarian, as discussed in Chapter 4 of this book. The key passage is as follows: "In the case of abstinences indeed – of things which people forbear to do, from moral considerations, though the consequences in the particular case might be beneficial – it would be unworthy of an intelligent agent not to be consciously aware that the action is of a class which, if practiced generally, would be generally injurious, and that this is the ground of the obligation to abstain from it" (220 [II, 19]).

(5) Another objection is that utilitarianism renders people cold and unsympathizing; that it chills their moral feelings toward individuals; that it makes them regard only the dry and hard consideration of the consequences of actions, not taking into their moral estimate the qualities from which these actions emanate. Mill's reply is that whether an action is done by "an amiable, a brave, or a benevolent man [or woman], or the contrary" is relevant, not to the estimation of actions, but of persons; and there is nothing in the utilitarian theory inconsistent with the fact that there are other things that interest us

in persons besides the rightness and wrongness of their actions (220–1 [II, 20–1]).

(6) The doctrine of utility is inveighed against as a *godless* doctrine. Mill's reply is that if it be a true belief that God desires, above all things, the happiness of his creatures, utilitarianism can be regarded as profoundly religious (222–3 [II, 22]).

(7) Utility is stigmatized as an immoral doctrine by giving it the name of "expediency," to contrast it with "principle." Mill's answer is that the expedient, in the sense in which it is opposed to the right, generally means that which is expedient for the particular interest of the agent or that which is expedient for some immediate object, some temporary purpose but that violates a rule whose observance is expedient in a much higher degree. The expedient, in this sense, he says, instead of being the same thing with the useful, is a branch of the hurtful. For example, telling a lie to avoid some momentary embarrassment weakens one's habits of truthfulness and the trustworthiness of human assertion. So the violation, for a present advantage, "of a rule of such transcendent expediency," is not expedient. Yet even the rule of truthfulness admits of exceptions, he says, such as when the withholding of some fact (as of information from a malefactor, or of bad news from a person dangerously ill) would save someone from great and unmerited evil and the withholding only can be effected by denial. "But in order that the exception may not extend itself beyond the need, and may have the least possible effect in weakening reliance on veracity, it ought to be recognised, and, if possible, its limits defined . . ." (223 [II, 23]).

(8) To the objection that there is not time, previous to action, for calculating and weighing the effects of any line of conduct on the general happiness, Mill replies that throughout all of human history mankind have been learning by experience the tendencies of actions. By this time they "have acquired positive beliefs as to the effects of some actions on their happiness; and the beliefs which have thus come down are the rules of

morality for the multitude, and for the philosopher until he has succeeded in finding better" (224 [II, 24]). Mill thinks that they do admit of improvement, but "to consider the rules of morality as improvable, is one thing; to pass over the intermediate generalization entirely, and endeavour to test each individual action directly by the first principle, is another.... The proposition that happiness is the end and aim of morality, does not mean that no road ought to be laid down to that goal, or that persons going thither should not be advised to take one direction rather than another" (224–5 [II, 24]).

(9) As a last objection dealt with in Chapter 2, it is claimed that the utilitarian will be apt to make his or her own particular case an exception to moral rules, and, when under temptation, will see a utility in the breach of the rule, greater than he or she will see in its observance. Mill's reply is that every moral code is subject to the common infirmities of human nature, with excuses for evildoing. Every moral creed tempers the rigidity of its laws for accommodation to peculiarities of circumstances, and at the opening thus made, self-deception and dishonest casuistry get in. Every system has cases of conflicting obligations. Mill thinks that utilitarianism is superior to others in that utility may be invoked to decide between obligations when their demands are incompatible (225–6 [II, 25]).

In Chapter 3, Mill is addressing the question of what motives there are to be moral. He points out that the question arises whenever a person is called upon to *adopt* a standard. Customary morality, which education and opinion have consecrated, presents itself as being *in itself* obligatory, and when one is asked to believe that morality *derives* its obligation from a more general principle round which custom has not thrown the same halo, the assertion is a paradox. The specific rules, such as not to rob or murder, betray or deceive, seem to be more obligatory than promoting the general happiness, which is proposed as their foundation. So the question, what motives there are to follow the utilitarian morality, will arise until the influences that form moral character have taken the same hold of the principle of utilitarianism as they have taken of some of the rules of morality that could be derived from that principle – until the feeling of unity with our fellow creatures shall be as deeply rooted in our character as the horror of crime is in an ordinarily well-brought-up young person. In the meantime, the difficulty is not peculiar to the doctrine of utility, but is inherent in every attempt to analyze morality and to reduce it to principles.

Mill's claim in this chapter is that all the same motives that now lead people to obey customary morality or to obey rules based on any other system of morals can lead them to obey utilitarian morality, and that there are additional sources of motivation as well.

Mill, following Bentham, uses the word "sanctions" to refer to the sources of motivation to be moral. Mill classifies them as "external" and "internal." Under the former heading are hope of favor and fear of displeasure from our fellow creatures and from the Ruler of the Universe (if one has a belief in the divine). These are the motives that Bentham analyzed as the political, the moral or popular, and the religious sanctions. Even if there were no other motive to be moral, these would operate, and these sanctions are consistent with utilitarianism. Other people, as well as oneself, desire their own happiness and commend conduct by which they think that their happiness is promoted; so hope of favor and fear of displeasure of others will conduce to behavior that promotes the happiness of others. And if people believe in the goodness of God, those who think that conduciveness to the general happiness is the criterion of good must believe that this is what God approves. Thus utilitarianism has available to it these external sanctions. Mill points out that we also have sympathy and affections for other people, and may have love or awe of God as well as hope or fear of favor or disfavor.

But it is the "internal" sanction that really interests Mill. This is the feeling of pain, attendant on the violation of duty, which is the essence of conscience. Mill thinks that conscience is *acquired* – "derived from sympathy, from love, and still more from fear; from all the forms of religious feeling; from the recollections of childhood and of all our past life; from self-esteem, desire of the esteem of others, and occasionally even self-abasement" (228 [III, 4]). Thus, Mill thinks that it is an internalization of the external sanctions complicated by various other associated feelings. He says that this complicated character of its origin gives it a sort of mystical character, which leads people to believe that it cannot possibly attach itself to any other objects than those that are found in our present experience to excite it. But Mill sees no reason why conscience may not be cultivated to as great intensity in connection with the utilitarian as with any other rule of morals.

Also, Mill thinks that his claim does not depend upon whether the feeling of duty is innate or acquired. If innate, it is still an open question as to what objects it naturally attaches itself, and Mill sees no reason why it should not be in regard to the pleasures and pains of others.

If, as Mill believes, moral feelings are acquired, the feelings might be analyzed away as arbitrary conditioning, if there were not a natural basis for the feelings. Mill believes that for a utilitarian conscience there is. It is the desire to be in unity with our fellow creatures, which he believes to be a universally powerful principle in human nature, and to become stronger with the influences of advancing civilization. Cooperating with others requires that collective interest be the aim of actions; one's own ends are at least temporarily identified with those of others, and this leads one to identify one's *feelings* more and more with their good, and to demonstrate these feelings to others. And even if one does not have such feelings, one has an interest in others having them in order to support their share of cooperation. Mill thus thinks that these feelings can be reinforced by external sanctions, and that as civilization goes on, and improvements in political life remove inequalities of legal privilege between individuals or classes, there is an increasing tendency for each individual to feel a unity with all the rest.

Even in the present imperfect state of society, where such social feelings are inferior to selfish ones, those who have such social feelings do not regard them as a superstition of education or a law despotically imposed by the power of society, but as an attribute that it would not be well for them to be without. This conviction Mill calls the "ultimate sanction" of the utilitarian morality.

In Chapter 4 Mill gives a psychological argument for the utilitarian doctrine "that happiness is desirable, and the only thing desirable, as an end; all other things being only desirable as means to that end" (234 [IV, 1]). This so-called "proof" of the principle of utility is one of the most controversial sections of the essay and is the subject of a chapter of the present work. Mill does not claim that it is a proof in the sense of a logical deduction from premises. It is merely claimed that the only evidence available to judge what is intrinsically good, when properly analyzed, supports the utilitarian theory of value, which Mill earlier called a "theory of life."

To be incapable of proof by reasoning, he says, is common to all first principles, those of knowledge as well as those of conduct. But the former, being matters of fact, may be subject to a direct appeal to the faculties that judge of fact – namely, our senses and our internal consciousness. For questions of practical ends, appeal must be made to the faculty of desire: "The only proof capable of being given that an object is visible, is that people actually see it. The only proof that a sound is audible, is that people hear it: and so of the other sources of our experience. In like manner, I apprehend, the sole evidence it is possible to produce that anything is desirable, is that people do actually desire it" (234 [IV, 3]).

Appealing to this evidence, Mill thinks that it is obvious that happiness is at least one thing that is desirable: "No reason can be given why the general happiness is desirable, except that each person, so far as he [or she] believes it to be attainable, desires his [or her] own happiness. This, however, being a fact, we have not only all the proof which the case admits of, but all which it is possible to require, that happiness is a good: that each person's happiness is a good to that person, and the general happiness, therefore, a good to the aggregate of all persons. Happiness has made out its title as *one* of the ends of conduct, and consequently one of the criteria of morality" (234 [IV, 3]).

More difficult is for Mill to be convincing that happiness is the *only* thing desirable as an end, and he admits that people do desire as ends things that "in common language, are decidedly distinguished from happiness. They desire, for example, virtue, and the absence of vice, no less really than pleasure and the absence of pain" (235 [IV, 4]). Utilitarians, Mill says, "believe that actions and dispositions are only virtuous because they promote another end than virtue"; still they recognize as a psychological fact the possibility of virtue's being, to the individual, a good in itself, without looking to any end beyond it (235 [IV, 5]).

Mill claims that this is consistent with the happiness principle because such a person "finds happiness" in the possession of virtue. Being a person of virtue is then a "part" of the person's happiness: "The ingredients of happiness are very various, and each of them is desirable in itself, and not merely when considered as swelling an aggregate. The principle of utility does not mean that any given pleasure, as music, for instance, or any given exemption from pain, as for example health, are to be looked upon as means to a collective something termed happiness, and to be desired on that account. They are desired and desirable in and for themselves; besides being means, they are part of the end" (235 [IV, 5]).

Mill thinks that virtue comes to be desired as an end by a process of association with pleasure and pain, and he gives other examples of things that thus come to be desired as ingredients of an individual's conception of happiness: money, power, and fame. In all these cases, what was once desired as an instrument for the attainment of happiness has come to be desired for its own sake, "as *part* of happiness. The person is made, or thinks he [or she] would be made, happy by its mere possession; and is made unhappy by failure to obtain it" (236 [IV, 6]). They are some of the elements of which the desire of happiness is made up. "Happiness is not an abstract idea, but a concrete whole, and these are some of its parts" (236 [IV, 6]).

Mill concludes from this analysis that there is in reality nothing desired as an end except happiness: "Whatever is desired otherwise than as a means to some end beyond itself, and ultimately to happiness, is desired as itself a part of happiness, and is not desired for itself until it has become so" (237 [IV, 8]). If the consciousness of the thing desired gave no pleasure or the consciousness of being without it gave no pain, then the individual would not desire it or would desire it only for the other benefits that it might produce for himself or herself or to persons whom he or she cared for (237 [IV, 8]). This is a psychological claim, "a question of fact and experience," that "can only be determined by practised self-consciousness and self-observation, assisted by observation of others" (237 [IV, 10]). And Mill thinks that these sources of evidence will declare that desiring a thing as an end and finding it pleasant, aversion to it and thinking of it as painful, are "two different modes of naming the same psychological fact" (237 [IV, 10]).

Mill believes that this psychological evidence provides a foundation for morality. If his psychological claim is true, then "happiness is the sole end of human action, and the promotion of it the test by which to judge of all human conduct; from whence it necessarily follows that it must be the criterion of morality, since a part is included in the whole" (237 [IV, 9]).

It remains for Mill to answer the objection that will is different from desire, and that a "person whose purposes are fixed" carries out these purposes without any pleasure in contemplating them or without any thought of pleasure expected to be derived from their fulfillment. Such a person may even carry them out when the pleasures are outweighed by the pains that pursuit of the purposes may bring. Mill admits this. But he dismisses it as not counting as evidence of what is desirable. He sees it as an instance of the power of habit. We may will from habit what we no longer desire for itself, or desire only because we will it. He claims that "will, in the beginning, is entirely produced by desire; including in that term the repelling influence of pain as well as the attractive one of pleasure.... Will is the child of desire, and passes out of the dominion of its parent only to come under that of habit." That which is the result of habit, he claims, "affords no presumption of being intrinsically good..." (238–9 [IV, 11]).

In Chapter 5, "On the Connexion between Justice and Utility," Mill is addressing the objection that justice is an idea distinct from utility and that it has feelings connected with it that are not connected with utility or happiness as the criterion of right and wrong. Mill recognizes that the subjective mental feeling (which Mill calls the "sentiment") of justice is different from that which commonly attaches to expediency or the general promotion of happiness. (Mill frequently uses the term "expediency" in this chapter to refer to general utility or simple promotion of happiness in contrast to the demands of duty or justice.) Except in extreme cases, justice is also far more imperative in its demands. He admits that this sentiment does not arise from the idea of utility. But in the course of the chapter he argues that what is moral in the sentiment does depend upon utility: that justice is a particular kind or branch of general utility and that there is even a utilitarian basis for distinguishing justice from other moral obligations and making the requirement more demanding. He argues that if justice is something distinct from utility, which the mind can recognize by simple introspection, it is hard to understand why there is so much controversy over what is just in punishment, in wages, or in taxation. If, on the other hand, justice is subordinate to utility, this is explicable. There will be as much difference of opinion about what is just as about what is useful to society.

First, however, he says that it is necessary to ascertain what is the distinguishing character of justice, or of injustice (for it is best defined by its opposite): what is the quality, or whether there is any quality, common to all modes of conduct designated as unjust and distinguishing them from such modes of conduct as are disapproved, but without having the particular epithet of injustice applied to them. He lists six candidates for this characterization.

In the first place it is considered unjust to deprive anyone of his or her personal liberty, property, or any other thing that belongs to him or her by law. Thus it is unjust to violate the *legal rights* of anyone.

Secondly, it is universally admitted that there can be unjust laws; so law cannot be the ultimate criterion of justice. Such laws may be regarded as violating a right, but because it cannot be a legal right, it is called a *moral right*.

Thirdly, it is considered just that each person obtain what he or she *deserves* – good if he or she does right, evil if he or she does wrong.

Fourthly, it is considered unjust to *break faith* with anyone.

Fifthly, it is considered inconsistent with justice to be *partial*, to show favor or preference for one person over another, in matters in which favor and preference do not properly apply.

Finally, another associated idea is *equality*. But Mill points out that what equality is required varies with variations in notions of utility. "Whoever thinks that government is necessary, sees no injustice in as much inequality as is constituted by giving to the magistrate powers not granted to other people" (244 [V, 10]).

With so much diversity of application, Mill examines the etymology of the word. He thinks that it points to an origin connected with conformity to law, but there are two qualifications in using this as an analysis of the concept. One is that already with the Greeks and Romans the sentiments of justice and injustice attached not to all laws but to such laws as *ought* to exist. The second is that nobody desires that laws should interfere with the whole detail of private life, yet everyone allows that in all daily conduct persons may and do show themselves to be just or unjust. But Mill says that even here the idea of a breach of law lingers. It would seem fit that acts that we deem unjust should be punished, even if we do not think it expedient that this should be done by tribunals.

Mill thinks that this idea of penal sanction, as the essence of law, is the generating idea of the notion of justice, but it does not distinguish justice from moral obligation in general: "We do not call anything wrong, unless we mean to imply that a person ought to be punished in some way or other for doing it; if not by law, by the opinion of his [or her] fellow creatures; if not by opinion, by the reproaches of his [or her] own conscience. This seems the real turning point of the distinction between morality and simple expediency. . . . There are other things, on the contrary, which we wish that people should do, which we like or admire them for doing, perhaps dislike or despise them for not doing, but yet admit that they are not bound to do; it is not a case of moral obligation; we do not blame them, that is, we do not think that they are proper objects of punishment" (246 [V, 14]).

To explain the difference between justice and other branches of morality, Mill appeals to the distinction between those duties in which a correlative *right* resides in some person or persons and those moral obligations that do not give birth to any right. Mill thinks that this distinction exactly coincides with that which exists between justice and the other obligations of morality. In the preceding survey the term "justice" appeared generally to involve the idea of a personal right. Whether the injustice consists in depriving persons of a possession, or in breaking faith with them, or treating them worse than they deserve, in each case the supposition involves a right in some person correlative to the moral obligation. This feature is the specific difference between justice, on the one hand, and generosity or beneficence. "Justice implies something which it is not only right to do, and wrong not to do, but which some individual person can claim from us as his [or her] moral right. No one has a moral right to our generosity or beneficence, because we are not bound to practise those virtues towards any given individual" (247 [V, 15]).

Turning to the feeling, which accompanies the idea of justice, Mill says that the two essential ingredients of it are the desire to punish a person who has done harm and the belief that there is some definite individual or individuals to whom harm has been done. He thinks that this desire is derived from two more basic sentiments that either are or resemble instincts: the impulse of self-defense and the feeling of sympathy. "It is natural to resent, and to repel or retaliate, any harm done or attempted against ourselves, or against those with whom we sympathize" (248 [V, 20]). This sentiment, in itself, however, has nothing moral in it. The natural feeling tends to make us resent indiscriminately whatever anyone does that is disagreeable to us; to make it moral, it must be exclusively subordinated to the social sympathies, and when moralized by the social feeling, it only acts in the directions conformable to the general good: "just persons resenting a hurt to society, though not otherwise a hurt to themselves, and not resenting a hurt to themselves, however painful, unless it be of the kind which society has a common interest with them in the repression of" (249 [V, 21]).

Having analyzed justice as the class of obligations that have correlative rights, Mill gives an analysis of what it is to have a right: "When we call anything a person's right, we mean that he [or she] has a valid claim on society to protect him [or her] in the possession of it, either by the force of law, or by that of education and opinion" (250 [V, 24]). When asked why society ought to recognize such rights, Mill says that he can give no other reason than general utility. If that does not convey a sufficient feeling of the strength of the obligation, it is because there goes into the feeling the animal element of self-defense as well as the rational element, and because it is an extraordinarily important and impressive kind of utility that is concerned – that of security. Security no human being can possibly do without. On it we depend for all immunity from evil and the whole value of every good beyond the passing moment (251 [V, 25]).

191

Next Mill argues against the notion that justice is independent of utility by showing that there is great controversy about
what policies, in punishment, wages, and taxation, are just and
unjust. If justice is something that the mind can recognize by
simple introspection, it is hard to understand why that internal
oracle is so ambiguous.

For instance, some say that it is unjust to punish anyone for
the sake of example to others; that punishment is just only
when intended for the good of the criminal. Others maintain
the extreme reverse, that to punish persons for their own benefit is unjust, because if the matter at issue is their own good, no
one has a right to control their judgment of it; but they may be
justly punished to prevent evil to others. And Robert Owen,[6]
who held that character is the product of circumstances for
which the individual is not responsible, affirms that it is unjust
to punish at all. There are also conflicting conceptions of the
proper amount of punishment. One theory is to exact literally
an "eye for an eye"; another is to make the punishment proportional to the moral guilt of the culprit; another is to inflict only
as much as will suffice to prevent the criminal from repeating
the act and others from imitating that misconduct.

Another example is the justice of wages. In a cooperative
industrial association, is it just or not that talent and skill should
give title to superior remuneration? One side argues against it
on the ground that all who do the best they can deserve equally
well. The other side argues that society receives more from the
more efficient laborers. Mill says that justice in this case has
two sides to it. "... [A]ny choice between them, on grounds
of justice, must be perfectly arbitrary. Social utility alone can
decide the preference" (254 [V, 30]).

Another example is justice in taxation. One opinion is that
justice demands that those with most ability to pay should pay

---

6 Robert Owen (1771–1858), British social reformer and socialist, put
   forward the idea that character is the product of environment in such
   works as *A New View of Society: or, Essays on the Formation of Character*.

more, perhaps at a graduated rate. Another opinion is to disregard means and take the same sum from each person on grounds that each receives equal benefit. It could be argued that each does not receive equal benefit, but between the two claims of justice in taxation, whether it should be proportional to benefit or proportional to ability to pay, Mill says "there is no other mode of extrication than the utilitarian" (255 [V, 31]).

Mill still recognizes an important distinction between justice and general utility. He thinks that justice that is grounded on utility is the chief part and the most sacred and binding part of morality. "Justice is a name for certain classes of moral rules, which concern the essentials of human well-being more nearly, and are therefore of more absolute obligation, than any other rules for the guidance of life. . . .

"The moral rules which forbid mankind to hurt one another (in which we must never forget to include wrongful interference with each other's freedom) are more vital to human well-being than any maxims, however important, which only point out the best mode of managing some department of human affairs. . . . It is their observance which alone preserves peace among human beings: . . . a person may possibly not need the benefits of others; but he [or she] always needs that they should not do him [or her] hurt" (255–6 [V, 32–3]).

Mill points out that many maxims of justice are simply instrumental in carrying into effect the principles of just punishment and reward. That a person is only responsible for what the person could voluntarily have avoided; that it is unjust to condemn any person unheard; that the punishment ought to be proportional to the offense; impartiality on the part of magistrates; these are all instrumental values.

Mill summarizes by saying that justice is the appropriate name for certain social utilities that are vastly more important, and therefore more absolute and imperative, than any others are as a class and that, therefore, ought to be, as well as naturally are, guarded by a sentiment "distinguished from the milder feeling which attaches to the mere idea of promoting human pleasure or convenience, at once by the more definite nature of its commands, and by the sterner character of its sanctions" (259 [V, 37]).

Thus, Mill feels that he has answered the objection that justice is distinct from utility. His claim is that the modes of conduct required by justice can be given a utilitarian justification and, in cases of conflict between competing theories of justice, even require a utilitarian arbitration. And although the sentiment attached to instances of justice is different from that which attaches to utility in general, the very existence of that distinct and stronger sentiment has a utilitarian support.

BIBLIOGRAPHY

A comprehensive bibliography of works on Mill can be found in *The Cambridge Companion to Mill*, John Skorupski, ed. (Cambridge: Cambridge University Press, 1998). The works listed in this bibliography are those cited in the text, and those not cited that pertain to Mill's utilitarian ethics.

Aiken, Henry David. "Definitions, Factual Premises, and Ethical Conclusions." *Philosophical Review* 61 (1952): 331–48.

Albee, Ernest. *A History of English Utilitarianism*. London: Sonnenschein; New York: Macmillan, 1902.

Alican, Necip Fikri. *Mill's Principle of Utility: A Defence of John Stuart Mill's Notorious Proof*. Amsterdam and Atlanta: Rodopi, 1994.

Anderson, Susan Leigh. *On Mill*. Belmont, CA: Wadsworth, 2000.

Anschutz, R. P. *The Philosophy of J. S. Mill*. Oxford: Oxford University Press, 1953.

Aristotle. *Nicomachean Ethics*. W. D. Ross, trans. Vol. 9 of *The Works of Aristotle*. London: Oxford University Press, 1925.

Ashmore, Robert B., Jr. "Deriving the Desirable from the Desired." *Proceedings of the American Catholic Philosophical Association* 44 (1970): 152–60.

Atkinson, R. F. "J. S. Mill's 'Proof' of the Principle of Utility." *Philosophy* 32 (1957): 158–67.

Baier, Annette. "Hume, David." *Encyclopedia of Ethics*. 2nd ed. 3 vols. Lawrence C. Becker and Charlotte B. Becker, eds. New York and London: Routledge, 2001.

Bain, Alexander. *John Stuart Mill: A Criticism with Personal Recollections*. 1882. Reprint, New York: Augustus M. Kelley, 1969.

Baker, John. "Mill's Captivating 'Proof' and the Foundations of Ethics." *Social Theory and Practice* 6 (1980): 299–310.

Baker, John M. "Utilitarianism and Secondary Principles." *Philosophical Quarterly* 21 (1971): 69–71.

Baumgardt, David. *Bentham and the Ethics of Today with Manuscripts Hitherto Unpublished*. Princeton: Princeton University Press, 1952. Reprint, New York: Octagon Books, 1966.

Bayles, Michael D. "Mill's 'Utilitarianism' and Aristotle's 'Rhetoric.'" *Modern Schoolman* 51 (1974): 159–70.

Bentham, Jeremy. *Constitutional Code*. Vol. 9 of *Works of Jeremy Bentham*. John Bowring, ed. Edinburgh, 1841.

———. *Book of Fallacies*. Vol. 2 of *Works of Jeremy Bentham*. John Bowring, ed. Edinburgh, 1843.

———. *Works of Jeremy Bentham*. 11 vols. John Bowring, ed. Edinburgh, 1838–43.

———. *An Introduction to the Principles of Morals and Legislation*. 1789. J. H. Burns and H. L. A. Hart, eds. London: University of London, Athlone Press, 1970.

Berger, Fred R. "Mill's Concept of Happiness." *Interpretation* 7 (1978): 95–117.

———. "John Stuart Mill on Justice and Fairness." In *New Essays on John Stuart Mill and Utilitarianism*, Wesley E. Cooper, Kai Nielsen, and Steven C. Patten, eds. *Canadian Journal of Philosophy*, supp. vol. 5 (1979): 115–36.

———. "Mill's Substantive Principles of Justice: A Comparison with Nozick." *American Philosophical Quarterly* 19 (1982): 373–80.

———. *Happiness, Justice, and Freedom: The Moral and Political Philosophy of John Stuart Mill*. Berkeley and Los Angeles: University of California Press, 1984.

Billings, John R. "J. S. Mill's Quantity-Quality Distinction." *The Mill News Letter* 7 (1971): 6–16.

Bradley, F. H. *Ethical Studies*. 1876. 2nd ed. London: Oxford University Press, 1927.

Brandt, Richard B. *Ethical Theory*. Englewood Cliffs, NJ: Prentice-Hall, 1959.

———. *A Theory of the Good and the Right*. Oxford: Oxford University Press, 1979.

———. *Facts, Values, and Morality*. Cambridge: Cambridge University Press, 1996.

Brink, David O. "Mill's Deliberative Utilitarianism." *Philosophy and Public Affairs* 21 (1992): 67–103. Reprinted in *Mill's Utilitarianism:*

Critical Essays, David Lyons, ed. 149–83. Lanham, MD: Rowman and Littlefield Publishers, 1997.

Britton, Karl. *John Stuart Mill*. 2nd ed. New York: Dover, 1969.

Bronaugh, Richard. "The Quality in Pleasures." *Philosophy* 49 (1974): 320–2.

———. "The Utility of Quality: An Understanding of Mill." *Canadian Journal of Philosophy* 4 (1974): 317–25.

Brown, D. G. "What Is Mill's Principle of Utility?" *Canadian Journal of Philosophy* 3 (1973): 1–12.

———. "Mill's Act-Utilitarianism." *Philosophical Quarterly* 24 (1974): 67–8.

———. "Mill's Criterion of Wrong Conduct." *Dialogue* 21 (1982): 27–44.

Carmichael, Peter A. "Mill and 'Desirable.'" *Philosophy and Phenomenological Research* 34 (1974): 435–6.

Carritt, E. F. *Ethical and Political Thinking*. Oxford: Clarendon Press, 1947.

Chamblin, T. S., and A. D. M. Walker. "Tendencies, Frequencies and Classical Utilitarianism." *Analysis* 35 (1974): 8–12.

Clark, George A. "Mill's 'Notorious Analogy.'" *Journal of Philosophy* 56 (1959): 652–6.

Cohen, Elliot David. "J. S. Mill's Qualitative Hedonism: A Textual Analysis." *Southern Journal of Philosophy* 18 (1980): 151–8.

Cohen, Stephen. "Proof and Sanction in Mill's Utilitarianism." *History of Philosophy Quarterly* (1990): 475–87.

Collingwood, R. G. *An Essay on Philosophical Method*. Oxford: Clarendon Press, 1933.

Coope, Christopher Miles. "Was Mill a Utilitarian?" *Utilitas* 10 (1998): 33–67.

Cooper, Neil. "Mill's 'Proof' of the Principle of Utility." *Mind* 78 (1969): 278–9.

Cooper, Wesley E., Kai Nielsen, and Steven C. Patten, eds. *New Essays on John Stuart Mill and Utilitarianism. Canadian Journal of Philosophy*, supp. vol. 5. Guelph: Canadian Association for Publishing in Philosophy, 1979.

Copp, David. "The Iterated-Utilitarianism of J. S. Mill." In *New Essays on John Stuart Mill and Utilitarianism*, Wesley E. Cooper, Kai Nielsen, and Steven C. Patten, eds. *Canadian Journal of Philosophy*, supp. vol. 5 (1979): 75–98.

Cowan, J. L. *Pleasure and Pain*. London: Macmillan; New York: St. Martin's, 1968.

Crisp, Roger. "Mill on Virtue as a Part of Happiness." *British Journal for the History of Philosophy* 4 (1996): 367–80.

———. *Routledge Philosophy Guidebook to Mill on Utilitarianism*. London and New York: Routledge, 1997.

Cupples, Brian. "A Defence of the Received Interpretation of J. S. Mill." *Australasian Journal of Philosophy* 50 (1972): 131–7.

Dahl, Norman O. "Is Mill's Hedonism Inconsistent?" *American Philosophical Quarterly*, Monograph 7 (1973): 37–54.

Dancy, Jonathan. "Mill's Puzzling Footnote." *Utilitas* 12 (2000): 219–22.

Den Uyl, Douglas, and Tibor R. Machan. "Recent Work on the Concept of Happiness." *American Philosophical Quarterly* 20 (1983): 115–34.

Dewey, John. *Ethics*. 1932. In vol. 7 of *John Dewey: The Later Works, 1925–1953*, Jo Ann Boydston, ed. Carbondale and Edwardsville, IL: Southern Illinois University Press, 1985.

Donner, Wendy. "John Stuart Mill's Concept of Utility." *Dialogue* 22 (1983): 479–94.

———. *The Liberal Self: John Stuart Mill's Moral and Political Philosophy*. Ithaca: Cornell University Press, 1991.

———. "Mill's Utilitarianism." In *The Cambridge Companion to Mill*, John Skorupski, ed. 255–92. Cambridge: Cambridge University Press, 1998.

Douglas, Charles. Introduction to *The Ethics of John Stuart Mill*, with introductory essays by Charles Douglas, ed. i–cxxvi. Edinburgh and London: Blackwood, 1897.

———. *John Stuart Mill: A Study of His Philosophy*. 1895. Folcroft, PA: Folcroft Library Editions, 1973.

Downie, R. S. "Mill on Pleasure and Self-Development." *Philosophical Quarterly* 16 (1966): 69–71.

Dryer, D. P. "Mill's Utilitarianism." In *Essays on Ethics, Religion and Society*, by John Stuart Mill. Vol. 10 of *Collected Works of John Stuart Mill*, J. M. Robson, ed. lxiii–cxiii. Toronto: University of Toronto Press, 1969.

———. "Justice, Liberty and the Principle of Utility in Mill." In *New Essays on John Stuart Mill and Utilitarianism*, Wesley E. Cooper, Kai Nielsen, and Steven C. Patten, eds. *Canadian Journal of Philosophy*, supp. vol. 5 (1979): 63–73.

Ebenstein, L. "Mill's Theory of Utility." *Philosophy* 60 (1985): 539–43.

Edwards, Rem B. "Do Pleasures and Pains Differ Qualitatively?" *Journal of Value Inquiry* 9 (1975): 270–81.

———. *Pleasures and Pains: A Theory of Qualitative Hedonism.* Ithaca: Cornell University Press, 1979.

———. "J. S. Mill and Robert Veatch's Critique of Utilitarianism." *Southern Journal of Philosophy* 23 (1985): 181–200.

———. "The Principle of Utility and Mill's Minimizing Utilitarianism." *Journal of Value Inquiry* 20 (1986): 125–36.

Ellis, Brian. "Retrospective and Prospective Utilitarianism." *Nous* 15 (1981): 325–39.

Falk, W. D. "'Ought' and Motivation." *Proceedings of the Aristotelian Society*, N. S. 48 (1947–8): 111–38. Reprinted in *Readings in Ethical Theory*, Wilfred Sellars and John Hospers, eds. 492–510. New York: Appleton-Century-Crofts, 1952.

Feagin, Susan L. "Mill and Edwards on the Higher Pleasures." *Philosophy* 58 (1983): 244–52.

Frankena, William. "Obligation and Motivation in Recent Moral Philosophy." In *Essays in Moral Philosophy*, A. I. Melden, ed. 40–81. Seattle: University of Washington Press, 1958.

———. *Ethics.* Englewood Cliffs, NJ: Prentice-Hall, 1963.

Fullinwider, Robert K. "On Mill's Analogy between Visible and Desirable." *Southern Journal of Philosophy* 10 (1972): 17–22.

Galle, Peter. "Gruzalski and Ellis on Utilitarianism." *Australasian Journal of Philosophy* 59 (1981): 332–7.

Gaus, Gerald F. "Mill's Theory of Moral Rules." *Australasian Journal of Philosophy* 58 (1980): 265–79.

Gerrard, Steve. "Desire and Desirability: Bradley, Russell and Moore versus Mill." In *Early Analytic Philosophy*, William W. Tait, ed. 37–74. Chicago: Open Court, 1997.

Gibbs, B. R. "Higher and Lower Pleasures." *Philosophy* 61 (1986): 31–59.

Goldinger, Milton. "Mill's Attack on Moral Conservatism." *Midwest Studies in Philosophy* 1 (1976): 61–7.

Gordon, Scott. "The Quality Problem in Utilitarianism." *The Mill News Letter* 10 (1975): 9–13.

Graff, J. A. "Mill's Quantity-Quality Distinction: A Defence." *The Mill News Letter* 7 (1972): 14–18.

Green, T. H. *Prolegomena to Ethics*. 1883. 5th ed., 1906. Oxford: Clarendon, 1929.

Griffin, James. *Well-Being*. Oxford: Oxford University Press, 1986.

Griffin, N. "A Note on Mr. Cooper's Reconstruction of Mill's 'Proof.'" *Mind* 81 (1972): 142–3.

Grote, John. *An Examination of the Utilitarian Philosophy*. Joseph Bickersteth Mayor, ed. Cambridge: Deighton, Bell, and Co., 1870.

Gruzalski, Bart. "Foreseeable Consequence Utilitarianism." *Australasian Journal of Philosophy* 59 (1981): 163–76.

Gunderson, Martin. "A Millian Analysis of Rights." *Ideas y Valores* 106 (April 1998): 3–17.

Habibi, Don. "J. S. Mill's Revisionist Utilitarianism." *British Journal for the History of Philosophy* 6 (1998): 89–114.

Hall, E. W. "The 'Proof' of Utility in Bentham and Mill." *Ethics* 60 (1949–50): 1–18.

Hancock, Roger. "Mill, Saints and Heroes." *The Mill News Letter* 10 (1975): 13–15.

Harcourt, Edward. "Mill's 'Sanctions,' Internalization and the Self." *European Journal of Philosophy* 6 (1998): 318–34.

Hare, R. M. *Moral Thinking: Its Levels, Method, and Point*. Oxford: Oxford University Press, 1981.

Harris, George W. "Mill's Qualitative Hedonism." *Southern Journal of Philosophy* 21 (1983): 503–12.

Harrison, Jonathan. "Utilitarianism, Universalisation, and Our Duty to Be Just." *Proceedings of the Aristotelian Society* N. S. 53 (1952–3): 105–34.

————."The Expedient, the Right and the Just in Mill's *Utilitarianism*." In *New Essays in the History of Philosophy*, Terence Penelhum and Roger A. Shiner, eds. *Canadian Journal of Philosophy*, supp. vol. 1 (1974): 93–107.

Harrod, R. F. "Utilitarianism Revised." *Mind* 45 (1936): 137–56.

Hearns, S. J. "Was Mill a Moral Scientist?" *Philosophy* 67 (1992): 81–101.

Himma, Kenneth Einer. "The Interpretation of Mill's Utilitarianism." *History of Philosophy Quarterly* 15 (1998): 455–73.

Himmelfarb, Gertrude. Introduction to *Essays on Politics and Culture*, by John Stuart Mill. Gertrude Himmelfarb, ed. New York: Doubleday, 1962; New York: Anchor Books, 1963.

Hoag, Robert W. "Mill on Conflicting Moral Obligations." *Analysis* 43 (1983): 49–54.

_____. "Happiness and Freedom: Recent Work on John Stuart Mill." *Philosophy and Public Affairs* 15 (1986): 188–99.

_____. "Mill's Conception of Happiness as an Inclusive End." *Journal of the History of Philosophy* 25 (1987): 417–31.

_____. "J. S. Mill's Language of Pleasures." *Utilitas* 4 (1992): 247–78.

Hoffman, Christopher A. "Desires and the Desirable." *Philosophical Forum* 25 (1993): 19–32.

Holbrook, Daniel. *Qualitative Utilitarianism.* Lanham, MD and London: University Press of America, 1988.

Hutcheson, Francis. *A System of Moral Philosophy.* 1755. Reprinted in part in *British Moralists*, L. A. Selby-Bigge, ed. Oxford: Clarendon Press, 1897.

Jenkins, Joyce I. "Desires and Human Nature in J. S. Mill." *History of Philosophy Quarterly* 14 (1997): 219–34.

Jones, Ernest. *The Life and Work of Sigmund Freud.* Harmondsworth: Penguin Books, 1964.

Jones, Hardy. "Mill's Argument for the Principle of Utility." *Philosophy and Phenomenological Research* 38 (1978): 338–54.

_____. "John Stuart Mill as Moralist." *Journal of the History of Ideas* 53 (1992): 287–308.

Joy, Glenn C., and Audrey M. McKinney. "On a Supposed Inconsistency in J. S. Mill's Utilitarianism." *Southwest Philosophical Studies* 14 (1992): 84–91.

Kamm, Josephine. *John Stuart Mill in Love.* London: Gordon and Cremonesi Publishers, 1977.

Kelly, P. J. "Utilitarian Strategies in Bentham and John Stuart Mill." *Utilitas* 2 (1990): 245–66.

Kleining, J. "The Fourth Chapter of Mill's *Utilitarianism.*" *Australasian Journal of Philosophy* 48 (1970): 197–205.

Kraut, Richard. "Two Conceptions of Happiness." *Philosophical Review* 88 (1979): 167–97.

Kretzman, N. "Desire as Proof of Desirability." *Philosophical Quarterly* 8 (1958): 246–58.

Kupperman, J. "Do We Desire Only Pleasure?" *Philosophical Studies* 34 (1978): 451–4.

Lachs, John. "Two Views of Happiness in Mill." *The Mill News Letter* 9 (1973): 16–20.

Lange, Berel and Gary Stahl. "Mill's 'Howlers' and the Logic of Naturalism." *Philosophy and Phenomenological Research* 29 (1968–9): 562–74.

Lecky, William Edward Hartpole. *History of European Morals*. 2 vols. 1869. 3rd ed. New York: D. Appleton, 1890.

Levi, A. W. "The Mental Crisis of John Stuart Mill." *Psychoanalytic Review* 32 (1945): 86–101.

Levin, David Michael. "Some Remarks on Mill's Naturalism." *Journal of Value Inquiry* 3 (1969): 291–7.

Long, Douglas G. "'Utility' and the 'Utility Principle': Hume, Smith, Bentham, Mill." *Utilitas* 2 (1990): 12–39.

Long, Roderick. "Mill's Higher Pleasures and the Choice of Character." *Utilitas* 4 (1992): 279–97.

Long, W. H. "The Legend of Mill's Proofs." *Southern Journal of Philosophy* 5 (1967): 36–47.

Loren, L. M. "Moore's Criticism of Mill." *Ratio* 9 (1967): 84–90.

Lyons, David. *Forms and Limits of Utilitarianism*. Oxford: Oxford University Press, 1965.

———. "Mill's Theory of Morality." *Nous* 10 (1976): 101–20.

———. "Mill's Theory of Justice." In *Values and Morals: Essays in Honor of William Frankena, Charles Stevenson, and Richard Brandt*, A. I. Goldman and J. Kim, eds. Dordrecht: Reidel, 1978.

———. "Benevolence and Justice in Mill." In *The Limits of Utilitarianism*, Harlan B. Miller and William H. Williams, eds. 42–70. Minneapolis: University of Minnesota Press, 1982.

———. *Rights, Welfare, and Mill's Moral Theory*. New York and Oxford: Oxford University Press, 1994.

———. "Human Rights and the General Welfare." *Philosophy and Public Affairs* 6 (1996–7): 113–29.

———, ed. *Mill's* Utilitarianism: *Critical Essays*. Lanham, MD: Rowman and Littlefield Publishers, 1997.

Mabbott, J. D. "Interpretations of Mill's *Utilitarianism*." *Philosophical Quarterly* 6 (1956): 115–20.

MacKensie, John S. *A Manual of Ethics*. 1883. 6th ed. London: University Tutorial Press, 1929.

Malinovich, Stanley. "The Happiness Criterion." *Philosophia* 2 (1972): 195–203.

Malthus, Thomas. *Principles of Political Economy*. 1820. Reprint, New York: Augustus M. Kelly, 1951.

_____. *An Essay on the Principle of Population*. 1798. Rev. ed., 1803. Reprinted as *An Essay on Population*, 2 vols. London: J. M. Dent; New York: E. P. Dutton, 1914. Reprinted as *Population: The First Essay*. Ann Arbor: University of Michigan Press, 1959.

Mandelbaum, Maurice. "On Interpreting Mill's *Utilitarianism*." *Journal of the History of Philosophy* 6 (1968): 35–46.

_____. "Two Moot Issues in Mill's *Utilitarianism*." In *Mill: A Collection of Critical Essays*, J. B. Schneewind, ed. 206–33. Garden City, NY: Doubleday, 1968.

Margolis, Joseph. "Mill's *Utilitarianism* Again." *Australasian Journal of Philosophy* 45 (1967): 179–84.

Marshall, John. "The Proof of Utility and Equity in Mill's *Utilitarianism*." *Canadian Journal of Philosophy* 3 (1973–4): 13–26.

_____. "Egalitarianism and General Happiness." In *The Limits of Utilitarianism*, Harlan B. Miller and William H. Williams, eds. 35–41. Minneapolis: University of Minnesota Press, 1982.

Martin, Rex. "A Defence of Mill's Qualitative Hedonism." *Philosophy* 47 (1972): 140–51.

Martineau, James. *Types of Ethical Theory*. 1855. 3rd ed. Oxford: Clarendon Press, 1901.

Mazlish, Bruce. *James and John Stuart Mill*. New York: Basic Books, 1975.

McCloskey, H. J. "An Examination of Restricted Utilitarianism." *The Philosophical Review* 66 (1957): 466–85.

_____. *John Stuart Mill: A Critical Study*. London and Basingstoke: Macmillan, 1971.

McGreal, Ian Philip. "Mill." Chap. 2 in *Analyzing Philosophical Arguments*. San Francisco: Chandler Publishing, 1967.

McNaughton, Robert. "A Metrical Conception of Happiness." *Philosophy and Phenomenological Research* 14 (1953–4): 172–83.

McNeilly, F. S. "Pre-moral Appraisals." *The Philosophical Quarterly* 8 (1958): 97–111.

Melden, A. I., ed. *Essays in Moral Philosophy*. Seattle: University of Washington Press, 1958.

Mill, James. *Analysis of the Phenomena of the Human Mind*. 2 vols. 1829; 2nd ed., John Stuart Mill, ed. 1869. Reprint, New York: Augustus M. Kelley, 1967.

Mill, John Stuart. *The Letters of John Stuart Mill*. 2 vols. H. S. R. Elliot, ed. London: Longmans, Green, 1910.

———. *Principles of Political Economy*. 1848; 6th ed., 1871. Vols. 2–3 of *Collected Works of John Stuart Mill*, J. M. Robson, ed. Toronto: University of Toronto Press, 1965.

———. *Auguste Comte and Positivism*. 1865. In *Essays on Ethics, Religion and Society*. Vol. 10 of *Collected Works of John Stuart Mill*, J. M. Robson, ed. Toronto: University of Toronto Press, 1969.

———. "Blakey's History of Moral Science." 1833. In *Essays on Ethics, Religion and Society*. Vol. 10 of *Collected Works of John Stuart Mill*, J. M. Robson, ed. Toronto: University of Toronto Press, 1969.

———. "Nature." In *Three Essays on Religion*. 1874. In *Essays on Ethics, Religion and Society*. Vol. 10 of *Collected Works of John Stuart Mill*, J. M. Robson, ed. Toronto: University of Toronto Press, 1969.

———. "Remarks on Bentham's Philosophy." 1833. In *Essays on Ethics, Religion and Society*. Vol. 10 of *Collected Works of John Stuart Mill*, J. M. Robson, ed. Toronto: University of Toronto Press, 1969.

———. "Sedgwick's Discourse." 1835. In *Essays on Ethics, Religion and Society*. Vol. 10 of *Collected Works of John Stuart Mill*, J. M. Robson, ed. Toronto: University of Toronto Press, 1969.

———. "Theism." In *Three Essays on Religion*. 1874. In *Essays on Ethics, Religion and Society*. Vol. 10 of *Collected Works of John Stuart Mill*, J. M. Robson, ed. Toronto: University of Toronto Press, 1969.

———. *Three Essays on Religion*. 1874. In *Essays on Ethics, Religion and Society*. Vol. 10 of *Collected Works of John Stuart Mill*, J. M. Robson, ed. Toronto: University of Toronto Press, 1969.

———. *Utilitarianism*. 1861. In *Essays on Ethics, Religion and Society*. Vol. 10 of *Collected Works of John Stuart Mill*, J. M. Robson, ed. Toronto: University of Toronto Press, 1969.

———. "Utility of Religion." In *Three Essays on Religion*. 1874. In *Essays on Ethics, Religion and Society*. Vol. 10 of *Collected Works of John Stuart Mill*, J. M. Robson, ed. Toronto: University of Toronto Press, 1969.

———. *The Later Letters of John Stuart Mill 1849–1873*. Vols. 14–17 of *Collected Works of John Stuart Mill*, Francis E. Mineka and Dwight N. Lindley, eds. Toronto and Buffalo: University of Toronto Press, 1972.

———. "Whewell on Moral Philosophy." 1852. In *Essays on Ethics, Religion and Society*. Vol. 10 of *Collected Works of John Stuart Mill*, J. M. Robson, ed. Toronto: University of Toronto Press, 1969.

————. *A System of Logic, Ratiocinative and Inductive*. 1843; 8ᵗʰ ed., 1871. Vols. 7–8 of *Collected Works of John Stuart Mill*, J. M. Robson, ed. Toronto: University of Toronto Press, 1974.

————. *On Liberty*. 1859. In *Essays on Politics and Society*. Vol. 18 of *Collected Works of John Stuart Mill*, J. M. Robson, ed. Toronto and Buffalo: University of Toronto Press, 1977.

————. "The Protagoras." 1834. In *Essays on Philosophy and the Classics*. Vol. 11 of *Collected Works of John Stuart Mill*, J. M. Robson, ed. Toronto, Buffalo, London: University of Toronto Press, 1978.

————. *An Examination of Sir William Hamilton's Philosophy*. 1865; 4ᵗʰ ed., 1872. Vol. 9 of *Collected Works of John Stuart Mill*, J. M. Robson, ed. Toronto and Buffalo: University of Toronto Press, 1979.

————. *Autobiography*. 1873. Published with parallel texts of the Early Draft, John M. Robson and Jack Stillinger, eds. In *Autobiography and Literary Essays*. Vol. 1 of *Collected Works of John Stuart Mill*, J. M. Robson and Jack Stillinger, eds. Toronto and Buffalo: University of Toronto Press, 1981.

————. *The Subjection of Women*. 1869. In *Essays on Equality, Law, and Education*. Vol. 21 of *Collected Works of John Stuart Mill*, John M. Robson, ed. Toronto and Buffalo: University of Toronto Press, 1984.

————. *Miscellaneous Writings*. Vol. 31 of *Collected Works of John Stuart Mill*, John M. Robson, ed. Toronto and Buffalo: University of Toronto Press, 1989.

————. *Utilitarianism*. Roger Crisp, ed. Oxford: Oxford University Press, 1998.

Miller, Dale E. "Internal Sanctions in Mill's Moral Psychology." *Utilitas* 10 (1998): 68–82.

Miller, Harlan B., and William H. Williams, eds. *The Limits of Utilitarianism*. Minneapolis: University of Minnesota Press, 1982.

Millgram, Elijah. "Mill's Proof of the Principle of Utility." *Ethics* 110 (2000): 281–310.

Mitchell, Dorothy. "Mill's Theory of Value." *Theoria* 36 (1970): 100–15.

Monro, David Hector. "Mill's Third Howler." In *Contemporary Philosophy in Australia*, R. Brown and C. D. Rollins, eds. 190–203. London: Allen and Unwin, 1969.

Moore, G. E. *Principia Ethica*. 1903. London and New York: Cambridge University Press, 1959.

Moser, Shia. "A Comment on Mill's Argument for Utilitarianism." *Inquiry* 6 (1963): 308–18.

Nagoka, Shigeo. "On Mill's Qualitative Distinction of Pleasures." *The Mill News Letter* 20 (1985): 15–26.

Nakhnikian, G. "Value and Obligation in Mill." *Ethics* 62 (1951): 33–40.

Nielsen, Kai. "Monro on Mill's 'Third Howler.'" *Australasian Journal of Philosophy* 51 (1973): 63–9.

Nowell-Smith, P. H. *Ethics*. Baltimore: Penguin Books, 1954.

Ossowska, Maria. "Remarks on the Ancient Distinction between Bodily and Mental Pleasures." *Inquiry* 4 (1961): 123–7.

Owen, Robert. *A New View of Society: or, Essays on the Formation of Character*. 1813; 4th ed., 1818. London: J. M. Dent and Sons, 1972.

Packe, Michael St. John. *The Life of John Stuart Mill*. London: Secker and Warburg, 1954.

Patten, S. C. "Some Are Base, Some Are Sublime: A Defence of Hedonistic Utilitarianism." *Journal of Value Inquiry* 14 (1980): 275–86.

Persson, Ingmar. "Mill's Derivation of the Intrinsic Desirability of Pleasure." *History of Philosopohy Quarterly* 17 (2000): 297–310.

Peterfreund, Sheldon P. "On Mill's Higher and Lower Pleasures." *Personalist* 57 (1976): 411–12.

Philips, Michael. "A Pleasure Paradox." *Australasian Journal of Philosophy* 59 (1981): 323–31.

Plamenatz, John. "John Stuart Mill." Chap. 8 in *The English Utilitarians*. 2nd ed. Oxford: Blackwell, 1958.

Plato. *Protagoras*. In *The Dialogues of Plato*. B. Jowett, trans. 1892. New :York: Random House, 1937.

Popkin, R. H. "A Note on the 'Proof' of Utility in J. S. Mill." *Ethics* 61 (1950–1): 66–8.

Quinton, Anthony. *Utilitarian Ethics*. New York: St. Martin's Press, 1973.

Raphael, D. D. "Fallacies in and about Mill's *Utilitarianism*." *Philosophy* 30 (1955): 344–57.

———. "J. S. Mill's Proof of the Principle of Utility." *Utilitas* 6 (1994): 55–63.

Rawls, John. "Two Concepts of Rules." *The Philosophical Review* 64 (1955): 3–32.

———. *A Theory of Justice*. Cambridge, MA: Harvard University Press, 1971.

Regan, Donald. *Utilitarianism and Co-operation*. Oxford: Oxford University Press, 1980.

Rescher, Nicholas. *Distributive Justice*. Indianapolis: The Bobbs-Merrill Company, 1966.

Rice, Philip Blair. *On the Knowledge of Good and Evil*. New York: Random House, 1955.

Riley, Jonathan. *Liberal Utilitarianism: Social Choice Theory and J. S. Mill's Philosophy*. Cambridge: Cambridge University Press, 1988.

————. "On Quantities and Qualities of Pleasure." *Utilitas* 5 (1993): 291–300.

————. "Is Qualitative Hedonism Inconsistent?" *Utilitas* 11 (1999): 347–58.

Robson, J. M. *The Improvement of Mankind: The Social and Political Thought of John Stuart Mill*. Toronto: University of Toronto Press, 1968.

————. Textual Introduction to *Essays on Ethics, Religion and Society*. Vol. 10 of *Collected Works of John Stuart Mill*, J. M. Robson, ed. Toronto: University of Toronto Press, 1969.

Robson, John M., and Michael Laine, eds. *James and John Stuart Mill: Papers of the Centenary Conference*. Toronto: University of Toronto Press, 1976.

Rogers, Reginald A. P. *A Short History of Ethics*. 1911. Reprint, London: Macmillan, 1964.

Rohatyn, Dennis A. "Hall and Mill's Proof." *Southwest Journal of Philosophy* 2 (1971): 113–18.

————. "A Note on Kaufmann and Justice." *The Mill News Letter* 6 (1971): 23–5.

————. "Mill, Kant, and Negative Utility." *Philosophia* 5 (1975): 515–22.

Ross, W. D. *The Right and the Good*. Oxford: Clarendon Press, 1930.

Russell, Bertrand. *A History of Western Philosophy*. London: George Allen and Unwin, 1946.

Ryan, Alan. "Mill and the Naturalistic Fallacy." *Mind* 75 (1966): 422–5.

————. *J. S. Mill*. London and Boston: Routledge and Kegan Paul, 1974.

————. *The Philosophy of John Stuart Mill*. London: Macmillan; New York: Pantheon Books, 1970; 2nd ed., New York: Macmillan, 1988.

Sabine, George H. *A History of Political Theory*. 3rd ed. New York: Holt, Rinehart and Winston, 1961.

Sayre-McCord, Geoffrey. "Mill's 'Proof' of the Principle of Utility: A More Than Half-Hearted Defense." *Social Philosophy and Policy* 18 (2001): 330–60.

Bibliography

Scarre, Geoffrey. "Happiness for a Millian." *British Journal for the History of Philosophy* 7 (1999): 491–502.

————. "Donner and Riley on Qualitative Hedonism." *Utilitas* 9 (1997): 355–60.

Schaller, Walter E. "Punishment and the Utilitarian Criterion of Right and Wrong." *Southern Journal of Philosophy* 29 (1991): 109–26.

Schneewind, J. B. "Concerning Some Criticisms of Mill's *Utilitarianism*, 1861–76." In *James and John Stuart Mill: Papers of the Centenary Conference*, John M. Robson and Michael Laine, eds. Toronto and Buffalo: University of Toronto Press, 1976.

————, ed. *Mill's Ethical Writings*. London: Collier-Macmillan; New York: Collier Books, 1965.

————, ed. *Mill: A Collection of Critical Essays*. Garden City, NY: Doubleday; London: Macmillan, 1968.

Selby-Bigge, L. A., ed. *British Moralists, Being Selections from Writers Principally of the Eighteenth Century*. Oxford: Clarendon, 1897.

Sellars, Wilfred, and John Hospers, eds. *Readings in Ethical Theory*. New York: Appleton-Century-Crofts, 1952.

Semmel, Bernard. *John Stuart Mill and the Pursuit of Virtue*. New Haven: Yale University Press, 1984.

Seth, James. "The Alleged Fallacies in Mill's 'Utilitarianism.'" *Philosophical Review* 17 (1908): 469–88.

————. *A Study of Ethical Principles*. 12th ed. New York: 1911.

Shaw, William H. *Contemporary Ethics: Taking Account of Utilitarianism*. Malden, MA and Oxford: Blackwell Publishers, 1999.

Sheldon, Mark. "Community, History and Proof." *The Mill News Letter* 14 (1979): 9–14.

Sidgwick, Henry. *Outlines of the History of Ethics*. 1886; 6th ed., 1931. London: Macmillan, 1954.

————. *Methods of Ethics*. 1874; 7th ed., 1907. London: Macmillan, 1967.

————. *Practical Ethics: A Collection of Addresses and Essays*. London: S. Sonnenschein; New York: Macmillan, 1898. Reprint, New York and Oxford: Oxford University Press, 1998.

Singer, Marcus G. "Actual Consequence Utilitarianism." *Mind* 86 (1977): 67–77.

————. "Incoherence, Inconsistency and Moral Theory: More on Actual Consequence Utilitarianism." *The Southern Journal of Philosophy* 20 (1982): 375–91.

_____. "Mill's Stoic Conception of Happiness and Pragmatic Conception of Utility." *Philosophy* 75 (2000): 25–47.

Skorupski, John. "The Parts of Happiness." *Philosophical Books* 26 (1985): 193–202.

_____. *John Stuart Mill*. London and New York: Routledge, 1989.

_____, ed. *The Cambridge Companion to Mill*. Cambridge: Cambridge University Press, 1998.

Slote, Michael. "Consequentialism." In *Encyclopedia of Ethics*, 2nd ed., 3 vols. Lawrence C. Becker and Charlotte B. Becker, eds. New York and London: Routledge, 2001.

Smart, J. J. C. "Extreme and Restricted Utilitarianism." *Philosophical Quarterly* 4 (1956): 344–54.

_____. "An Outline of a System of Utilitarian Ethics." In *Utilitarianism: For and Against*, J. J. C. Smart and Bernard Williams, eds. Cambridge: Cambridge University Press, 1973.

Sobel, J. Howard. "'Everyone,' Consequences, and Generalization Arguments." *Inquiry* 10 (1967): 373–404.

Soles, David E. "Yet Another Paper on Mill's Proof." *Southwest Philosophy Review* 14 (1998): 29–44.

Sorley, W. R. *The Ethics of Naturalism*. 2nd ed. Edinburgh, 1904.

_____. *A History of British Philosophy to 1900*. 1920. Reprint, Cambridge: Cambridge University Press, 1965.

Sosa, Ernest. "Mill's *Utilitarianism*." In *Mill's* Utilitarianism: *Text and Criticism*, James M. Smith and Ernest Sosa, eds. Belmont, CA: Wadsworth Publishing Company, 1969.

Spence, G. W. "The Psychology behind J. S. Mill's 'Proof.'" *Philosophy* 43 (1968): 18–28.

Stephen, Leslie. *The English Utilitarians*. 3 vols. 1900. Reprint in one vol., New York: Peter Smith, 1950.

Stewart, Robert Scott. "Art for Argument's Sake: Saving Mill from the Fallacy of Composition." *Journal of Value Inquiry* 27 (1993): 443–53.

Stocker, Michael. "Mill on Desire and Desirability." *Journal of the History of Philosophy* 7 (1969): 199–201.

Stout, A. K. "But Suppose Everyone Did the Same." *Australasian Journal of Philosophy* 32 (1954): 1–29.

Strasser, Mark. "Mill's Higher and Lower Pleasures Reexamined." *International Studies in Philosophy* 17 (1985): 51–72.

_____. "Actual versus Probable Utilitarianism." *The Southern Journal of Philosophy* 27 (1989): 585–97.

———. *The Moral Philosophy of John Stuart Mill: Toward Modifications of Contemporary Utilitarianism*. Wakefield, VT: Longwood Academic Publishers, 1991.

Sumner, L. W. "More Light on the Later Mill." *The Philosophical Review* 83 (1974): 504–27.

———. "The Good and the Right." In *New Essays on John Stuart Mill and Utilitarianism*, Wesley E. Cooper, Kai Nielsen, and Steven C. Patten, eds. *Canadian Journal of Philosophy*, supp. vol. 5 (1979): 99–114.

———. "Welfare, Happiness, and Pleasure." *Utilitas* 4 (1992): 199–223.

Sutherland, J. "An Alleged Gap in Mill's Utilitarianism." *Mind* 11 (1886): 597–9.

Sylvester, Robert P. "Pleasures: Higher and Lower." *Personalist* 56 (1975): 129–37.

Taylor, Helen. Introductory Notice to *Three Essays on Religion*. 1874. In *Essays on Ethics, Religion, and Society*. Vol. 10 of *Collected Works of John Stuart Mill*, J. M. Robson, ed. Toronto: University of Toronto Press, 1969.

Ten, C. L. "Mill and Utilitarianism." *Utilitas* 13 (2001): 112–22.

Thomas, Laurence. "Moral Psychology." In *Encyclopedia of Ethics*, 2nd ed., 3 vols. Lawrence C. Becker and Charlotte B. Becker, eds. New York and London: Routledge, 2001.

Thomas, William. *Mill*. Oxford: Oxford University Press, 1985.

Toulmin, S. E. *An Examination of the Place of Reason in Ethics*. Cambridge: Cambridge University Press, 1950.

Urmson, J. O. "The Interpretation of the Philosophy of J. S. Mill." *Philosophical Quarterly* 3 (1953): 33–40.

———. "A Defence of Intuitionism." *Proceedings of the Aristotelian Society* 75 (1974–5): 111–19.

Waldron, J. "Kagen on Requirements, Mill on Sanctions." *Ethics* 54 (1994): 310–24.

Wall, Grenville. "Mill on Happiness as an End." *Philosophy* 57 (1982): 537–41.

Walter, Edward. "Revising Mill's Utilitarianism." *Journal of Social Philosophy* 12 (1981): 5–11.

———. "Mill on Happiness." *Journal of Value Inquiry* 16 (1982): 303–9.

———. "A Concept of Happiness." *Philosophy Research Archives* 13 (1987–8): 137–50.

Warke, Tom. "Multi-Dimensional Utility and the Index Number Problem: Jeremy Bentham, J. S. Mill, and Qualitative Hedonism." *Utilitas* 12 (2000): 176–203.

Warnock, Mary. *Ethics Since 1900*. London: Oxford University Press, 1960.

––––––. Introduction to *Utilitarianism* and *On Liberty*, by John Stuart Mill, with an Introduction by Mary Warnock, ed. 2nd ed. 1–16. Malden, MA and Oxford: Blackwell Publishing, 2003.

Wedar, Sven. *Duty and Utility: A Study in English Moral Philosophy*. Lund: Berlingska Boktryckeriet, 1951.

Wellman, Carl. "A Reinterpretation of Mill's Proof." *Ethics* 69 (1958–9): 268–76.

Wertz, S. K. "Composition and Mill's Utilitarian Principle." *Personalist* 52 (1971): 417–31.

West, Henry Robison. "Act-Utilitarianism and Rule-Utilitarianism." Ph.D. diss., Harvard University, 1964.

––––––. "Reconstructing Mill's 'Proof' of the Principle of Utility." *Mind* 81 (1972): 256–7.

––––––. "Mill's Naturalism." *Journal of Value Inquiry* 9 (1975): 67–9.

––––––. "Mill's Moral Conservatism." *Midwest Studies in Philosophy* 1 (1976): 71–80.

––––––. "Mill's Qualitative Hedonism." *Philosophy* 51 (1976): 101–5.

––––––. "Mill's 'Proof' of the Principle of Utility." In *The Limits of Utilitarianism*, Harlan B. Miller and William H. Williams, eds. Minneapolis: University of Minnesota Press, 1982.

––––––. "Consequentialism." In *The Encyclopedia of Philosophy: Supplement*. 101–2. New York: Simon and Schuster Macmillan, 1996.

––––––. "Mill, John Stuart." In *The Encyclopedia of Philosophy: Supplement*. 346–7. New York: Simon and Schuster Macmillan, 1996.

––––––. "Mill, John Stuart." In *Encyclopedia of Ethics*, 2nd ed., 3 vols. Lawrence C. Becker and Charlotte B. Becker, eds. 1098–1104. New York and London: Routledge, 2001.

White, Morton. "Desire and Desirability: A Rejoinder to a Posthumous Reply by John Dewey." *Journal of Philosophy* 93 (1996): 229–42.

Wilson, Fred. "Mill's Proof That Happiness Is the Criterion of Morality." *Journal of Business Ethics* 1 (1982): 59–72.

––––––. "Mill's 'Proof' of Utility and the Composition of Causes." *Journal of Business Ethics* 2 (1983): 135–58.

Bibliography

Wittgenstein, Ludwig. *Philosophical Investigations*. G. E. M. Anscombe, trans. 3rd ed. New York: The Macmillan Company, 1971.

Wolf, Jean Claude. *John Stuart Mill's 'Utilitarismus.'* Freiburg and Munich: Alber, 1992.

Zimmerman, Michael J. "Mill and the Consistency of Hedonism." *Philosophia* 13 (1983): 317–35.

Zinkernagel, Peter. "Revaluation of J. S. Mill's Ethical Proof." *Theoria* 18 (1952): 70–7.

INDEX

Albee, Ernest, 69, 71
Alican, Necip Fikri, 120, 122
A priori school of morality,
    30–32, 42–47, 170
Aristotle, 127, 128
Atkinson, R. F., 125
Austin, John, 9, 11, 12

Bacon, Francis, 16–17
Baier, Annette, 42
Bain, Alexander, 14
Baker, John M., 76
Baumgardt, David, 144
Bentham, Jeremy, 5, 8, 11, 12,
    13, 22–27, 33, 45, 70, 79,
    91, 92, 97, 99, 101–102,
    103, 104–108, 131, 144, 183
  Book of Fallacies, 106
  Rationale of Judicial Evidence,
    13
  Introduction to the Principles of
    Morals and Legislation, 104
Bentham's hedonic calculus,
    25–26, 91
Berger, Fred R., 76, 77
birth control, 41
Bradley, F. H., 71, 120
Brandt, Richard, 2, 32, 74
British empiricism, 16–17
Brown, D. G., 76, 118
Burns, J. H., 22
Butler, Joseph, 32

Carritt, E. F., 1
Chamblin, T. S., 76
Christianity, 5, 37
civilization, 40
Coleridge, 14
Comte, August, 15
conscience, 97–98, 108, 184
consequentialist theories, their
    variety, 33–34
contractarianism, 1
Copp, David, 76, 82
Coulson, Walter, 37
courage, 39
Crisp, Roger, 4, 78
Cupples, Brian, 76

de Tocqueville, 16
dignity, sense of, 50
Donner, Wendy, 73, 132
Dryer, D. P., 76
Dumont, Etienne, 12

East India Company, 13, 18
Edwards, Rem B., 52, 77
Ellis, Brian, 80
Ethical Theory, 74
externalism, 109–110

Falk, W. D., 109
Fourier, Francois, 15
Frankena, William, 31, 32, 108
free will, 111–114, 159
Freud, Sigmund, 138–139

213

Galle, Peter, 80
Gaus, Gerald F., 77, 84, 92
God's commands, 6, 20, 35–37, 46, 128
Gomperz, Theodor, 44
Green, T. H., 72
Griffin, James, 33, 138
Grote, George, 85
Grote, John, 70, 119
Gruzalski, Bart, 79

Hall, E. W., 125
Hancock, Roger, 76
Hare, R. M., 2
Harrison, Jonathan, 75, 76
Harrod, R. F., 75
Hart, H. L. A., 22
Hartley, David, 9
hedonism, 5, 6
    ethical hedonism, 23
    qualitative hedonism, 48–73
    psychological hedonism, 23, 26, 101–103, 128–140
Herford, Edward, 41
Himmelfarb, Gertrude, 16
Holbrook, Daniel, 66
Hume, David, 42
Hutcheson, Francis, 48, 51–52

instinct, 39, 40
internalism, 109–110
intuitionism, 34, 42, 44–45, 128
intuitionists, 1, 20, 43
intuitive school of morality, 30–32, 170

Jones, Henry, 141
Jowett, B., 29
justice, 4, 6, 39, 146–168
    distributive justice, 161–163

Kamm, Josephine, 16
Kant, 30–31, 111, 170, 171

Levi, A. W., 90
liberty, 40
Lindley, Dwight N., 37
Locke, John, 16–17
lying, 1, 92–93
Lyons, David B., 74, 76, 77, 82, 86, 93, 94

Mabbott, J. D., 76
Malthus, 40
Mandelbaum, M., 133
Marshall, John, 142
Martin, Rex, 73
Mayor, Joseph, 119, 125
Mazlish, Bruce, 14
McCloskey, H. J., 75, 120
Mill, James, 5, 8, 10, 11, 99, 101, 103, 104, 108, 131
    Analysis of the Phenomena of the Human Mind, 9, 99–100, 103
    Elements of Political Economy, 9
    Fragment on Mackintosh, 31, 84
    History of British India, 8
Mill, John Stuart
    Analysis of the Phenomena of the Human Mind, by James Mill, with notes by J. S. Mill, 20, 58, 67–68, 99–101, 133
    Auguste Comte and Positivism, 19–20, 83
    Autobiography, 8, 9, 11, 15, 20, 22, 44, 160
    "Bentham," 15
    "Blackey's History of Moral Science," 35, 42
    Considerations on Representative Government, 16, 18–19
    "Coleridge," 15

Essays on Some Unsettled Questions of Political Economy, 16–17

Examination of Sir William Hamilton's Philosophy, 20, 111–117

"Nature," 22, 37

mental "crisis," 13–14

On Liberty, 15, 18, 40, 78–79

Principles of Political Economy, 15, 16–17, 40, 108

"Protagoras," 30

"Remarks on Bentham's Philosophy," 86, 92, 106, 131

"Sedgwick's Discourse," 35, 42, 43, 80, 81

Subjection of Women, 41

System of Logic, 2, 16–17, 40, 44, 55, 60, 80, 89, 90, 103, 109, 121, 125, 129, 160, 174

"Theism," 22, 37

Three Essays on Religion, 22, 37

Utilitarianism, its composition, 19

"Utility of Religion," 22, 36

"Whewell on Moral Philosophy," 43, 44, 45, 94, 123, 133

Mineka, Francis E., 37

Mitchell, Dorothy, 122

Moore, G. E., 33, 60, 120, 124

moral sense, 6, 42, 43, 45, 46

motives, 86, 96–117, 178–179, 182–183

natural, 43

Nature, 6, 20, 37–42, 46, 128

Nicomachean Ethics, 127

Nowell-Smith, P., 75

overpopulation, 40–41

Owen, Robert, 15, 159–160

Packe, Michael St. John, 14, 41

Parliament, 18, 21

philosophical radicals, 9

Plato's *Protagoras*, 29–30

pleasures

animal, 52–53

attitude theory of pleasure, 54–56, 57–59

bodily, 52–53, 176

competent judges of pleasures, 64, 65, 66

family resemblances of pleasures and pains, 59–61, 68

"first-order" pleasures, 62, 67

hedonic tone theory of pleasure, 54

higher faculties and superior pleasures, 61–69, 86, 135, 175–176

human, 52–53

intrinsic value of pleasures, 63

mental, 52–53, 176

qualitative differences, 48–73

"second-order" pleasures, 62, 67

sensation of pleasure, 55–56, 57–59

superiority of higher pleasures, 61–69

theories of pleasure, 54–69

poverty, 40

progressive morality, 43, 46

proof of the principle of utility, 4, 6, 118–145, 172, 185–188

Protagoras, 29–30

psychology

introspective, 53, 58, 59

moral, 99–117

psychology (*cont.*)
   psychological egoism, 103
punishment, 159–161, 192

Qualities of pleasure, 48–73

Rawls, John, 1, 34, 75, 81, 150,
   153, 164–168
Regan, Donald, 75, 93
Rescher, Nicholas, 147
Retribution, 114–115
Ricardo, David, 9, 10
rights, 4, 6, 85, 156–157, 164,
   166, 189, 191
Riley, Jonathan, 64, 72
Robson, J. M., 8, 19, 169
Ross, W. D., 1
rules of thumb, 81

Sabine, George H., 120
Saint Simonians, 15
sanctions, 4, 6, 26–27, 96–99,
   183–185
Scarre, Geoffrey, 64
Schneewind, J. B., 70, 119
Seth, James, 72
Shaw, William H., 2
Sidgwick, Henry, 70, 101
Singer, Marcus, 79–80
Skorupski, John, 85, 87
Slote, Michael, 34
Smart, J. J. C., 2, 4, 75, 79
Smith, Adam, 10
Sobel, J. Howard, 93
Socrates, 29–30
Sosa, Ernest, 73
Stephen, Leslie, 64
Stillinger, Jack, 8
Stout, A. K., 75
Strasser, Mark, 80
Sumner, L. W., 55, 77, 87
supererogation, 6, 83

sympathy, 42, 191

Taylor, Harriet, 15–17, 18
Taylor, Helen, 37
teleological principle, 31
tendency of actions, 4, 80, 174
Theory of Justice, A, 1, 164–168
Thomas, Laurence, 111
Toulmin, S. E., 75
truth telling, 1, 90, 92–93

Urmson, J. O., 34, 76
utilitarianism
   act-utilitarianism, 3, 4, 6,
      74–95, 180
   actual consequence
      utilitarianism, 4, 80
   foreseeable consequence
      utilitarianism, 4
   moral code rule-utilitarianism,
      74–75
   rule-utilitarianism, 3, 6,
      74–95, 180
   utilitarian generalization,
      74–75
   utilitarianism, defined, 3, 4,
      24, 173, 176
Utilitarianism: For and Against, 4

Venn, John, 75, 93
virtue, 39

Wall, Grenville, 125
Walker, A. D. M., 76
Ward, William George, 39
West, Henry R., 31, 61, 75, 84,
   93, 123
Whewell, William, 45–46, 60, 93
Wittgenstein, Ludwig, 59
women's suffrage, 21
women, subjection of, 42
Wordsworth, William, 14